TOXIC PEOPLE

10 WAYS OF

DEALING WITH PEOPLE

WHO MAKE YOUR LIFE

MISERABLE

LILLIAN GLASS, PH.D.

SIMON & SCHUSTER

NEW YORK LONDON TORONTO SYDNEY TOKYO SINGAPORE

SIMON & SCHUSTER
ROCKEFELLER CENTER
1230 AVENUE OF THE AMERICAS
NEW YORK, NY 10020

DESIGNED BY BARBARA M. BACHMAN

MANUFACTURED IN THE UNITED STATES OF AMERICA

1 3 5 7 9 10 8 6 4 2

LIBRARY OF CONGRESS CATALOGING-IN-PUBLICATION DATA
GLASS, LILLIAN
TOXIC PEOPLE : 10 WAYS OF DEALING WITH PEOPLE WHO MAKE YOUR LIFE MISERABLE / LILLIAN GLASS.
P.   CM.
INCLUDES BIBLIOGRAPHICAL REFERENCES AND INDEX.
1. INTERPERSONAL CONFLICT.   2. ADJUSTMENT (PSYCHOLOGY)   3. INVECTIVE.
4. INTERPERSONAL COMMUNICATION.   I. TITLE.
BG637.I48G57   1995
158'.2—DC20   95-1431
CIP
ISBN 0-684-80315-1

To all the Toxic People I have known throughout my life: those who have been rude and disrespectful to me, who have not believed in my aims, and who have tried to thwart my purposes: I bless you and release you, and I thank you for providing me with data for this book.
It only goes to prove that
The Pen Is Indeed Mightier Than the Sword!

ACKNOWLEDGMENTS

I wish to thank the following people:

My bright, beautiful, and bubbly superagent, Jan Miller, who made this all possible.

Dean Williamson, Jan's associate, for his positive encouragement.

Bob Asahina, the greatest editor, for his wisdom, intelligence, and enthusiasm.

Sarah Pinckney for her terrific editing skills, wonderful insight, and kind words.

Rosalie Glass, my best friend and mother, who always makes me smile and whose teachings permeate this book.

All my dear and special friends throughout the world, for their love, kindness, positive thoughts, and best wishes.

Contents

"Sticks and stones can break my bones, but words can never hurt me." Most of us grew up with this seemingly innocent childhood saying. We may have shouted it at the top of our lungs in order to drown out the ugly words of some childhood tormentor—a nasty girl or rude boy who was taunting us, badgering us, or hurling insults at us on the playground. Until now, we probably never gave this childhood mantra a second thought.

When we dissect this rhyme, we find both truth and untruth in it. While it is certainly true that sticks and stones can break one's bones, it is not true that words will never hurt you. Words will *definitely* hurt you.

Throughout my years of private practice as a communication specialist and a voice, speech, and image consultant, I have seen the incredible importance of words. I have seen what devastating effects ugly words, ugly actions, and nasty people have on other people's lives. I have discovered how incredibly fragile we human beings are. We are so emotionally tender that we not only remember ugly things that happened to us as children but tend to live our lives based on words we heard and actions we saw in childhood.

After all, why else would so many of us have to seek psychotherapy as adults in order to help rid ourselves of the poor self-esteem inculcated in us as children?

When a middle-aged man is stuck in a rut with his job and feels that he can't get out, he realizes that it was his teacher's words "You'll never amount to anything" and "You're not good enough" that hold him back today.

When a young woman consults a therapist because of an eating disorder, she discovers that it was her hostile childhood classmates' calling her a "fat cow" that put her on the road to anorexia.

When a little girl commits suicide, it is discovered that the constant teasing and harassment of her toxic peers led her to it.

It is amazing to see how many of these messages become engraved on our psyches and affect our self-esteem. How emotionally tender human beings are!

The tormentors who hurl negative verbal garbage that hurts us, scars us, and sometimes even immobilizes us are "toxic people." A toxic person can be anyone—childhood classmate, brother or sister, parent, lover, husband or wife, boss or coworker.

A toxic person is anyone who has poisoned your life, who is not supportive, who is not happy to see you grow, to see you succeed, who does not wish you well. In essence, he or she sabotages your efforts to lead a happy and productive life.

Many psychologists suggest closing the door, letting go, and completely losing contact with a horrible person in your life, for the sake of improving and regaining your own mental health so that you can get on with your life. Though this may be an effective approach for many people, it is only *one* way to deal with a toxic person. I have discovered that there are many other available options, and I will describe them in this book.

As a communication specialist, I have spent literally thousands of hours hearing hundreds of people, ranging in age from four to eighty-seven, telling me what makes them unhappy. I found that the number one cause of my clients' unhappiness was that certain toxic people made their lives a living hell. Perhaps the philosopher Sartre was right when he said, "Hell is other people."

As I listened to countless testimonies, I discovered that there are indeed people who are hazardous to others' mental, emotional, and physical health. I have seen people who were literally skin and bones because they were in abusive marriages. I have seen people end up in hospitals with bleeding ulcers because they were working for nasty, hostile bosses. I have seen parents lose their jobs and suffer financial setbacks because of an unruly teenager who stole and took drugs. I have seen a person's life become consumed by toxic friends who replaced almost every one of her thoughts with a negative one. I have heard a little girl tell me, "I hope I die, because my mommy doesn't love me." She felt this way because her mother was hardly ever around. And when she *was* home, she yelled constantly at her daughter and told her what a bad girl she was.

Listening to these stories, I began to take notes. I saw numerous patterns emerge, and I learned some very interesting things. First of all, there were different types of toxic people (thirty, to be exact). Second, someone who is toxic to one person may not necessarily be toxic to another. I also learned that there were different ways to handle specific types of toxic people that could enable one to get along better and cope with them.

After offering my clients specific advice on how to communicate with the toxic people in their lives, I noticed how their lives turned around. My clients saw how effectively the techniques that I taught worked, time after time. It did not matter who the toxic perpetrator was—a nagging mother, a jealous husband, an abusive teacher, a harassing boss, or even a rude waiter, a pompous doctor, or a condescending salesperson. Whoever those people were, my clients now had the tools to handle them. They suddenly felt less stressed and not as depressed, more empowered, and much happier, when around the toxic person. I used these techniques in my own life, and I found that more and more of my days were happier. I no longer had to hold my feelings in or agonize about whether or not I said the right thing. I no longer had to beat myself up over what I "should have said" or what I "should have done" when a toxic person said something ugly to me.

I decided to take my knowledge about dealing with toxic people on the road. As an international motivational speaker, I brought up the topic in my lectures, and I found that *everyone* could relate to it. No matter where they lived in the world, what they did for a living, how rich or poor they were, *all of them* had some toxic person who made their life miserable. At the question-and-answer session after my speeches, audience members shared their personal experiences with me as they asked how they might handle specific toxic people in their lives.

I received countless letters from people all over the world (including Australia, Germany, Indonesia, Israel, India, England, Africa, Singapore, and Saudi Arabia), sharing with me how well the techniques they had learned from my seminar worked for them. They were comforted in the realization that (*a*) they were not the problem and (*b*) they were not alone. It was a relief to know that others had toxic people in their lives as well. They felt strength in knowing that they no longer had to be victims. They discovered that there was finally a way to handle the terrible situations they were in, and they expressed joy in their newfound freedom.

My research also led me to other cultural traditions. I found that Indonesians nail a barong, a wooden mask of a monsterlike face, with sharp teeth and bulging eyes, over their doorways in order to rid their rooms of toxic evil spirits. The Chinese put the foo dog, a stone carving of a lionlike dog, outside their homes to ward off such spirits. The Japanese place pillars of salt outside the entryway of homes and businesses in order to avert evil forces. To deter toxic spirits and the ill wishes of toxic people, a Hindu in India will place a lit candle in the palm of his hand and encircle his face three times while spitting three times. Many Persians will burn a dried vegetable called *esfand* over flames in order to rid their homes of an evil eye or the energy of a toxic person. Similarly, people from India will often cut a turnip and throw it away, symbolically discarding a toxic person from their life. Many Chinese carry a small pocket knife as a symbol to cut or kill evil spirits, while Chinese babies often wear bells on their feet when they begin to walk, to frighten malevolent spirits.

When Persians have received a toxic comment that they feel could trigger the "evil eye," they will touch or point to a sharp pin they wear. Babies in various Latin American countries will sometimes have a sandstone or a black onyx bead pinned to their diaper to protect them from the "evil eye." In Italy, a golden ram's horn charm worn around the neck symbolizes protection against the evil eye, or *malocchio,* while in many Eastern European countries, as well as in African cultures, a glass bead that looks like an eye is a symbolic amulet worn to keep away a hex from a toxic or jealous person.

In various Asian cultures, a mirror is attached strategically to a building in order to deflect evil influences. Some Eastern Europeans carry sachets of salt and pepper—salt to "burn" the eyes of anyone looking askance at them and pepper to "sneeze out" any evil or toxic thoughts against them. Red items may be placed in their homes, or red objects worn on their bodies.

Certain Arab cultures also believe in the power of the evil eye. The people never speak of any happiness in their lives, for fear that the "evil spirit" may take it from them. This is also true in certain Jewish traditions, the word *kineahora* being uttered to avoid an evil eye after speaking about something positive.

In Singapore and in Malaysia, a *bomoh* or medicine man uses a series of chants and various herbs, while in China a Taoist medium and in Mexico a *curandero* are summoned to do the same thing—to lift the spell of the evil eye transmitted by a toxic person.

Many Africans and Caribbeans stick pins in various parts of voodoo dolls' anatomy in hopes the toxic people in their lives feel the pain.

Buddhism teaches that evil demons attack people who do not protect themselves by wearing various talismans or using magical nostrums designed to break the spell that threatens life.

No matter what culture we come from, we *all* share similar feelings and similar emotions, from happiness to sadness to fear to doubt to anger to surprise to boredom to love, as anthropologists have discovered. *All* of us want to experience kindness and respect from others. *All* of us want to hear kind words that will give us a meaningful place on this earth. Unfortunately, in today's hostile and all too often ugly world, society's pressures and our own insecurities and feelings of inadequacy limit our treating one another with the dignity and respect we all deserve.

Knowing how to defuse the toxins that are verbally hurled at us can help us to eliminate the hate, anger, and prejudice that infect our world, with brother unnecessarily hating brother. Each day, we see how improper handling of toxic people in our lives can lead to self-destruction.

As of today, you will *never* need to be a victim of not knowing how to handle a toxic person. You will *never* have to be the target of other people's verbal darts. This book will guide you in making sure that you know what to say and how to say it to people who get under your skin. You will learn that you have options and new tools to cope with some of the most miserable people in your life.

This book is a survival guide not only to help you interact better with the nasty people in your life but to prevent you from becoming a toxic person to others and to yourself. The purpose of the book is twofold. In the first section, the Toxic People Quiz and the presentation of thirty "Toxic Terrors" will enable you to identify the actual toxic people in your life and teach you how to treat them. You will learn to recognize some common toxic comments that toxic people make and to understand why they make them.

The second part of the book will teach you ten successful methods for handling a toxic person effectively and easily, so that you no longer have to let your bad feelings fester inside you. You will learn the best techniques to use with certain people in your daily life, as well as with each of the thirty Toxic Terrors. You will learn, too, how to revitalize a toxic relationship—or to close the door for good.

This book will make you laugh and may even make you cry as you identify with the people in the stories—real people whom I have interviewed throughout my travels and have worked with in my private practice.

You no longer have to suffer stomach pains or hives, overeat or undereat, develop heart disease or even cancer, as you hang on to negativity, anger, and hatred, thinking obsessively about that toxic person in your life. You will learn the quick, easy, and effective tools and devices that have helped so many of my clients handle toxic people. These techniques can now help *you* to live a happier and more productive life.

Finally, this book is also designed to help you become a better person, not toxic to others—or to yourself. By learning how to handle negative people and become more stress-free and communicative, you will in turn have the opportunity to develop richer, more productive personal and business relationships. As your self-esteem increases, you will become happier, more loving, and more lovable. You may even find your finances improving. Equipping yourself to handle the pressures of toxic people, you will become freer and more creative. Thereby you will be able to take more risks and have a richer life.

When you learn how to get the monkey off your back and the hurt out of your heart, magical things will happen to you. You will begin to see the world as having a new set of possibilities. By incorporating the tools in this book, you won't have to be the victim of a toxic person ever again.

CHAPTER 1

Is There a Toxic Person in Your Life?

- **Toxic People Quiz**

- **Emotional Symptoms**

- **Behavioral Symptoms**

- **Physical Symptoms**

- **Communication Symptoms**

- **What Your Answers Mean**

TOXIC PEOPLE QUIZ

•

To start you thinking about toxic people, I have composed the Toxic People Quiz. It shows the wide range of effects a toxic person might have on you and how every area of your life can be affected. Even without doing individual evaluations by means of the quiz, you will learn how to identify the toxic people in your life.

To begin, think of a person whom you do not particularly like, who makes you miserable, and whom you have difficulty getting along with. Answer *yes* or *no* to the following questions in four categories: Emotional Symptoms, Behavioral Symptoms, Physical Symptoms, and Communication Symptoms.

Emotional Symptoms

1. Do you feel emotionally numb after you talk to this person?

2. Are you in a bad mood after being around the person?

3. Do you feel that the person "deep down" doesn't like you, even though he or she never says mean things to you?

4. Do you come away feeling devalued when you have been around this person?

5. Do you feel "dirty" after being with this person?

6. Do you feel emotionally empty when you're around the person?

7. Do you feel less than intelligent or less than qualified after talking to this person?

8. Do you often get sad or depressed in this person's presence or afterward?

9. Do you feel unattractive after being with the person?

10. Do you feel tense or nervous around the person?

11. Do you feel angry and irritable around the person?

12. Do you lack energy after being around the person?

13. Does this person make you feel disgusted?

14. Do you feel like escaping emotionally through food, alcohol, drugs, or sex?

15. Do you find yourself bingeing or starving as a reaction to this person?

16. Does the person ignore you around others, so you feel like a "nonperson"?

17. Does this person annoy or hurt you by making you the butt of jokes, then laugh it off and say, "I was just kidding"?

18. Do you feel betrayed by the person?

19. Do you feel constantly judged by the person—you can do no right?

20. Do you feel that this person constantly puts you down or belittles you, especially in front of others?

21. Do you lack respect for the person or does he or she disrespect you?

22. Do you feel emotionally abused by the person?

23. Do you feel that things are hopeless after being around the person?

24. Does the person make you feel like crying more often than not?

25. Do you feel emotional relief when you are away from the person?

26. Do you ever fantasize about seeing him or her suffer or be hurt and feel joy at the prospect?

27. Would you rejoice if you never had to see the person again?

Behavioral Symptoms

28. Do you want to get away from him or her physically?

29. Do you drink more than usual or take drugs after being around this person?

30. Do you find yourself overeating or not eating at all when you are or have been around the person?

31. Do you have the urge to punch or do bodily harm to the person at times?

32. Do you plan ways to avoid the person?

33. Does the person try to sabotage you by doing things behind your back?

34. Does the person depersonalize you or negate your importance?

35. Does the person treat you differently in public than in private?

36. Do you act uncharacteristically submissive or aggressive in the person's presence?

Physical Symptoms

37. Does the person give you a headache?

38. Do you scrunch up your face, knit your brow, and tense your nostrils whenever you are around or even think about this person?

39. Do you feel nauseous when with the person or afterward?

40. Do you cringe whenever you're around the person?

41. Do you have difficulty catching your breath?

42. Is there tension in your neck and back?

43. Does your heart beat faster as though you are having a panic attack?

44. Have you gained or lost a significant amount of weight after being around the person for a while?

45. Do you sweat more around the person?

46. Is there a tightness in your throat when you talk to this person?

47. Do you lack energy or feel physically weak around the person?

48. Do you have a cough or a tickle in your throat whenever you're around this person?

49. Do you develop skin blotches or hives from being around the person?

50. Are you repulsed or do you recoil when the person touches you?

51. Does this person touch you aggressively?

52. Do you not want to touch or be physically near this person?

53. Do you have eye tics when you are around the person?

54. Do his or her mannerisms annoy or disgust you, causing you embarrassment?

55. Do you want to run away from this person and never see him or her again?

Communication Symptoms

56. Do you find that you walk on eggshells, are afraid to be yourself, and choose your words carefully when you talk to this person?

57. Is the person condescending toward you?

58. Is the expression on your face tense when you talk to the person?

59. Does the person speak harshly or aggressively to you?

60. Do you use a harsh or hostile tone in talking to this person?

61. Do you find that the person makes ugly or snide comments to you?

62. Does the sound of his or her voice repel you?

63. Do you find yourself lashing out verbally when talking to this person?

64. Do you stutter or stammer around the person?

65. Do you often yell or scream at the person?

66. Does the way he or she communicates nonverbally (i.e., with gestures, posture, and facial expression) turn you off?

67. Does the person make negative, sarcastic comments to you, followed by "I was only kidding" when he or she sees your reaction?

68. Are you often at a loss for words when talking to the person?

69. Do you find yourself not wanting to talk to the person on the phone?

70. Do you clam up when you're around the person?

71. Do you find yourself taking issue with everything the person says?

72. Does the person negate almost everything you say?

73. Do you feel at peace or relieved when you haven't spoken to the person for a while?

74. Does this person abuse you verbally?

75. **Does the person often use foul language around you?**

76. **Do you use foul language around this person?**

77. **Do you feel that his or her value system is so opposed to yours that you cannot even talk to him or her?**

78. **Do you feel you are speaking two different languages and can't communicate?**

WHAT YOUR ANSWERS MEAN

•

Yes answers to even a few of these questions mean that you are dealing with someone who is toxic to you.

As you can see from the quiz, toxic people may affect different areas of your well-being. And different toxic people may affect you differently. They can change the way you behave and the way you feel.

From this quiz you can see that sometimes when you don't feel good emotionally or physically, it could be the result of dealing with a toxic person!

In the next chapter, I'll cover the behavior of toxic people, showing how they operate and what their effect is on you. If you had trouble thinking of a toxic person, the next chapter will clarify the characteristics.

CHAPTER 2

TOXIC BEHAVIOR

- Toxic Speech

- Putting Their Feet and Everything Else into Their Mouths

- Backhanded Compliments—What Did They Really Say and Mean?

- Making Toxic Comments to Ourselves

- The "I Was Only Kidding" Syndrome

- Listen Carefully

- Swear Words Are Not the Only Toxic Word Triggers

As you saw from the questions in Chapter 1, toxic people can affect any area of your well-being. Despite the fact that they come in a range of types, they all share certain qualities in their behavior and motivation. In this chapter, I'll take a look at some of their distinguishing behavior, specifically their toxic language. In Chapter 3, I'll cover what motivates their actions.

T O X I C   S P E E C H

•

"I was shocked."
"I was humiliated."
"I couldn't believe what I heard."
"I was dumbfounded."
"I was numb."
"What a jerk!"
"How insensitive!"
"Can you believe what he said?"

These are some of the reactions I hear every day in my practice after a client has relayed a comment made by a toxic person. In every case, my client feels hurt. In every case, my client is angry. In every case, my client is shocked at how rude and insensitive a particular person was.

Usually, the client will try to rationalize it, saying things such as: "Well, it's her problem" or "He's just a jerk" or "She must be unhappy" or "He's probably jealous." No matter how hard my client tries to justify the toxic person's negative comment, it still hurts. It continues to hurt long after it is said. Toxic comments resonate in people's thoughts.

Whoever said "Sticks and stones can break my bones, but words can never hurt me" was dead wrong. Negative words and comments hurt, destroy, and maim the psyche.

Seven-year-old Amy Hagadorn from Fort Wayne, Indiana, wrote a letter to Santa Claus. Born with cerebral palsy, she wanted kids not to make fun of her because of the way she walked and talked.

That this little girl suffered not just from her physical condition but from the cruel and ugly words of her classmates is heartbreaking. All she wanted was what everyone else wants and deserves—acceptance and kindness.

Hostile words can cut you quicker and deeper than any sword. While a sword wound may heal after a few weeks, leaving only a hint of a scar, verbal wounds can persist a lot longer and leave a deep scar that lasts forever.

People say rude, ugly, and insensitive things for a variety of reasons—to make themselves feel better, because they are jealous, because they are having a bad day, because they can't stand you, because they are ignorant. However, when you are the victim of their verbal barbs, you rarely think about their reasons for saying them or where their head is. Instead you feel the punch and you definitely hurt.

A very dear friend of mine was forty-two and had still not met the man of her dreams. She was a very loving and maternal person who was financially successful and wanted to have a child.

Chloe could not find anybody to have a child with and did not want any legal problems with custody, so she decided to go to a sperm bank. Nine months later, Chloe gave birth to a baby, who is now a bright, articulate, gorgeous, delightful little girl.

Chloe never minded answering any questions that her friends or acquaintances had about her situation or the potential problems of having a fatherless child. What she did mind was strangers who, having heard about what she did, asked her intimate questions.

One day she went out on a double date. Her date, who fully accepted what Chloe had done, shared the sperm bank story with the other couple. The woman, whom Chloe had just met, immediately remarked in a hostile and rude tone, "Ugh, I could never do that—that's disgusting. What if the sperm had AIDS in it? Besides, what are you going to tell your child when she asks who her father is?" She chuckled and said sarcastically, "Are you going to tell her that her father was a test tube full of sperm?"

Chloe was in shock, as was everyone at the table. At first she wanted to punch the woman in the face. Then she wanted to say, "Look, lady, how are you going to tell your own child that you are as ugly on the inside as you are on the outside?" Instead, in order to preserve her dignity and to spare the other guests further embarrassment, she calmly remarked, "When my daughter is old enough I will tell her the truth." Then, as she did not want to spend another millisecond with this rude and obnoxious woman, she asked her date to take her home.

People often make toxic comments not because they want to but because they are ignorant or think they are being cute and funny. In fact, they end up appearing thoughtless and insensitive. Although I firmly believe that most people do not aim to hurt others or to make them feel unhappy, when they do get out of line they definitely need to be put in their place.

Even though Chloe's immediate reaction of wanting to hit the woman may have been a good fantasy, asking how she would tell her own child she was as ugly inside as outside would have been an even better and more productive response.

Deflecting negative comments made by toxic people is a skill you'll learn later with my Ten Techniques.

PUTTING THEIR FEET AND EVERYTHING ELSE INTO THEIR MOUTHS

•

In Chloe's case, the rude woman obviously had a problem dealing with someone's decision to have a baby created by sperm from a sperm bank. The situation brought out a hostile reaction in her.

However, most people are not as openly vindictive or hostile. Instead they are ignorant and insensitive, which is why they usually end up putting their feet and everything else into their mouths. People say stupid things when they do not mean to. Most of the time, people are just curious. They want to know, but they don't have the class or the couth to be diplomatic in gathering the information. These are not bad, mean, or evil people. They are merely unconscious of others' feelings as they let out their uncensored stream of consciousness. Whether their remarks are rude or insensitive or hurtful never crosses their mind.

When they do finally become conscious that what they said was stupid, it is often too late.

This has happened to most of us at one time or another. We have been on either the giving or the receiving end of a foot put in the mouth at another's expense, much as Amy experienced.

Amy had recently put on weight because she had been so busy she had not been able to keep to her once rigorous exercise schedule. At a luncheon one day, she ran into Danielle, whom she hadn't seen in a while. Instead of looking Amy in the face and saying hello, Danielle reached down and patted Amy's stomach, saying, "So when is the baby due?" Amy was in shock; how much weight she must have put on for Danielle to say such an awful thing!

Though Amy was burning up inside, she managed to smile as she removed Danielle's hand from her stomach and replied, "The baby is due when I get married and get pregnant someday." Danielle was as red as a beet. If there had been a hole next to her, she would gladly have crawled in and covered it up behind her.

Yet, how many of us haven't made undiplomatic comments without meaning to. This happened to a dear friend of mine, Roxanne, who was finally fixed up with Rob, her dream date, whom she'd had a crush on for several years.

A mutual friend set them up when Rob divorced his wife. The date went well until Rob said, "I have to tell you, Roxanne, you look a lot like my sister." Roxanne was taken aback at his comment but smiled and cocked her head curiously. Rob then pulled out a photo of his sister to show her. Upon seeing the photo, Roxanne blurted out, "Oh, no way—she's so ugly." Rob's smiling face turned to stone as he quickly put the photo back into his wallet. He hardly spoke a word to her as he drove her home. Roxanne tried to apologize the entire way home, but Rob was silent and numb. He didn't hear a word she said, and that was the end of their potential relationship.

BACKHANDED COMPLIMENTS—WHAT DID
THEY REALLY SAY AND MEAN?

•

When people give you a compliment, they are, in essence, giving you a gift. A compliment is a key that can unlock communication— a key that can open up a channel of understanding between two people. When it is sincere and spoken in a kind and nurturing tone, it can be the cement that binds a relationship.

However, when it is insincere, spoken with sarcasm, jealousy, or meanness, or when kind words are followed by a harsh verbal slap in the face, it is called a backhanded compliment.

I was in Dallas, Texas, once, to give a lecture. The limousine to take me to the lecture hall had pulled up, and my female escort and I were about to get in. We both noticed a penny on the ground in front of the limousine.

My escort immediately remarked, in a Dallas twang, "My, my, there's a penny. You'd better pick it up—it'll bring you good luck. And you'll definitely need all the luck possible today." What a nasty person! I immediately thought to myself. Had she said, "My, my, there's a penny. You'd better pick it up—it will bring you good luck," in a pleasant tone, my reaction would have been completely different. Perhaps I would have wanted to speak with her on the ride to the lecture. Because of her backhanded compliment, I didn't even bother with her.

Somebody may say nice things to you in one breath: "You're really so attractive. I love the way you're dressed. You really are put together well," and then completely contradict it: "but your hair looks so messy—you should really wear it up." This is typical of backhanded compliments. They start out pleasantly, making you feel great, and end up ugly, causing you to feel awful.

You may think that the person means well and intends to say loving, supportive things to you, but these backhanded compliments are really conveying: "I can't stand you" or "I'm jealous of you" or "I don't like you" or "You don't have it all" or "Who do you think you are?" or "You need to be put in your place" or "You're no better than I am."

The tone of voice is a surefire giveaway of a person's actual feelings about you. It is often not *what* is said but *how* that can reflect people's sincerity. Sarcastic tones, loud tones, and monotones often express hostile feelings.

MAKING TOXIC COMMENTS TO OURSELVES
•

Sometimes we are so used to having toxic comments hurled at us by others that we begin to feel comfortable with them. Therefore we continue where our verbal tormentors have left off and say horrible things to ourselves.

How many times have we told ourselves that we were fat, dumb, ugly, or disgusting? "I did such a dumb thing—I'm so stupid." "I look so horrible—I'm such a pig."

I call these self-denigrating statements "poison brain food." The more often you say awful things to yourself, the more they become ingrained in your mind and become part of how you think about yourself.

I remember the old wives' tale "If you make an ugly face, it might freeze and stay that way." Perhaps your mother or grandmother said it to stop you from making silly faces. After a while you realized that this was nonsense—your face never did freeze—so you continued to make ugly and funny faces.

However, as you grew older, it turned out that the "old wives" tale was right! If you constantly frown or have a negative expression on your face, your facial muscles will indeed develop that way. This is one reason why some people look much older than their chronological age.

Similarly, those who walk around with an upbeat expression develop more pleasing, happy faces.

What your elders said about your face "freezing that way" definitely holds true for your thoughts about yourself and your words to yourself.

If you say, "I can't do it" or "I'm not good enough," you definitely won't ever do it, and you will never be good enough.

If in the recesses of your mind you say, "I can never shoot this basket," "I can never hit this golf ball right," "I can never lose weight," "I can never have a healthy relationship," "I'll never be rich," "I can never find a good job," I guarantee that *you won't.* Your words will always return to haunt you, becoming a self-fulfilling prophecy.

If you continue to say ugly things about yourself, others will pick up on it and follow suit. After all, if you make these toxic statements, they must be true, since you know yourself best. When you put it out in the universe that "I am a jerk" or "My thighs are so fat" or "My hair is awful," you are giving others permission to say the same things to you and to treat you as badly as you treat yourself.

When I was an undergraduate, we had a rule in the dormitory: if a guy told you he was a jerk, you should believe him, because he probably was. After all, who knew better than he? Those young ladies who negated the comments made by self-proclaimed "jerks" and replied, "No you're not. You're a sweet guy," always found out that the guy was right. Eventually he did turn out to be a jerk.

Sometimes we say negative and toxic things about ourselves in order to sound humble. Whatever culture we may come from, our parents have ingrained it in us not to brag or get "bigheaded." In reality, our self-deprecation is not perceived positively as humility. Instead it is perceived negatively, and others have a lowered opinion of us.

One of my clients was devastated by her boyfriend's affectionate name for her, "Thunder Thighs." "After all," she told me, "if he said how horrible my thighs looked, unsolicited, they must be in bad shape, and everybody probably thinks they look horrible too."

"Unsolicited?" I questioned. I pointed out that practically everything she talked about had to do with her body and especially her "fat" thighs and how she hated them.

"Really?" she asked. "I had no idea I bring it up that much."

"Absolutely," I replied. "You talk about it so much—so openly and so freely—that others feel comfortable about joining in, thereby adding injury to insult. Your boyfriend isn't trying to be mean; instead he's teasing you about your thighs because you have left the door wide open."

That was a rude awakening for her, as she had never previously been conscious of her negativity about herself.

Constantly saying toxic things about yourself can affect not only your personal relationships, as we have just seen, but your business relationships as well.

The great lesson to learn here is that what you say about yourself definitely makes a difference in how people perceive you and what they in turn say about you.

THE "I WAS ONLY KIDDING" SYNDROME

•

Has anyone ever said something shocking or bizarre to you, watched your face turn red with anger or contort in disgust, and immediately, in an attempt to negate the hostile comment, claimed that he or she was "only kidding"? Meanwhile you feel as though you have just been flattened by a steamroller.

Sigmund Freud's theory that there are no jokes, "only truth," readily applies in these instances. People who say or do a mean thing to you, then tell you that they were "only kidding," are revealing a lot. They are telling you how negatively they really feel about you.

People who use the "I was only kidding" syndrome often want to get your attention or elicit a reaction from you. They may succeed in doing so, but your reaction is likely to be so negative that you may never want to deal with them again.

When Joseph, the man you are dating, smiles and asks how old your dog, Scruffy, is, you smile back and fondly reply, "Five years old." To his response: "Isn't that old enough to be put to sleep?" your brow furrows, your eyes squint, and your face contorts in disgust, as you blurt out, *"What?"* You then see a big grin on Joseph's face as he tries to defuse your anger by saying, "I was only kidding!" In reality, Joseph does not like Scruffy. In fact, he subconsciously wishes Scruffy would disappear, especially when Joseph is trying to kiss you and the dog jumps all over him. When he is trying to make love to you and Scruffy is all over the bed, Joseph would not be too upset if your pet died then and there.

His hostile statement followed by "I was only kidding" reflects his animosity toward your dog and resentment at having to share your affection with the little creature. When you confront Joseph on the matter, he makes you feel as though it's your fault, saying, "What's wrong with you—can't you take a joke?" thereby arousing your guilt for lacking a sense of humor.

Often the "I was only kidding" jokester—the one who has perpetrated the verbal crime—puts *you* on the defensive. Usually, he or she feels so insecure and so hurt, is so unable to express vulnerability and to communicate feelings, that he or she lashes out at you—making you the "bad" person for getting angry at negative things said to *you*. After all, he or she was "only kidding."

Ursula found out just how much anger and insecurity Gil harbored toward her when he said he was "only kidding" after telling her that he thought she was sexier-looking before she had her breast implants. Ursula was devastated, and nothing Gil said could negate his initial comment. He did not succeed in putting her on the defensive or making her feel guilty as he asked, "Come on, don't you have a sense of humor—what's wrong with you?" Instead she pursued it relentlessly, until they got into a screaming match and Ursula finally insisted on breaking off their engagement.

Then, after hours of tension, tears, and trying to get to the truth, Gil admitted that he was scared of losing Ursula. He felt that now that she had bigger breasts and dressed more provocatively, she made more men's heads turn. Gil got jealous and insecure, fearful of being supplanted by another man, whom she might find more attractive. In actuality, he liked her new breasts but felt so threatened about their effect on other men that he resorted to putting a verbal dagger in Ursula's chest, then abruptly pulling it out with "I was only kidding." She was left staggering and in a state of complete shock.

It was only through Ursula's relentless confrontation that they were able to resolve the matter. This resolution allowed her verbal stab wound to heal.

Whenever you hear "I was only kidding," what you are really hearing is "I am not kidding: I am resentful, insecure, or just plain angry at you"—and that is no joke.

LISTEN CAREFULLY

•

Toxic people reveal what they really mean through their toxic comments.

Faith, one of my clients, was an attractive and talented actress who really believed in herself. Unfortunately, her agent, Jake, didn't share her confidence, and he revealed himself in a toxic comment he made to her. My client had gone on an audition, and apparently the casting agent said to Jake, "I don't think she has any talent." Jake relayed this to Faith in an undiplomatic way and floored her. She then replied, "Well, Jake, just don't give up on me. We're in this for the long haul." Jake replied, "Oh, don't worry. I won't—yet." A few seconds of silence followed that word "yet." Though Faith didn't like hearing it, the truth came to light.

The up side of this story is that Faith dumped Jake before he dumped her. She ended up getting one of Hollywood's top agents, and now her career is going full speed ahead.

You have to listen not only to what you *want* the person to say but to what is *actually* said. Words are not cheap. Words are very powerful. They can teach you so much when you pay attention and listen to every one of them. You will be surprised at the hidden intentions you can decode.

SWEAR WORDS ARE NOT THE ONLY TOXIC WORD TRIGGERS

•

Sometimes people don't even have to say much. They just have to start a sentence with such words or phrases as: "You should" or "Why didn't you"; "You should have," "You'd better," or "Why can't you"; "I don't agree," "No way," "I can't believe that," or "That's not true," in order to inflame tempers and trigger defensive responses.

Nothing they add to the sentence matters. Just hearing these toxic word triggers can turn listeners off, causing them either to tune out or to become verbally aggressive toward a speaker.

Whenever you hear a toxic word trigger, you may be dealing with a highly critical and judgmental toxic person, as Christina discovered. Christina told Mary that she had found a new spiritual path. Mary's response was, "Well, you should try Buddhism if you really want to follow the spiritual path," completely negating Christina's interest in her new belief system. Christina clammed up, not even wanting to talk to her so-called friend for the rest of the evening.

If you hear toxic word triggers, just remember that you are not too far away from having your negative feelings toward the person surface.

The effect one's words can have upon another is expressed in the Bible, in Proverbs 18:21: "Death and Life are in the power of the tongue."

Indeed, hundreds of crimes have been perpetrated on those who uttered toxic words. We keep hearing news accounts of people's words triggering a violent crime against them. Nowadays, saying toxic things to people may cost you your life.

Toxic words by others can result, too, in senseless death at one's own hand. Sometimes verbal torments, constant harassment, and barrages of toxic words are just too much to handle. A person who can no longer take it may do what fifteen-year-old Megan Pauley of New Hampshire did. Megan's suicide note said that she could no longer endure the harassment by her peers and felt it was better to die than to live with the painful verbal torture. Unfortunately, Megan's case is not an isolated incident. Teenage suicide is on the rise around the globe, and peer pressure and low self-esteem are significant contributors.

Even though there has been increasing pressure to "fit in" and "be accepted" over the years, the punishment today for being different—even to the extent of not wearing the right labels—is more brutal and violent than ever before.

Teenagers aren't the only ones who suffer when they are constantly blasted by toxic taunts and comments. Adults feel the pain too, maybe even more so.

When I was doing my postdoctorate in medical genetics at Harbor UCLA Medical Center, I worked a great deal with dwarfs, or little people. One day I was escorting a little woman to an examination room. As we passed through the hospital lobby, two young children began making jokes about her, laughing hysterically. The mother joined in. I turned to these people and said, "I'm surprised at you! How dare you laugh at this woman because she's a small person? There is nothing funny about her." Embarrassed, they immediately stopped laughing, and the little woman turned to me and said, "You know, Dr. Glass, I appreciate so much what you did in trying to defend me, but I have to tell you, I'm used to it. I've heard it all my life."

Her words broke my heart. Why should anyone have to be *used* to hearing ugly verbiage fired at them like an angry dragon's breath. It is a tragic commentary on a society that laughs at others' misfortunes. This has nothing to do with humor. It reflects a moral sickness.

One cannot taunt, heckle, or demean people for their entire lives and expect them to take it. If the victims don't turn such attacks inward and ultimately become destroyed, they will often reach a breaking point and direct the hostility outward. One day, having just had all they can take, they may end up doing something horrific to others.

Therefore it comes as no surprise to read about a New York City subway motorman who, after numerous attempts to stop his coworkers from baiting and taunting and viciously teasing him about his stuttering, ended up wounding one of them, killing another, and finally killing himself.

Christ's comment in the New Testament, Matthew 15:11, best sums it up: "It is not that which goes into the mouth that defiles a man, but that which comes out of a mouth is what defiles a man."

If you use toxic words to another person, you *must* take full responsibility for the consequences. Know that *your words may never be forgotten.*

True, you may be so angry that you're going to explode, and you need to yell and use toxic words. You can yell, scream, rant and rave and say the ugliest things, but when you do so, realize that you are taking a chance of losing a friend forever, because *hurtful words are remembered* and *cannot* be taken back.

Too often we hurl toxic words at others like random bullets. We *have* to be responsible for what we say and how we use our verbal bullets. Like real bullets, toxic words not only can wound but can literally kill others—or ourselves.

CHAPTER 3

WHAT MAKES TOXIC PEOPLE ACT THE WAY THEY DO?

- Jealousy—The Root of All Toxicity

- Why Do They Hate You When You're Beautiful or Successful?

- Why Do They Like You Only When You're Successful or You Look Good?

- Why Do They Hate You When You Fail?

- Why Do They Hate You After They Know You?

- You Can't Please Everyone, So You've Got to Please Yourself

JEALOUSY—THE ROOT OF ALL TOXICITY

•

Jealousy is a primitive response. After all, why do dogs bark at a small child whom you are cooing over and admiring? Why are some wild animals willing to kill others in their pack who have more food than they do? Why do verbal and toilet-trained three-year-olds stop talking, regress into baby talk, or even begin to wet and soil their pants when a new infant arrives home?

It's because of jealousy and its concomitant envy—the discontent and feelings of inadequacy brought about by another's possessions, success, or love, and the desire to have them for oneself. While toxic people behave the way they do because they may be jealous of you, it is important to acknowledge that jealousy can cause you to behave in a toxic way also.

I witnessed an archetypical example of jealousy in action when I was nine years old and watched a children's television show that featured a children's beauty pageant. Two little contestants were standing in front of the cameras, holding hands anxiously as the drum roll was heard in the background, heralding the host's announcement of the next beauty queen. Finally, the big moment came and the name of the winner was called. At that point, the loser clenched her fist and punched the winner right in the face—in front of everyone. The winner began to cry hysterically because she'd been punched. The loser was crying hysterically because she'd lost. I, at home, was hysterical too, because I thought it was the most comical thing I had ever witnessed in my life, especially when the host failed to pry the girls apart and their respective mothers were screaming at each other and at the host, who was trying to regain his composure and some control of the show.

The little loser's reaction was a very basic response to watching someone else get what one wants. In essence, she felt jealous and angry for losing, so she lashed out at the winner.

Looking back on this incident as an adult, I find it isn't funny at all. Instead I see it as a blatant illustration of that negative element of the human condition that afflicts too many people, young and old—jealousy.

A male client of mine who was handsome, smart, and athletic got fixed up on a date with a lovely, attractive young woman. Since they were attracted to each other, they arranged a second date, this time to play racquetball. The woman, a former nationally ranked champion, kept winning, and he became angrier and angrier. Finally, he hit her deliberately in the head with a ball when she was standing with her back to him. Although he made it appear an accident and apologized profusely, he was inwardly happy that she was hurt and had to stop the game. Telling me the story, he smirked and snickered as he tried to show how clever he had been in preventing himself from being shown up by a "woman."

I was nauseated by this story. I saw that his weak character had been overcome by jealousy toward this woman who happened to be a better athlete than he was. He could not handle the fact that she outshone him, so he did just what the four-year-old "losing" beauty contestant did: he hit her.

Beatings due to jealousy are often not just physical but mental as well, involving mind games, cruel words, and nasty behavior.

As we go through life we see that there are haves and have-nots or, as we have come to view them most commonly, winners and losers. Sometimes we win, sometimes we lose at various things in life. There is no better feeling than that which winning produces, no worse feeling than losing. We feel depressed, victimized, and unworthy, often taking it out on ourselves by eating or drinking too much, escaping through drugs or through diversions that can get us in trouble. Many times we take out our anger and frustration at losing on others, usually people who are closest to us or whom we love the most. Their negative reactions to our treatment of them makes us feel worse about ourselves and perpetuates the cycle of our conviction that we are losers.

Looking at others "winning" reinforces our feelings of frustration. When we do happen to look outside ourselves and see our neighbor who "won," we end up feeling even worse about ourselves. After all, he has a big house, a kid at Harvard, a wife who loves him, a new sports car. He is in great physical shape, dresses well, has a lot of money, and takes vacations with his family twice a year to various places around the globe. He has great parties at his home, with lots of people who really seem to like him, and he and his wife always look as though they're having loads of fun. He is always smiling, and everyone you talk to seems to like him, so why do you hate his guts?

It is because he has it *all,* or at least you *think* he has it all. Instead of feeling happy for him, more inspired and motivated to do better yourself, you, along with many of us, will seek to destroy him.

You may seek to destroy your neighbor with sarcastic statements, discouraging responses, or sugar-on-your-lips, salt-in-your-eyes claims of happiness at his success. Your face and body language betray your words. The "winner" isn't deaf, dumb, or blind. He definitely knows what's going on, and it hurts him. It makes him feel extremely uncomfortable. It especially hurts someone you supposedly love or one who considers you a friend.

Jennifer told her dearest friend, Marilyn, a secret she had told no one else—that she was pregnant. The two women had had countless conversations, griping about their ticking biological clocks and discussing their desire for babies. Then Jennifer succeeded in getting pregnant. She couldn't wait to tell Marilyn, sure that she would be overcome with joy for her.

What a surprise Jennifer received! Instead of showing happiness, Marilyn swallowed hard and, with a pained and stiff expression, managed to say, "Wow, that's really great, I'm really excited for you!" in a monotone. Her words clearly belied her feelings. It didn't take a genius to figure out that Marilyn was not thinking about Jennifer's happiness and the baby she was going to have. Instead she was thinking about the baby she did not have. Marilyn was obviously jealous of her friend, and Jennifer definitely felt it. But rather than do what most people would—let her anger hurt their friendship, Jennifer gave Marilyn a huge hug.

Feelings of jealousy and envy usually surface when we experience inadequacy—when we lack something or feel that another person has more.

Jealousy is the key element that ends most relationships. In an informal survey of 105 people I conducted, in which people were asked the question "What broke up your friendship with a good friend?" over 75 percent attributed the rupture to their ex-friends' jealousy. This is particularly evident in intimate relationships if one of the parties fears that the other will leave him or her behind. Jealous, the person gets possessive and often lashes out verbally or physically.

In interviews with several psychologists and marriage and family counselors, I asked, "Why do spouses usually beat up on each other?" The consensus was that it is usually due to feelings of inadequacy by a spouse who feels so jealous of his or her mate and so insecure that violence is resorted to in order to gain more control over the relationship. Sometimes the violence is verbal and manifests itself as criticism.

Perhaps this is the reason for so many high-powered and well-respected businessmen, running huge companies and handling thousands of employees, who have verbally abusive wives at home. These women constantly nag and criticize them in order to achieve whatever power they can in the domestic realm and to knock them off their pedestals.

Criticism can be a good thing when offered with kind words in a loving, helpful tone. Also significant is who is criticizing you and why. Is it so that you can better yourself? Is it undertaken with sincerity and with your best interests at heart? If so, then you will not harbor negative feelings toward the one who is offering you criticism. In fact, you may even gain a greater respect for that person for telling you the truth. Often the constructive critic will couch criticism in positive tones and use polite words of encouragement and endearment.

On the other hand, there will be people who criticize you without having your best interests at heart. They lash out at you because they really don't like you or are jealous of you and they derive pleasure from telling you what is wrong with you.

Whoever points a finger at you in criticism must always look at him- or herself. After all, though one finger is pointing toward you, there are three fingers pointing backward at him- or herself. Therefore someone who is critical of you needs to examine his or her reasons.

A completely honest person will usually find a motive of jealousy, as you most likely have something he or she wants or lacks.

WHY DO THEY HATE YOU WHEN YOU'RE BEAUTIFUL OR SUCCESSFUL?

•

A few years ago, an advertising campaign for a shampoo featured gorgeous actress Kelly LeBrock (*The Woman in Red*) tossing her beautiful hair from side to side and saying, "Don't hate me because I'm beautiful." She went on to describe the virtues of the product, which she insisted was the reason for her beauty. I'm sure the shampoo helped, but I doubt it was the reason she was so beautiful. Yet it was an effective advertising campaign, as it made you warm up to the woman who made so bold a statement and it secured your attention for the rest of the ad.

Ours is a society that puts a top premium on physical appearance. Perhaps it starts in Hollywood, where the "beautiful people" live, and then permeates the country and the world.

Hollywood is an extreme and unfortunate shrine to humankind's physical appearance. Hollywood is definitely not a democracy. You are judged there on how you look and speak and who you are. Your life depends on it. I have seen beautiful, robust, voluptuous nineteen-year-old girls come into my Beverly Hills office crying hysterically because some producer or director told them they need to lose twenty pounds if they want the job. They starve themselves. They eat uncontrollably out of frustration and then force themselves to vomit. They take laxatives. They have liposuction and nose jobs. They get their teeth bonded and veneered. They get their breasts lifted and implanted, their skin peeled—all in the pursuit of beauty. Ironically, when they finally achieve the right weight, the right nose, the right teeth, and the right complexion, they run the risk of being "too beautiful" and getting rejected for the role they seek.

People harbor conflicted emotions toward those who are beautiful. This tends to become hatred or resentment for someone who *becomes* beautiful. Others feel very uncomfortable with a newly achieved attractiveness if they aren't secure about themselves.

Frieda, forty-five, was born with a hole in the roof of her mouth, a cleft palate, which was never surgically repaired. It was difficult to understand her very nasal speech. She had made an appointment after hearing me on a talk show. When she came into my office, I observed how poorly groomed she was. Her teeth were rotted, and she looked as though she hadn't bathed recently. She had long, stringy, greasy hair; outdated glasses; and a poor complexion. Very overweight, she wore unflattering clothing.

Besides her speech, I decided to help her improve her "total image." As a factory worker on an assembly line, she didn't have the funds to pay for an image makeover, so I enrolled the help of my plastic surgeon friend Dr. Henry Kawamoto and my dentist friend Dr. Henry Yamada, who agreed to use her as a "teaching case." After I'd explained her situation to others who could help her, my dermatologist friend took care of her skin problems; my hairdresser friend gave her an easy-to-manage, flattering haircut; and my optometrist friend gave her a visual exam and a pair of attractive eyeglasses, all for free. I contributed hours and hours of therapy to improve her speech and communication skills, not to mention hours of confidence-building and positive-thinking pep talks, so that she could do more with her life and live out her dreams. I put her on a healthy diet and an exercise program and taught her how to enhance her facial features with makeup. Finally, I took her to a discount designer clothing store and showed her how to shop for a few top-quality items that she could mix and match and how to accessorize these outfits.

Frieda looked great, sounded great, felt great, and now she was ready to get on with a new life.

Several months later, I received a disturbing phone call from Dr. Kawamoto. Frieda had come to his office as part of her postsurgical follow-up examination; her speech mechanism was now working properly, he said, but her speech had regressed. He also reported that she looked as she had prior to the surgery—unkempt, overweight, and poorly dressed—and wondered what had happened to the fabulous makeover.

Shocked, I immediately called Frieda and heard the monotonous, nasal tone we had worked hours and hours to eliminate. I said, "Frieda, what happened to you? We both worked so hard to help you improve your speech and your image." Without hesitation, she replied, "Well, my friends like me better the way I was before."

I felt as though someone had kicked the wind out of me. Not only did it sadden me to think of the devoted efforts and numerous hours thrown down the drain, but I was devastated that Frieda hadn't achieved the courage, inner strength, or knowledge to realize that these toxic people who now liked her the way she was before weren't really her friends. Instead they had been threatened by her newfound beauty and self-confidence.

Unfortunately, there are too many people like Frieda's so-called friends, who are so threatened by one's positive changes that they attempt sabotage. This is most common when a person is trying to break a drug, alcohol, or food dependency.

On the other hand, there are toxic people who will like you only when you are looking or feeling great.

WHY DO THEY LIKE YOU ONLY WHEN YOU'RE SUCCESSFUL OR YOU LOOK GOOD?

•

Tara hated the three-hundred-pound man Zane had become during their eight years of marriage. The weight eventually turned her off sexually. She could hardly breathe with his weight on top of her body and was disgusted by his labored breathing, his sweating, and his gross appearance. Every chance she got, she nagged him to lose weight. She used every possible approach, from cajoling him to threatening him. All her efforts failed. When one day he couldn't fit into his car, he finally enrolled in a residential weight-loss program, where he lost one hundred fifty pounds.

When Zane emerged from the program, he was even more handsome than he'd been when he and Tara first married. He had more manly features and a beautiful head of thick, distinguished-looking salt-and-pepper hair. He worked out with weights and became a hunk. Women went nuts over Zane and began to flirt with him unmercifully. People who previously wouldn't give him the time of day were initiating conversations with him. Friends invited him out more, and his lighting business improved.

Zane started getting cocky, infused with self-assurance. Tara, scared, thought: I created a monster. She didn't know how to handle the new and improved Zane. At first she was seductive and clamored constantly to make love; his response was lukewarm. Enraged at his rejection, she went back to her old nagging ways, only this time it was about the way Zane dressed, how much money he spent, and other petty things. Zane recalled how horribly she had treated him when he was fat, and this time he would not tolerate it. He resented the fact that she tried to be sexual with him only after he was thin. He had no second thoughts when it came to filing for divorce.

We can all relate to Zane's experience. People do not want to be liked just because they look good. If they discover this to be the case—as after a physical change for the better—it leads to anger and resentment.

There was a marvelous example on *Donahue* of how you resent the heck out of someone when he or she reacts positively to you only because you look good. The *Donahue* staff put a beautiful thin woman into a latex "fat suit," dressed her in large-size clothing, and filmed her meeting a blind date at a restaurant. Within a few minutes of their meeting, the man started talking about how this girl should get into an exercise program and should eat only certain foods. He got more and more repulsive by the minute as he continued to talk down to this woman, blatantly referring to her weight throughout dinner. He even ordered for her, determining what she could and couldn't eat.

The next day the man appeared on the *Donahue* stage, where he thought he was going to be a member of a "Would you date a fat person?" panel. He was prepared to talk about his experiences and give his opinions.

Suddenly a gorgeous slender woman came out of the audience and sat next to him on the stage. Donahue asked the man if this was the type of woman he would date. The man smiled and put his arm around her in a lecherous manner, at which the woman pushed him away and practically punched him in the nose.

Needless to say, this slender beauty was the woman who had worn the "fat suit." She got angrier and angrier as she related her experiences with the man while she was "fat." Despite this, the man kept trying to put his arm around her. Finally, she yelled to Phil, "Tell this jerk to keep his hands off me or I'll walk off the stage."

This man proved repellent to everyone who watched the show. It was an ugly and painful experience to witness, first, rudeness to a person on the basis of appearance alone and, then, seductive treatment when the same individual looked good.

Anger is only natural here: nobody wants to feel loved merely because he or she looks good. Unfortunately, this is all too prevalent in our society.

WHY DO THEY HATE YOU WHEN YOU FAIL?

•

In Hollywood, an actor who is on top is invited to all the "A" list parties, has seats at the best restaurants, and is photographed relentlessly by paparazzi. When this same person stars in a TV show or film that turns out not to be a success, what happens is fascinating. The volume of party invitations decreases, there is a shortage of good seats in restaurants, and the paparazzi lose interest.

One of my clients had a number one hit record. Her concerts were packed, and offers to do television and film were abundant. She was at a party every night and treated like the belle of the ball. Then her next album flopped, and people turned mean and ugly overnight. She never regained her top-dog status. The Hollywood truism is that you are only as good as your last picture. People there will not give you the time of day when you fail.

In the "real world" too, people can treat you unfairly just because you have failed. After resenting you for your success, they can end up hating you for your failure.

Why is it that when people are down, it is so easy to hop on the bandwagon and kick them even lower?

Donald Trump had it all—he was rich, famous, confident, and intelligent, had social status and a gorgeous wife. The press couldn't adulate him enough—until he had an affair with Marla Maples. It wasn't a discreet affair: Marla and Ivana, Donald's wife at the time, confronted each other on the ski slopes of Aspen in front of Donald—and the world.

After that incident it appeared as though Donald's star had fallen into the toilet. He no longer had the Midas touch. He lost millions of dollars as well as his good reputation, and he lost his wife. Ivana emerged as the victor—carving out a successful life for herself with a line of clothing, with books and lectures, and with an active social life and a new man. Everyone appeared to take her side.

People were mad at Donald for the way he had handled his life. He had been their hero. Even though he finally married "the other woman," many people felt that Marla hooked Donald because she got pregnant.

Why was the public so ready to rejoice in Donald's failure and to continue kicking him when he was down? People became embroiled in the Trump soap opera because Donald was a hero who fulfilled the American Dream and then blew it. He disappointed those who lived through him, vicariously, and thought he had the ideal life to which they could aspire. Having represented someone we could look up to, he turned out to be just like us, so we were angry. We wanted a hero.

In essence, people cannot stand you for failing because your failure brings out the potential for failure in them.

The toxic comments people make about the homeless or the obese, about people who have lost their jobs, their homes, or their health, or those who have had a series of tragedies in their lives, arise from fear. It is the There-But-for-the-Grace-of-God-Go-I syndrome. People are afraid that similarly bad things could happen to them. Instead of showing compassion and lending a hand, they find it much easier to deal with the pain by converting it to hostility or avoiding it in hopes that it will go away. This way they mitigate any feelings of vulnerability that might surface in them.

WHY DO THEY HATE YOU AFTER THEY KNOW YOU?

•

We have all heard the maxim "Familiarity breeds contempt." In fact, familiarity should breed love. Why do people who know you best end up treating you worst? Why is it that people behave so much better to perfect strangers than to those they are close to? It all boils down to a lack of self-esteem.

Remember the Groucho Marx joke: "I wouldn't want to be a member of any club that would have *me* as a member"? Anyone who would want him as a friend, he thought, surely didn't have very good judgment!

Though we laugh at this self-deprecating humor, it is not funny. All too often, this sentiment infects families, friendships, and marriages in today's society.

If you feel awful about yourself or unworthy of being loved, how can you love anyone else? In my practice, I have heard countless stories about people who, beginning a friendship or relationship, are giving, loving, open, and generous, then turn into terrorists.

My client Dolores had such a Jekyll-and-Hyde experience with a man who, during their engagement, treated her like a queen. Dominic showered her with surprise gifts. He took her to the finest restaurants and attended to all her needs. He was affectionate, called her five times a day just to tell her he loved her, ran baths for her, and prepared candlelight dinners.

After they married, everything changed. Dominic became selfish, bored, sullen, negative, and downright hostile. It was only after extensive marital counseling that Dominic could reveal that he felt he didn't deserve Dolores. He had tried to sabotage their relationship by doing horrible and insensitive things. Having worked hard to get her in his life, now he was working just as hard to get rid of her. With the additional help of individual therapy, Dominic was able to improve his self-esteem and self-love, so that he could transfer these positive feelings to his relationship with Dolores.

Dominic and Dolores were lucky ones who were able to salvage their relationship, but in most instances a person who is motivated by self-hatred or insecurity can never really feel good about anyone else in his or her life, whether it be in an intimate relationship, a working relationship, or a family relationship. This is why so many families are able to treat outsiders with respect, dignity, and kindness but behave rudely, hatefully, and disrespectfully toward each other. They give those who are closest to them the same self-loathing and disrespect they give themselves. It all boils down to an absence of self-respect, self-love, and self-esteem.

You Can't Please Everyone, So You've Got to Please Yourself

•

Toxic people hate you when you succeed and when you are beautiful. They also hate you when you fail. Thus you can't win for losing, and you lose for winning. People are going to either like you or dislike you for your successes or your failures, and there is *nothing* you can do about it.

The late Ricky Nelson, a 1950s teen idol, tried to make a comeback in the early 1970s and was literally booed off the stage in Madison Square Garden when he didn't play his old nostalgic songs. It was an error in judgment: the audience had come to hear the old familiar songs. In his pain, he ended up writing a song about the experience, "The Garden Party," which became one of the best-selling songs of the decade.

"You can't please everyone, so you've got to please yourself," said the song. These words should be branded on everyone's mind, to be called upon for comfort whenever one feels ostracized or alienated. Techniques I'll teach you later in this book will enable you to deal with toxic actions taken as a result of jealousy or low self-esteem.

So many of us go through life trying to please everyone and trying to have everyone like us when, in reality, there will be certain people who may never like us. We may be toxic to these people for no known reason. In turn, their actions are toxic to us.

People need to be taught from the start—in childhood—that it doesn't matter why they are picked on: whether because they are too fat or too thin, too tall or too short, too blond or too dark- or light-skinned. They must learn early on that as long as they love and accept themselves, however they look and whatever their characteristics, it doesn't matter what anyone else thinks or says about them.

If we continued to think like this into our adult years, we would certainly be a lot happier and experience fewer disappointments, as we wouldn't have to try to please anyone but ourselves.

Perhaps actor Bill Cosby's comment best summarizes this point: "I don't know the key to success, but the key to failure is trying to please everybody." How right he is!

CHAPTER 4

IDENTIFYING THE TOXIC PEOPLE IN YOUR LIFE

- Your First Realization That Someone May Be Toxic to You

- Who Is Toxic?

- Why Are There Toxic People?

- Toxic People and Illness

- Toxic Mood Contagion

- Bringing Out the Worst in You

- One Man's Friend Is Another Man's Toxin

- Toxic People in Your Past

- Who Is Toxic to Me

YOUR FIRST REALIZATION THAT SOMEONE
MAY BE TOXIC TO YOU

•

Several years ago, I conducted a seminar in Sacramento, California, for a group of government officials. At one point, I said, "If there are people in your lives who do not support you and who do not treat you with the respect and dignity you deserve, get them out of your life. Do not allow them to be a part of your daily life."

After the seminar, a tall, handsome gentleman came up to me with tears in his eyes and said, "Dr. Glass, how can you say that you must let these types of people go from your life? What about the friends I've had for the past twenty or thirty years? Doesn't that count for anything?"

Although I was sensitive to his concerns, I replied, "Sir, there is no sentimentality when somebody is abusing you, dragging you down, and not letting you be the best you can be. Sentimentality is for sweetness, love, and for people who are positive forces in your life. Sentimentality is reserved for people who treat you with kindness, dignity, and respect. Sentimentality is not for people who sabotage you and do not allow you to grow."

The man continued to challenge me as he persisted in trying to defend his position that one shouldn't let go of toxic people. He clung to the belief that if people have been in your life for a long time, playing a big part in it, you simply must not let them go.

I asked him, "Is there somebody specific in your life about whom you are thinking when you tell me that you should not let go of someone toxic?"

"Well, yes," he timidly replied. "What if that toxic person is my wife? Does that mean I have to get rid of my wife?"

Tears began to roll down his cheeks as he said, "Throughout your talk I kept thinking about my wife. Ever since we got married, twenty years ago, she has constantly berated me. She tells me what a loser I am and that I can't do anything right—that I have two left hands and two left feet. She's always yelling at me." He went on to confide that their sex life was virtually nonexistent because she told him he was a horrible lover. Her criticism of him was constant, and even when something good happened to him, such as a raise or an award, she would not praise him. Instead she never failed to put him down and to take the wind out of his sails whenever he was happy about something.

He revealed that they had tried therapy, but she continued to beat him up verbally. I told this gentleman that if he had tried every possible alternative to save his marriage and it still wasn't working, he needed to consider whether he wanted to live another twenty years with disrespect and abuse. I assured him that he did not have to be victimized any longer. He had choices, and he needed to make some definite changes in his life.

At long last, he woke up. He realized that his wife was not an ally, not a friend, but rather an extremely toxic person, infecting his life and tearing down what was left of his already fragile self-esteem.

For the first time in his life, this man was honest with himself. It left him emotionally distraught. Being honest with yourself is a scary experience, especially after years of self-deceit or ignoring or denying the situation. It can be especially unnerving to face reality and realize finally that the person whom you may have thought you loved may be toxic to you and even hazardous to your health, mentally, physically, and emotionally.

WHO IS TOXIC?

•

A toxic person is someone who seeks to destroy you. A toxic person robs you of your self-esteem and dignity and poisons the essence of who you are. He or she wears down your resistance and thus can make you mentally or physically ill. Toxic people are not life-supporting. They see only the negative in you. Jealous and envious, they are not happy to see you succeed. In fact, they get hostile whenever you do well. Their insecurities and feelings of inadequacy often cause them to sabotage your efforts to lead a happy and productive life.

Just as they come in all shapes and sizes, toxic people express themselves in different ways.

Anyone can be a toxic person. Socioeconomic group, age, cultural heritage, religion, or educational level don't matter. Nor does IQ. A toxic person might be a genius.

Toxic people may be found in every area of your life. You may have them in your family or in your business.

Some may be hostile and ugly to your face, while others may say and do things behind your back. Some may even have sugar on their lips, saying sweet, positive, loving words to you, while having salt in their eyes, looking at you with burning envy, negativity, and hostility.

We can learn a lot from the great philosopher Confucius, whose teachings influenced the Chinese empire and civilization throughout East Asia. In the fifth century B.C., he made this succinct statement: "When friends are pretentious, fawning, or opportunistic, they are harmful." This is one definition of a toxic person.

As with many of Confucius's truths, it applies significantly to modern times and our own culture. Toxic people were harmful two and a half thousand years ago, and toxic people are still harmful today in every aspect of our lives.

WHY ARE THERE TOXIC PEOPLE?

•

It is my general belief that most people are good, not evil. Human beings are born innocent, sweet, loving, happy, open, receptive, and harmless. Research has shown that babies are not born with hate and envy.

We will never know if people are toxic as the result of their environment (how they were raised), their specific biological makeup (their genetic composition), or a combination of both factors. We will never know with certainty why someone turns toxic and someone else does not.

Bernie, a Hollywood producer, came from a very rough home. His father physically tortured him and eventually ended up in prison for killing a neighbor. His mother was a perennial victim, severely abused by Bernie's father. Consequently, Bernie grew up with little or no respect for women—or for anyone else.

Though he made a name for himself in show business, he managed to alienate practically everyone along the way, burning bridges, cheating people out of tens of thousands of dollars, and never repaying debts. He was a miserable father to his children and a horrible husband to his wife, verbally, emotionally, and physically abusing them all.

When he died of stomach cancer recently, Bernie left not only a trail of debts but a trail of enemies as well. The day he died, his secretary telephoned some major celebrities whom Bernie knew, asking them to deliver the eulogy at his funeral. Everyone turned her down. In fact, nobody agreed even to attend the funeral.

His children were ecstatic to find out he had finally died, while his spiritual ex-wife was glad to hear that he was finally at peace. His secretary also felt relief at his death, as she would no longer have to put up with his overt hostility. The only thing she was unhappy about was the inconvenience of finding another job.

When Bernie's secretary shared this story with me, she said that after making over two hundred fifty phone calls and discovering that absolutely no one would attend her boss's funeral service, she had "cremated his ass," and nobody, she felt sure, ever gave Bernie a second thought.

Upon dying, a person should be remembered with warm memories, as we think of his or her positive and loving impact on other people's lives. Unfortunately, all that Bernie left behind was a legacy of toxins, which had polluted every life he touched.

If a person is toxic as the result of a horrible upbringing and a dearth of parental love, it should not matter to you. What really matters is whether or not the person is toxic to *you*. Whatever a person's reputation or toxicity to others, the only thing to concern you is that you be treated with the dignity and respect that *you* deserve.

TOXIC PEOPLE AND ILLNESS

•

If you are around a toxic person for a long time and you let this person's poison eat at you, you may be subject to psychosomatic illness. The individual's negativity can wear down your physical resistance. By not utilizing any of the techniques described later in this book, by repressing your anger and not confronting the toxic person, you could develop a serious, even fatal illness.

Anger and hostility affect the production of the hormone norepinephrine. A person who feels constant stress or hostility may produce an overabundance of this hormone, which causes high blood pressure as well as blockages that lead to heart attacks or strokes. There is also, as researchers have confirmed, a high correlation, in cases of cancer and heart disease, with repressing negative emotions.

According to Dr. Deepak Chopra in his book *Ageless Body, Timeless Mind,* survival rates for cancer and heart disease are lower among people in psychological distress. Recently I came across a quote from comedian Woody Allen: "One of my problems is that I internalize everything. I can't express anger; I grow a tumor instead." When I read this, I did not laugh. His quote was all too real and all too true as, sadly, I recalled my client Madelyn, a former makeup artist. I believe that Madelyn's tendency to keep anger inside contributed to her developing a brain tumor. Madelyn came to see me for speech therapy after surgery for removal of the tumor left her tongue and vocal cords paralyzed. During one of our sessions, I asked her what her life had been like before the brain tumor was discovered.

She told me she had kept everything in—she never told anyone she was angry or hurt. She denied her angry feelings because she felt guilty and did not want to hurt anyone's feelings.

"You know, Dr. Glass," she said one day, "I learned so much from this experience. Never again will I be a wimp and not tell people they are getting on my nerves. I *am* angry, and for the first time in my life I am giving myself permission to *be* angry. I don't have to be the good, quiet little girl. I feel like I want to do that scene in the film *Network* where Peter Finch yells out the window, 'I'm mad as hell and I'm not gonna take it anymore.'"

Madelyn went on, "I am mad as hell at my father, who never cared about me or showed me any love or affection. I am angry at my best girlfriend, who always feels that she has to be one up on me and compete with me, especially when there are men in the picture. And I am full of rage at my boyfriend, who really hasn't been there for me throughout my illness. All he cares about is himself, not me."

As she told me this, she began to sob spasmodically. Between sobs she cried out that she felt a great relief that she had never experienced before. For the first time in her life, Madelyn was able to discharge her emotions—especially her anger.

How said that it took a brain tumor to make Madelyn realize her anger at the toxic people in her life.

Developing a brain tumor is quite extreme, but being around a toxic person can contribute to a wide range of psychosomatic illnesses. You may experience headaches, nausea, backaches, throat tension, skin disorders, asthmatic attacks, or an allergic cough whenever you are around the person. You may also react with such psychological discomforts as lethargy, or mental illness such as depression. Most often you will feel as though your energy has been zapped after you have been around a toxic vampire. These states of emotional depletion can lead to various self-destructive behaviors: overeating, bulimia, anorexia, or alcohol or drug abuse.

You may not want to make waves or challenge the situation. You may say, "Oh, it's nothing—it doesn't bother me," but end up acting self-destructively in order to cope with the pain inside.

Roger, who had not seen his parents for several years, took his new fiancée back east at Christmastime to meet them. After a delicious family Christmas dinner, Roger, his fiancée, his parents, and all his brothers and sisters and their children sat under the tree and exchanged gifts. Roger, knowing that his father was a golf fanatic, had taken the time to select with care a very expensive cashmere golf sweater.

When he presented the gift, his father tore open the wrapping, looked at the gift, and handed the box back to Roger, saying coldly, "I don't need this." Roger, numbed by the incident, dutifully took the gift from his father, and they exchanged no more words for the entire evening. No one showed any emotion, and the incident seemed to be forgotten.

Later that evening, Roger's fiancée, Darlene, said, "I can't believe how horribly your father treated you! Aren't you angry? Aren't you upset? Aren't you hurt by what he did?"

"No," said Roger. "It's no problem, I'm not angry. That's just the way he is. It didn't bother me at all." Darlene was both surprised and appalled, her fury at his father's treatment of him now extended to Roger for denying his feelings.

Watching her fiancé suppress his emotions was a preview of things to come. Darlene began to notice that whenever they got into an argument, Roger would shut down, never expressing his feelings but just walking away. This drove her to reconsider whether she wanted to be married to Roger and share a life of noncommunication. She became frustrated when Roger, after months of her pleading with him, refused to go into therapy with her so that they could learn how to communicate with each other. He continued to deny that there was a problem and insisted that there was nothing wrong with him. Darlene finally came to her senses and denied Roger the opportunity to continue their relationship. She found him toxic because he refused to let her know how he was feeling.

It came as no surprise to Darlene when she got a call that Roger, aged thirty-eight, had been taken to the hospital after suffering a heart attack. His heart was dying literally as well as figuratively. Heavy with anger and pain, it finally stopped beating. Roger had been an angry man. He was angry at his father. He was angry at Darlene for leaving him. But most of all, he was angry at himself for not being able to express his anger, until it was too late.

Keeping anger, pain, and humiliation in, and not expressing it to others, can lead to serious physical problems.

TOXIC MOOD CONTAGION

•

Have you ever been in a bad mood and not known why? Maybe it was because you were around a toxic person. People who are sensitive to others may mimic the voice, posture, and facial expressions of a toxic person, thereby taking on some of the internal characteristics as well.

Remember when your mother told you that if you lie down with dogs you'll catch fleas? Well, the same holds true with negative mood contagion. If you are around a person who is always in a bad mood, eventually you will catch that person's mood. You will even become a source of mood contagion yourself, infecting the moods of others, as happened with Alex and his brother, Walt.

Walt, once successful, went bankrupt and his wife left him. He left New York for California, to move in with his brother until he got back on his feet. Walt not only brought all his clothes and belongings to Alex's house; he brought all his negative energy and bad moods, too.

"Everything has gone wrong since he came to live with us," Alex confided to me. "I always feel down and in a bad mood. My wife and I are constantly fighting. I feel antsy, unhappy, and depressed. My energy, which is usually high, is low, and I feel drained, angry, tired. I have trouble sleeping, and I'm eating like a pig. I got on the scale yesterday morning and found I've gained twenty pounds since Walt has been here. It's only been seven weeks."

As Alex shared this story with me, I asked him why he didn't find another place for Walt to stay. He replied that he didn't want to hurt Walt and would feel too guilty if he asked him to leave. I then asked Alex how he would feel if his marriage ended, his work suffered, and he lost his home and everything he had worked so hard for.

He got my point and said, "What's a little guilt after all?" When he returned from our session, he had a heart-to-heart talk with Walt. He gave him some money and told him that he would have to move out and be on his own. Apparently there was no problem after all, as Walt was more than happy to oblige.

When Walt left, it was as though a black cloud had lifted from Alex's head. He noticed that his wife and children were generally in better spirits also. The house had a lighter, brighter, more energetic aura. Alex became more productive as his energy level increased. He got on the treadmill every morning and soon lost the twenty pounds he had gained during Walt's stay.

Whenever Walt called him, however, Alex would get into a sullen mood all over again, his energy zapped. Convinced now of

Walt's toxic mood contagion, he made a conscious decision to curtail his communication with his brother; he would no longer be his caretaker and bail him out of trouble, as he had done all his life. In essence, he decided that he would no longer be victimized by Walt's constant negative energy.

If, like Alex, you find yourself sucked into a bad mood when around a toxic person, it is in your best interest to stay as far away as possible. Just as Alex did, you will discover that you will laugh more, sing more, smile more, and generally have a better outlook on life.

BRINGING OUT THE WORST IN YOU

•

Being around a toxic person sometimes brings out the worst in you. For instance, you may become very quiet. At the other extreme, you might act testy, taking offense at everything that person says, lashing out verbally, or even making snide comments to him or her.

Carla and Peter were coworkers. They shared the same office space, and each always knew what the other was doing. Carla was usually in an upbeat, positive mood, except when she got a call from her toxic ex-boyfriend, Larry, whom she had dumped on numerous occasions. Larry was disgustingly persistent in trying to win back Carla's affections. She decided never to answer his calls and told her secretary to just take a message. Periodically, however, Larry would get through to Carla.

Whenever one of these unfortunate calls got through, Peter would immediately know it was Larry on the other end of the phone. He would see Carla's face scrunch up, her eyebrows knit, her forehead furl, her lips tighten, and her nostrils flare.

You have probably noticed this yourself in friends or colleagues who receive a phone call from someone they are not fond of or do not want to talk to. Though they may sound pleasant to the caller, you see them tighten their cheeks, purse their lips, roll their eyes, frown, nod their heads, or even gesture with their hands as if to say, "Let's get this over with." You may watch them mock the caller, making it apparent to you that they are talking only reluctantly to that person.

Peter was always shocked to listen to his sweet and cheery office mate Carla coldly and boldly tell her ex that he was a total loser who repelled her. Also surprising were the "fuck you"s coming out of her usually polite mouth. Thank goodness her sharp, biting tone was never used with anyone else.

Larry brought out the worst in Carla and induced reactions that were not normal for her. Carla was not proud of the way she spoke to Larry, as doing so lowered her self-esteem, but she couldn't help herself: he was the source of her anger.

You can be a wonderful person and consider yourself a kind, sensitive, caring, gentle soul, but if you are around the wrong person—a toxic person—you can turn into someone whom even *you* don't recognize. Therefore it is important to know that there are people who *can* and *do* bring out the worst in you and make you act so negatively that you may be ashamed of your actions.

ONE MAN'S FRIEND IS ANOTHER MAN'S TOXIN

•

A person who is toxic to you is not necessarily toxic to everyone else. Toxicity may be specific and interactive. You may react adversely to certain people who rub you the wrong way, based on your particular personality makeup. You may find it difficult to be around loud, boisterous, or bossy people; your best friend, on the other hand, may not be able to stomach uptight, judgmental people but, unlike you, has no problem with the loud and boisterous.

The following scenario clearly illustrates how a toxic person is perceived differently, depending on the point of view. Three of my female friends—Shoshana, Nancy, and Alicia—and I were having lunch when Shoshana told us that she was dreading her sister-in-law's upcoming visit. I responded, "Is she quiet, sullen, and moody?" Alicia then interjected, "Is she loud and obnoxious?" Nancy queried, "Is she selfish and two-faced?" Shoshana answered that she was indeed "selfish and two-faced."

Afterward I couldn't help sharing my observation with my small lunch group. What was innately toxic to me ("quiet, sullen, and moody") was very different from what was toxic to Alicia ("loud and obnoxious") and again different from toxic traits that got to Shoshana and Nancy ("selfish and two-faced"). Everyone chuckled in acknowledgment of my point. Though we all find certain traits to be toxic, each of us finds certain traits more toxic than others.

As Sly and the Family Stone sang in the 1970s, "different strokes for different folks." What is one person's pain is another's pleasure. Similarly, one person's trash is another person's treasure.

The important thing to recognize is that those traits that are specifically toxic to you are not necessarily toxic to anyone around you.

Both Carla and Larry are thought of as wonderful people. If you ask Carla's friends if she is a toxic person, they will most likely laugh at you and say, "No way. Carla is the sweetest, kindest, most generous woman alive." Similarly, if you ask Larry's friends if he is toxic, they will tell you that he is the "nicest, warmest guy, with a great attitude and a terrific sense of humor."

However, Larry brings out the worst in Carla. To Carla, Larry is controlling, abusive, vulgar, and slimy. Carla, in turn, becomes curt, verbally abusive, and hostile to Larry, thereby bringing out the worst in him. These two seemingly wonderful individuals are extremely toxic to each other and need to stay as far away from one another as possible if they don't want to damage their self-esteem.

The idea of traits that are toxic to some and not to others was perhaps most apparent to me on a recent lecture tour I did in Australia to promote my book *He Says, She Says: Closing the Communication Gap Between the Sexes.*

After a breakfast lecture to over three hundred people in Brisbane, a woman came up to me and the Australian publicist assigned to me by the publisher. The woman proceeded to share her experiences of how "awful" men were. She had a pinched look about her, a rigid posture, and she hardly moved her lips when she spoke. My first thought was: What a prissy, uptight woman. I wanted to say, "Why don't you just lighten up, lady? Maybe if you would relax and not take yourself so seriously, men would find you more attractive and you wouldn't have so many horror stories about them."

Unable to listen to her any longer, I walked away to get a breath of fresh air, leaving her for my publicist to deal with. A few moments later, the publicist joined me, and I revealed that I had found the woman toxic. The publicist's reaction surprised me. "Well, I really liked her," she said. "In fact, we exchanged phone numbers and plan to get together for lunch when I get back."

As my tour continued throughout Australia, the publicist described the personalities of the various interviewers I would encounter and what I could expect from them. It turned out that whomever she had a negative comment about I ended up adoring. She characterized a certain radio interviewer in Sydney as an "eccentric woman" who rambled on and on, someone I would probably detest. I met her and thought she was great. Instead of seeing her the way my publicist depicted her, I found her to be a highly intelligent, beautifully sensitive, and spiritually connected human being. In fact, we hit it off so well that she invited me to have lunch on her boat the next time I come to Sydney.

At the radio station, we encountered an Aboriginal man who was also scheduled to be interviewed. I had never met an Aboriginal person before, and the publicist proceeded to fill me in on how ignorant and self-destructive these people were. After a short conversation, this man, a guitarist in an Aboriginal band, and I became fast friends and exchanged addresses so that I could send him my book and he could send me his album.

I had to conclude that anyone about whom the publicist had anything negative to say would turn out to be someone I would probably love. Another confirmation that what is toxic to one person is not always toxic to another. And vice versa.

You need to reserve your judgment whenever someone tries to fill your head with disparaging comments about another person. That they don't like the person is no guarantee that you won't. Don't take a negative statement made about someone as fact or gospel. An alleged toxic person may become your best friend.

TOXIC PEOPLE IN YOUR PAST

•

Throughout your life, you have met people whom you did not particularly care for. In fact, there may be those you find so odious that the mere thought of them makes you ill. Although we have been taught that we should all love one another and not categorize people, this is, in practice, not a reality. The reality is that there *are* certain categories of people who are toxic to *you*. You may find yourself periodically having it out with the same type of person as you go through life.

Although Chuck has been married four different times, to four different women—Lori, Mandy, Tawny, and Lisa—his friends tease him that he has really married the same woman each time: each wife was just as spoiled and selfish as the others.

Perhaps you have never really thought about it before, but there are definite reasons why you do not like certain people. As you go through life, you may find that these people are detrimental to your specific personality makeup.

To discover which type of people are particularly toxic to you, do the following Who Is Toxic to Me exercise.

WHO IS TOXIC TO ME

•

1. **Make a list of five men and five women who have made your life difficult throughout the years. Reflect on everyone who has been in your life from childhood to the present.**

2. **Consider why you do not care for these people. Next to their names, list three or four negative characteristics these people possess. If you are having trouble coming up with characteristics, refer to the following list for help in describing their characters.**

3. **Compare your lists and see how many negative traits each of these people share.**

Abusive
Acrid
Acrimonious
Adamant
Adversarial
Affectionate
Aggressive
Aloof
Amoral
Angry
Annoying
Apathetic
Argumentative
Arrogant
Ass-kissing
Attacking
Backstabbing
Belittling
Bickering
Bitchy
Blaming
Blunt
Bold
Boring
Bossy
Brash
Brazen
Brown-nosing
Bubbly
Bulldozing
Bullshitting
Calm
Can't be alone
Cheap
Clandestine
Clinging
Cold

Commitaphobic
Competitive
Complaining
Condescending
Confrontational
Conniving
Conservative
Conspiratorial
Contradicting
Controlled
Controlling
Corny
Cowardly
Crass
Crazy
Critical
Crude
Cruel
Crying
Cursing
Defeatist
Defensive
Defiant
Delicate
Demanding
Denying
Deprecating
Depressed
Desperate
Difficult
Dirty
Dishonest
Disloyal
Disrespectful
Dissatisfied
Distant
Ditsy

Dogmatic
Double-crossing
Doubting
Dull
Dumb
Duplicitous
Effusive
Eggheaded
Egomaniacal
Egotistical
Emotional
Emotionless
Empty
Enigmatic
Evasive
Evil
Exacting
Exhausting
Fake
False
Fanatical
Fastidious
Fault-finding
Fearful
Fearless
Flamboyant
Forceful
Fragile
Frightened
Frightening
Gossipy
Gregarious
Gross
Guilt-ridden
Harsh
Hasty
Hateful

Helpless
Holier than thou
Honest to a fault
Hot and cold
Hurtful
Hyperactive
Hyperkinetic
Hypocritical
Ignorant
Immature
Independent
Indifferent
Indirect
Indiscreet
Inexpressive
Infantile
Inflammatory
Insane
Insecure
Insensitive
Intense
Interfering
Intimidated
Intimidating
Invasive
Irrational
Irritable
Irritating
Jealous
Jocular
Jovial
Judgmental
Know-it-all
Lackadaisical
Lawless
Lecherous
Lethargic

Lewd
Liberal
Lifeless
Limited
Loner
Loose
Loser
Loud
Lying
Macabre
Macho
Maniacal
Manipulative
Martyr-like
Masochistic
Mean
Mean-spirited
Meddling
Mercurial
Messy
Meticulous
Miserly
Moralizing
Morose
Mousy
Mysterious
Narcissistic
Nasty
Negative
Nerdy
Neurotic
Nitpicking
Noncon-
frontational
Nosy
Not serious
Obnoxious

Obstinate
Old-fashioned
Overaccommodating
Overenthusiastic
Overneat
Paranoid
Passive-aggressive
Perfectionist
Petty
Phony
Pollyanna
Pontificating
Precise
Pretentious
Prissy
Promiscuous
Provocative
Prudish
Pugnacious
Pushy
Questioning
Quick-witted
Quiet
Raunchy
Rebellious
Repressed
Ridiculing
Rigid
Saccharine
Sadistic
Sarcastic
Secretive
Seductive
Self-destructive
Self-important
Selfish
Self-righteous

Serious	Stubborn	Ungenerous
Sexual	Submissive	Unimaginative
Shady	Sunny	Unkempt
Shallow	Superficial	Unladylike
Shameless	Superior	Unmanly
Sharp-tongued	Superstitious	Unpredictable
Sheepish	Suspicious	Unrealistic
Shy	Talkative	Unreasonable
Silly	Tenacious	Unstable
Skeptical	Testy	Untrustworthy
Slavish	Threatened	Uptight
Slick	Threatening	User
Sloppy	Timid	Victim-like
Slow	Troublemaking	Violent
Smart	Turncoat	Volatile
Sneaky	Two-faced	Vulgar
Snobby	Unappreciative	Weak
Snotty	Unaware of others	Whiny
Sobersided	Unbelievable	Wimpy
Socially inept	Unclean	Wisecracking
Solemn	Uncommunicative	Wishy-washy
Speedy	Underhanded	Worrisome
Spineless	Unemotional	Worthless-feeling
Stick-in-the-mud	Unevolved	Yelling
Stingy	Unfriendly	

You may be surprised to see how many negative characteristics are shared by the people who are toxic to you.

I had one of my clients, Jessica, do this exercise, and the results were most revealing. Here is her list of toxic women and toxic men who have caused her the most grief throughout her life.

Women Jessica Did Not Like and Their Negative Characteristics

  1. **Sheri (project consultant in her company)—judgmental, clandestine, two-faced, jealous**

2. **Sharon (her college roommate)**—two-faced, judgmental, up-tight, self-righteous

3. **Jan (her friend since childhood)**—negative, judgmental, self-righteous

4. **Susan (colleague at work)**—negative, judgmental, jealous

5. **Diane (her attorney)**—two-faced, dogmatic, judgmental, self-righteous

Men Jessica Did Not Like and Their Negative Characteristics

1. **Gerald (her college professor, sophomore year)**—wimpy, wishy-washy, two-faced, loser

2. **Charles (her department head, first job)**—cold, unemotional, conspiratorial, clandestine

3. **Mark (her cousin)**—wimpy, wishy-washy, two-faced, loser

4. **Stephen (her first boyfriend)**—wimpy, wishy-washy, stingy, frightened, loser

5. **Barry (her superior at work)**—weak, wimpy, wishy-washy, loser

As you can see, the traits which Jessica finds toxic in women do not duplicate those for men. Therefore, it is essential to make separate lists for both the men and women in your life.

Jessica cannot stand two-faced, judgmental, jealous, and self-righteous women, and she has very little tolerance for wimpy, wishy-washy, weak men. In her female category, Sharon and Diane are interchangeable, as are Jan and Susan. But all the women share negative traits. The same is true for Jessica's male category. While Gerald and Barry have identical negative traits, all the men's characteristics are similar and toxic to Jessica.

After you do this exercise, look for overlapping traits in the men and the women you listed. Are there patterns? Are certain people's traits so similar that they are interchangeable?

From this exercise you can identify traits which signal that people will possibly be toxic to you and perhaps cause you a great deal of emotional distress.

Now that you have identified common characteristics in those who are toxic to you, you can be on the lookout for them in new people you meet.

It is in your best interest to steer clear of these types of people, or, if this is not possible, to use the Ten Techniques (see Chapter 6) in dealing with them.

It is OK not to like everyone, as this exercise clearly shows. It is healthy to discriminate against people who are harmful to your well-being and to your particular personality. Not everyone is or should be welcome in your life. As Confucius advised: "Don't associate with anyone who is not as good as you are." This may strike you as a very undemocratic thing to say, yet it can be adapted to terms that make sense in today's world, where it is advisable to surround ourselves with people who are good *for* us.

The notion that we should love everyone and that everyone should love us is a naive one in this day and age. Most of us have been brought up to think in those terms, but it is not realistic. Not *everyone* is going to like you, and *you* are definitely not going to like everyone. Though I think that I'm a nice person and most people who encounter me seem to feel the same way, that does not mean that everyone likes me—or even likes being around me. I know that my constant high energy, my doing ten different things at once, and my emotional delivery may put some people off, just as it turns many people on.

Even if your heart is in the right place, your intentions are honorable, and you are trying your hardest, you may still be toxic to another person for any number of unknown reasons. You have to realize that there will be people out there who will not like you and there is very little you can do about it.

If you accept the notion (reluctantly or not) that not everyone will like you, just as you won't like everyone, you will find it a lot easier to deal with all the toxic people in your life.

CHAPTER 5

THE THIRTY TYPES

OF

TOXIC TERRORS

- The Cut-You-Downer

- The Chatterbox

- The Self-Destroyer

- The Runner

- The Silent but Deadly Volcano

- The Gossip

- The Angry Pugilist

- The Gloom and Doom Victim

- The Smiling Two-Faced Backstabber

- The Wishy-Washy Wimp

- The Opportunistic User

- The Bitchy, Bossy Bully

- The Jokester

- The Unconscious Social Klutz

- The Mental Case

- The Bullshitting Liar

- The Meddler

- The Penny-Pinching Miser

- The Fanatic

- The Me, Myself, and I Narcissist

- The Eddie Haskell

- The Self-Righteous Priss

- The Snooty Snob

- The Competitor

- The Control Freak

- The Accusing Critic

- The Arrogant Know-It-All

- The Emotional Refrigerator

- The Skeptical Paranoid

- The Instigator

Sound Familiar?

Why is it that some animals take to certain people, wagging their tails, licking and jumping up on them, while some animals are repelled by other people, barking and snarling, growling or ignoring them?

On a very basic level, cats, dogs, and other creatures can instinctively discriminate between whom they like and whom they don't like—who is toxic to them and who is not, who is a threat and who is not, who is fearful of them and who is not.

We are animals also, however more evolved. Instinctively, we too know whom we like and whom we cannot stand. We may not be able to verbalize why we do not particularly like another person; it may be a gut feeling.

In my practice as a communication specialist, I have spent thousands of hours listening to stories about toxic people. As I heard story after story, I began to discover different patterns of people. Based on the accounts I heard throughout the years, I came up with thirty types of toxic people, whom I have termed Toxic Terrors.

These Toxic Terrors definitely do not know how to win friends or influence people. In fact, many of their traits are so offensive that others loathe being around them.

When you read the descriptions and case examples of the Toxic Terrors, you may be surprised to recognize many people whom you know, and whom you may not like, in the various categories. I've listed some of their traits, which you have encountered in the Who Is Toxic to Me exercise, so you can see whom to especially avoid. You may find that toxic people fall into several of these categories. You may even be surprised to see yourself in some of the categories.

If you do happen to see yourself, don't get too upset. Remember that *knowledge is power.* Knowing that you practice a type of toxic behavior and being aware of what you are doing will give you the power to do something about it and begin to change your toxic traits. You will learn how to make such changes later on in this book.

THE CUT-YOU-DOWNER

•

- **They pick friends—to pieces.**

- **Cars don't run down as many people as they do.**

- **They are the "knife" of the party.**

- **They have a tongue that could clip a hedge.**

The Cut-You-Downer is arrogant, mean, belittling, bitchy, hateful, self-righteous, condescending, threatened, superior, insecure, offensive, critical, sarcastic, disrespectful, underhanded, and fault-finding.

Cut-You-Downers have so little self-esteem that they will find fault with you and with everyone else they see. They get a thrill out of belittling and taunting others. They love to ridicule people, especially strangers. Sitting in a restaurant or at an airport with you, they will comment, "Look at how fat that person is" or "What an ugly man!" You, too, are an object of their cutting and sarcastic comments.

Cut-You-Downers often give backhanded compliments. They will make a statement with a negative barb, such as: "That dress doesn't make you look fat at *all*," which leaves you wondering if you *do* look fat. The Cut-You-Downer is the type of person who, when you receive a raise, will comment on how good the company is about giving employees automatic raises as a form of incentive. If you lose weight as the result of a strict diet, the Cut-You-Downer will say, "You shouldn't lose too much weight or you'll get sick." Nothing is ever good enough for this type, who will find a cloud in every silver lining.

Cut-You-Downers have to cut you down so they can build themselves up. These people, insecure and full of self-loathing, feel threatened by you and by others around them. The only way that Cut-You-Downers can hold their heads up is by tearing everyone else's head off—cutting others down to their size. They look for faults in you and others because they see the world through "crooked eyes," as my friend Yogi Bikram Choudhury says.

Ken is the epitome of a Cut-You-Downer. Going out to dinner with him can be such a harrowing experience that you lose your appetite. He'll say, "Look at the way that man's eating—what a pig." "That waitress's ass is as big as a house." "See that girl over there? Her tits are fake. They're so big they'll probably explode all over the dinner table." Ken's scenario drives him into uncontrollable laughter as he continues to make grosser and more hostile comments about this poor woman, her breasts, her date, their meal, and everyone in the entire restaurant.

THE CHATTERBOX

•

- **What she needs is lockjaw.**

- **He buys dozens of books on How to Speak in Public—what he needs is one on How to Shut Up.**

- **She is a source of constant ear-itation.**

- **The reason you haven't spoken to him in weeks is that you can't interrupt him.**

- **She has a voice that is hard to extinguish.**

- **It takes two hours to tell you that he's a man of few words.**

The Chatterbox is too talkative, ignorant, selfish, irritating, unaware of others, narcissistic, disrespectful, uncommunicative, and boring.

Chatterboxes are talkaholics who won't shut up. These toxic types impose their free-flowing stream of consciousness on everyone who happens to be around, hardly ever making much sense. They will call you up and go on and on and on. It is as though Chatterboxes are having conversations with themselves and you don't even exist. These people will talk about everything and everyone, for usually they have no boundaries. Having "diarrhea of the mouth," these chronic talkers usually engage in idle chatter about their lives, their family's lives, or the lives of strangers, people they don't know and don't even care to know. Their insignificant, endless stories are of little interest to anyone. They may spend a good fifteen minutes describing everything they bought at the grocery store. Lacking social awareness, they are so consumed with telling their story that they pay little or no attention to your looks of annoyance, impatience, or disgust. Chatterboxes are too selfish to acknowledge anyone else's right to talk.

By not letting you get a word in edgewise, the Chatterbox manipulates you into doing what you don't want to do: to listen to the Chatterbox.

THE SELF-DESTROYER

•

- **They do serve one purpose in life—as horrible examples.**

- **Every time a scary cigarette-smoking report comes out, she smokes an extra pack.**

- **Every time he hears that a certain food has been found not to be good for you, he will be sure to eat more of it.**

The Self-Destroyer is victim-like, unrealistic, weak, unstable, sabotaging, rejecting, negative, threatened, selfish, lifeless, desperate, unappreciative, macabre, depressed, defiant, rebellious, and out of control.

Self-Destroyers hate themselves so much that they constantly tear themselves down. They harp on what's wrong with them and repeatedly berate themselves. They usually say things like "I'm so stupid," "That was dumb of me," or "I'm the worst." In essence, Self-Destroyers try to cut themselves down before anyone else has a chance to do it. They can never accept compliments and will negate any nice or kind words that come their way. They can be so full of self-loathing that they will become alcoholics, foodaholics, drug abusers, or sexaholics. The bottom line is that Self-Destroyers don't think they are worthy of good things or deserve anything positive in life. Their self-esteem is at the bottom of the barrel.

Untimely death can be the ultimate tragic outcome for the Self-Destroyer, as it was for the young actor River Phoenix. Phoenix had the whole world ahead of him, but he didn't think enough of himself to continue living his life. He ended up destroying himself with an overdose of cocaine and heroin, dying on the sidewalk in front of a club while people stepped over him.

When life goes wrong for these toxic types, they lash out at themselves. In essence, such a person has a death wish. It is difficult being around the Self-Destroyer, watching him or her destruct right in front of your eyes, as Bernadette found out.

Bernadette dated Theodore for over a year. She met him when he was going through a particularly tough time in his life, involving a divorce and a job change. She was his support system and was always there for him during his crises. The couple got along very well, except that Bernadette always fussed at him for eating, drinking, and smoking too much. As a result, when Theodore finally asked her to marry him, she had to think twice before she was willing to take on the task.

Bernadette noticed that whenever anything went wrong for Theodore or he felt the least bit stressed, he would do self-destructive things to himself. For example, he would reach for a bottle of bourbon and drink it all, or he would eat masses of junk food in one sitting—five peanut-butter-and-jelly sandwiches on white bread, potato chips, pretzels and candy bars and peanuts. To top it off, he would chain-smoke two to three packs of cigarettes a day.

Bernadette encouraged him to take his anxiety out on the treadmill, to take a walk or work out at the gym, and to eat healthy food instead of junk food. She offered to send him to a rehab center to stop his drinking and smoking. Though Theodore was a great guy and she loved him dearly, she finally told him, "I want to marry you, not bury you." She would not commit to marrying him until he cleaned up his act.

He began a counseling program, got a trainer, stopped drinking and smoking, and saw a nutritionist, her conditions before she would consider marrying him. This lasted six months, but he was unable to escape his self-destructive mode.

One day Bernadette received a call from the emergency room at the local hospital. Theodore was dead of a heart attack, aged forty-two.

This rather extreme story shows us not only the potential tragic consequences of being a Self-Destroyer but the emotional turmoil undergone by those in the orbit of such a toxic person.

THE RUNNER
•

- **He is the kind you ask to stay with you when you want to be alone.**

- **She is always close to you, until you try to touch her.**

- **As soon as she starts giving her side of an argument, he shuts off his hearing aid.**

The Runner, a weak wimp who can't confront, is wishy-washy, rejecting, cowardly, noncommunicative, intimidated, dishonest, in denial, cowardly, disloyal, disrespectful, mercurial, fearful, unmanly, unwomanly, unreliable, alone, and socially inept.

The Runner's way of coping with any type of stress is to run from it. Unable to handle something, he or she disappears, as Gus did.

Gus was jogging in place near a stoplight, waiting for it to turn green. Suddenly he noticed that the man who had been standing next to him had dropped to his knees, apparently in the throes of a heart attack. Instead of calling for help and seeing if he could do anything for the man, Gus continued on his way—escaping from the situation as quickly as possible.

Gus wasn't coldhearted; he was so consumed with fear, so traumatized, that he couldn't cope with the situation and literally ran away from it.

The Runner cannot take a stand on anything. In fact, Runners are "commitaphobics," so weak that they cannot cope with any negative stressful situation.

After dating Dick for three years, Bree wanted a commitment for marriage. When she confronted Dick about it, he freaked out. He didn't know how to respond to the ultimatum, so he did the thing he did best: he ran away, never to be heard from again.

When Bree came into my office, devastated by what Dick had done, her first inclination was to blame herself, berating herself for bringing up the subject of marriage. I told her that if Dick's inclination was to run every time there was a crucial or difficult situation, refusing to sit down and communicate with her, she was a lot better off without him. Though she agreed with me intellectually, she continued to feel hurt and devastated.

Since Runners never stick around for a conflict, they don't ever see the trauma they cause by running away from problems.

THE SILENT BUT DEADLY VOLCANO

•

- **He hasn't paid attention to her in years—but he'll shoot any man who does.**

- **She pretends to be burying the hatchet when she's really digging up the dirt.**

- **They are sure to leave pussyfoot prints on the sands of time.**

The Silent but Deadly Volcano is unstable, noncommunicative, conspiratorial, picky, fault-finding, unreliable, weak, enigmatic, sneaky, irrational, mercurial, mysterious, resentful, wimpy, and out of control.

These are some of the scariest people to be around, because you never know where you stand with them. In essence, they are walking time bombs. The Silent but Deadly Volcanoes may appear to be very much in control, acting calmly, smiling and behaving in a cordial manner all the time. They will never let you know that there is a problem brewing or that they are upset with you or anyone or anything. Never will they speak up or tell you that you have done something they think is wrong. They are mild-mannered Caspar Milquetoast types, who would not think of harming a flea.

Then all of a sudden the volcano erupts and lava spews in every direction. For example, you may say hello or look at them the wrong way and trigger a reaction. They may explode in a horrible rage, shouting a barrage of insults and blaming you for everything that ever went wrong in their life. This behavior is not only shocking but frightening as well.

Dr. Rearden, a prominent researcher, had this experience with his assistant of three years. Linda was quiet and mild-mannered, a tiny-boned, delicate woman who kept to herself and tended to her business, very serious about her work. She seemed to blend into the woodwork, acting like a meek little mouse and shying away from her fellow workers. Whenever she had to, she nodded hello cordially, even though it was a big effort for her.

Dr. Rearden was rather demanding, an energetic, upbeat man with a lot on his plate, much of which required immediate attention. He would often yell to Linda from his office: "Get me that number immediately" or "Get me the report now" or "Call the Institute of Health—now" and "Do it immediately" and "I need it right away!" Linda did not seem to be fazed, as she obediently carried out his commands for three years.

Then one day, acting his usual self, Dr. Rearden yelled out, "Hey, Linda, I need this report immediately. Drop everything else." Linda stormed into his office, her eyes like a wild animal's. With her veins pulsing in her head and neck and her face turning red, she screamed at the top of her lungs: "I'm sick of this and I'm sick of you. Who do you think you are? Just because you are famous and in *Newsweek,* that doesn't make you God. I'm not impressed with you! I hate your guts!" After knocking all the papers off the doctor's desk and kicking over the wastebasket, she stormed out—never to be seen again.

Everyone in the office was stunned. Dr. Rearden, speechless, was frightened, not only for his own well-being but for Linda's and that of anyone in her path.

The Silent but Deadly Volcano is so full of inner rage that you may be afraid of suffering bodily harm, which is not something to take lightly. Extreme cases of this type are the people who end up on shooting sprees, killing innocent bystanders for no apparent reason at all. Whenever their acquaintances are interviewed on television in the aftermath of the destruction, you always hear the same comments: "He was so nice." "Nobody would ever have suspected he could do such a horrible thing." "She was so mild-mannered."

The Silent but Deadly Volcano is the scariest of all the toxic types, because you never know when or where an explosion will occur. Volcanoes hold things in and are tightly wound up, as they keep a running mental record of everything that upsets them or hurts their feelings.

THE GOSSIP

•

- **They are good at letting the cat out of the bag.**

- **They pick up more dirt with a telephone than they do with a vacuum cleaner.**

- **They have a keen sense of rumor.**

The Gossip is indiscreet, insecure, fault-finding, false, duplicitous, belittling, quick to place blame, brazen, bullshitting, clandestine, hypocritical, competitive, hurtful, self-righteous, shallow, sharp-tongued, skeptical, sneaky, imposing, adversarial, conspiratorial, critical, disloyal, meddling, mean-spirited, offensive, and angry.

. . .

The Gossip (or yenta, in Yiddish) loves to spread stories—even embellishing them—and may invent stories of his or her own.

The Gossip is basically a nosy person whose biggest pleasure is telling you about someone else's misfortunes. She might relish telling you a story about how your mutual friend's husband was caught cheating on his wife. She might laugh as she tells you how your friend threw a lamp at her husband's head and cut his forehead.

Gossips generally have very little going on in their own lives. Primarily, they have a need to be accepted and to feel important. They feel that bringing you privileged information will endear them to you.

A client of mine who is a Gossip candidly admitted that the reason she loves gossip is that it makes her feel important. Her friends look forward to receiving their weekly "dirt" report from her and encourage her to keep on gossiping.

Though they enjoy digging up other people's dirt, gossips will *never* divulge anything about themselves. In fact, their lives are the only thing they are secretive about. These hypocrites suck you in with their charm and cordiality, making you feel they are your best friend as they pump you for information. The reason they never reciprocate with information about themselves is that they would not want you to do to them what they are doing to you.

Because of her job, Lynnette is privy to the comings and goings of many rich and famous people. She uses this information to make herself feel more important. Initially she is sweet and engaging and shows interest in your life. She seems a true friend. Instead, as you find out later, Lynnette is your secret enemy—a snake lying in wait to milk you for some valuable "juice" that she can dispense to everyone she talks to.

She starts out by opening up, sharing intimate gossip about people you have in common or even about her rich and famous clients. So you let your guard down. You think you are the only one to whom she is telling these very private things, because she really likes, respects, and trusts you, considers you a very special person and her most intimate confidante.

Well, guess what? Not only is Lynnette definitely telling every-body what she just told you; she will now tell everybody what you told her: your information becomes part of her gossip mill.

In dealing with a Gossip, the most important thing to remember is: He who brings carries. That is, anyone who brings information about others is definitely carrying information about you to others, so beware and be aware.

THE ANGRY PUGILIST

•

- **They are so disagreeable that their own shadows can't stand them.**

- **He had three phones installed so he could hang up on more people.**

- **They are mean, selfish, loudmouthed, and uncouth, but in spite of it all, there is something about them that repels you.**

- **He has an approach like a dentist's drill.**

The Angry Pugilist is difficult, disrespectful, controlling, con-frontational, hateful, arrogant, attacking, bitchy, brash, bulldozing, hurtful, intense, intimidating, sadistic, sharp-tongued, volatile, ma-cho, out of control, maniacal, stubborn, self-destructive, crude, law-less, loud, uncommunicative, threatening, offensive, and depressed.

Angry Pugilists live their life with a chip on their shoulder, con-stantly daring you to try to knock it off. They are always on the of-fensive—ready for a fight or an argument.

They love to play devil's advocate, even if they agree with you. Whatever you say, they will say the opposite.

They consistently provoke people, for no apparent reason. It's their own insecurity and their desperate need to show how impor-tant or how smart they are that lead them to initiate arguments.

Everything and everyone seem to irritate them. They are universally critical. These are people who often get physically violent, punching holes in walls or doors with their fists.

Angry Pugilists are furious all the time for no reason, even if you are doing what they want. They will manage to find fault, attacking you before you attack them. Their biggest fear is that you will say or do something to make them feel inadequate, so they beat you to the punch, starting fights so that they can achieve some control over a situation.

Angry Pugilists typically had a difficult time growing up. As adults, they often feel that life has played dirty tricks on them. Their bravado masks their supersensitivity.

A certain good actress has never achieved the star status she deserves, because she has difficulty getting along with everyone. She is her own worst enemy; everyone dreads working with her. Directors, fellow actors and actresses, and even production companies can't stand her.

Why? It is because she is always poised for a fight. She is perpetually ready to pounce on somebody for no reason at all or to disagree with anyone who is in authority. As a result, she has sabotaged her once promising career.

Angry Pugilists tend to be disrespectful and insubordinate. They will fight with anybody. They are into challenging you, daring you, and ultimately defying you, just to prove that they are right, even if they don't know what the heck they are talking about.

THE GLOOM AND DOOM VICTIM

•

- **They are misfortune-tellers.**

- **They are so fond of hard luck they run halfway to meet it.**

- **Their usual greeting is "Good moaning."**

- **They're always pulling tomorrow's cloud over today's sunshine.**

- **They can find fault even in paradise.**

- **He's on the right track but getting run over sitting there.**

The Gloom and Doom Victim is masochistic, guilt-ridden, worrisome, sabotaging, resentful, rigid, selfish, rejecting, sad, negative, petty, fault-finding, paranoid, stubborn, whiny, weak, defeatist, unimaginative, self-destructive, fearful, solemn, cowardly, depressed, macabre, skeptical, unappreciative, suspicious, morose, lifeless, lethargic, lackadaisical, defensive, and depressed.

Gloom and Doom Victims are depressing to be around. Their energy really zaps you as they tell you how horrible life is, has been, and will be for them. They aim to make you feel sorry for them, but they have no interest in any advice you offer.

Their preference is to wallow in self-pity, certain that the world has done them in and everybody has done them wrong. Nothing ever goes right for them. Perhaps it is because they always see the glass as half empty rather than half full.

Gloom and Doom Victims will blame everyone but themselves when anything goes wrong in their lives, much like the Angry Pugilist.

In fact, they are just like the Angry Pugilist in their feelings of inadequacy and their conviction of life's unfairness. But instead of taking it out with their fists and sharp tongues, they resort to tears and gloomy expressions. They blame the weather, they blame their personal lives, they blame their business lives, they blame their childhoods. Forever victims, they enjoy self-pity and seek the pity of others with their poor-helpless-soul routine.

Gloom and Doom Victims are also perpetual worriers. They make up scenarios in advance. For example, they just know they will have a horrible time at a party, that nobody will talk to them there, and that everything will go wrong before they even step out of the house.

After you have been around the Gloom and Doom Victim for a short while, you will become depressed and exhausted. You may feel like either crying or going to sleep, as they drain you of all your energy. Any advice you try to give them is futile; they will always answer with "Yeah, but" and proceed to tell you why their problems won't submit to your solutions. After all, they continue to see the negative, hopeless side of things, and nothing you can do or say can change that.

Unfortunately, Gloom and Doom Victims are all too prevalent in our society. Turn on any morning or afternoon talk show and you will see somebody whose husband has been beating her, or who is stuck in a bad marriage, who is too poor, too fat, too miserable, or too hopeless to deal with life. Watching these people on a daily basis can not only irritate us but leave us depressed and tired.

THE SMILING TWO-FACED BACKSTABBER

•

- **With friends like them you don't need enemies.**

- **They don't knock before they enter your home—but they knock plenty after they leave it.**

- **They roll out the carpet for you one day and pull it out from under you the next.**

- **They are the kind who will borrow your pot and then cook your goose.**

- **They talk in stereo—out of both sides of their mouth.**

The Smiling Two-Faced Backstabber is clandestine, sneaky, slick, secretive, uncommunicative, dishonest, seductive, sabotaging, selfish, phony, duplicitous, enigmatic, fake, conspiratorial, evasive, hypocritical, lying, mean-spirited, meddling, superficial, cowardly, untrustworthy, a double-crosser, and a turncoat.

Most of us find the Smiling Two-Faced Backstabber the most toxic of all the terrors. In fact, in Dante's *Inferno,* the final circle of hell was reserved for perpetrators of the most heinous sin of all—betrayal. Nothing hurts more than to learn that you have been betrayed by someone you trusted. This is the office of the Smiling Two-Faced Backstabber.

These toxic people are extremely passive-aggressive, smiling hypocritically and pretending to be your best friend while sneaking behind your back and stabbing you. Confucius, an authority on social protocol, deplored such types, declaring: "It is shameful to befriend someone while concealing a grudge."

These chameleon-like toxic people are scary, for they change depending on what they think you need to hear. They step on your toes to get ahead, willing to do whatever it takes to get whatever they want.

Sharon and Laura went to school together, and both majored in graphic design. They were supposedly dear friends. After college, Laura wanted a certain position badly and confided her desires to Sharon, explaining who the players were and what her strategy would be to acquire the job. Sharon, Laura's most trusted confidante, asked detailed questions to indicate that she was interested and supportive. In reality, she was gathering data for herself. She ended up going to the company behind Laura's back, applying for the job, and getting it. When Laura found out, she was devastated. Sharon could not care less. She continued to smile, having little remorse for what she did to Laura.

You can never trust Smiling Two-Faced Backstabbers. They will use your confidences against you at times when you least expect it. They are plotters who are always looking for an edge over you. Deep inside, they resent you but don't have the guts to confess that they are angry or upset or even envious.

Smiling Two-Faced Backstabbers are evasive and will never tell you what is on their mind. What's on your mind is what's on theirs, and in this they're like the Gossip.

Smiling Two-Faced Backstabbers are people who have salt in their eyes, sugar on their lips. They may say sweet and tender and supportive things, but they're really remorseless vipers.

THE WISHY-WASHY WIMP

•

- **They are always on the fence to avoid offense.**

- **He has the guts of a skeleton.**

- **She is so indecisive that her three-year-old hasn't been named yet.**

- **She is a person of conviction after she knows what someone else thinks.**

- **He is as cautious as two porcupines making love.**

The Wishy-Washy Wimp is passive-aggressive, weak, quiet, brown-nosing, uncommunicative, dependent, indirect, intimidated, ass-kissing, fearful, insecure, untrustworthy, secretive, scared, sheepish, guilt-ridden, tentative, threatened, conservative, disloyal, indecisive, desperate, lifeless, mousy, spineless, submissive, socially inept, nerdy, indecisive, cowardly, a stick-in-the-mud, a loser, and a yes-man.

Wishy-Washy Wimps are passive-aggressive individuals who are spineless wonders, lacking guts and backbone. They bend in whatever direction the wind is blowing and have difficulty making any decision. Often quiet and agreeable, they at first seem likable yes-men and yes-women. However, dislike sets in later on, as it becomes clear that their "yes" means "no."

They may say one thing one day, the opposite another day. In fact, they don't really know what they are doing, nor does anyone around them, which makes them extremely difficult and frustrating to work with.

Mark typifies the Wishy-Washy Wimp. Promoted and put in charge of a division of his company, he ended up getting fired in record time, because he was unable to make any decisions. He would listen to pros and cons, then do nothing.

Lacking inner substance and unwilling to stick up for anything or anybody, including themselves, they think that if they stall long enough their problems will go away or the decisions will make themselves. They waste time because they are so insecure about their abilities and can never take the risk of being wrong. When forced into making decisions, they get angry.

The Wishy-Washy Wimp is so paralyzed by fear and anxiety that he or she cannot make a move if there is pressure to perform. Even an action to save another person's life might be avoided.

Wishy-Washy Wimps cannot handle confrontation. They see themselves as victims, so they never want to make waves or cause any trouble. Seeking comfort, they crawl into the woodwork of life.

THE OPPORTUNISTIC USER

•

- **She is always around when she needs you.**

- **He'll steal the teeth out of your mouth and then come back for your gums.**

- **When the money stops talking, she starts walking.**

- **He is a human gimme pig.**

The Opportunistic User is selfish, interfering, manipulative, backstabbing, brown-nosing, secretive, indirect, ass-kissing, disloyal, conspiratorial, dishonest, sneaky, unappreciative, underhanded, tenacious, and seductive.

A classic example of Opportunistic Users involved a Beverly Hills doctor and a widowed socialite. Though the socialite's multimillionaire husband left her millions of dollars when he died, he left her more millions of dollars of debt. In reality, she was poor as a church mouse, though she looked like the richest princess in town.

To continue living the good life she was accustomed to, she went on a mission to find a rich man and set her sights on a certain Beverly Hills doctor, who she assumed was rich.

The doctor was also looking for a rich mate—someone to bail him out of his eight malpractice suits, his failed business ventures, his insurance fraud investigation, and his waning practice, the result of his soured reputation in the community. He had heard Emily was filthy rich, which made her the woman of his dreams.

When they spotted each other across a crowded room, it was love at first sight, for their respective millionaire reputations had preceded them. The fantasy of the rich life danced through both their minds as, one month later, they walked down the aisle after exchanging wedding vows. I am sure that they both chuckled to themselves when the "for richer or poorer" line was recited by the minister.

What a surprise they got months later, when each discovered that the other had debts rather than money. Tensions rose, tempers flared, and the marriage ended as fast as it had begun.

Opportunistic Users are out for themselves alone. They are fair-weather friends who want you in their life only when it is convenient for them—when they can benefit. These people will do anything to get ahead. If they can't benefit from someone or have benefited all they can, they discard the person like a used paper towel, without a second thought.

THE BITCHY, BOSSY BULLY

•

- **When he wants your opinion he gives it to you.**

- **She's as overbearing as a woman giving birth to quadruplets.**

- **He is like a crocodile: when he opens his mouth, you'd better be prepared to have him chew you up.**

- **After she sharpens her teeth, she sharpens her tongue.**

The Bitchy, Bossy Bully is abusive, acrimonious, adversarial, forceful, out of control, angry, argumentative, harsh, rejecting, rude, nagging, demanding, sharp, irrational, sadistic, cruel, difficult, defiant, crass, arrogant, infantile, intimidating, crude, fault-finding, pugnacious, macho, pushy, offensive, mean-spirited, mercurial, maniacal, loud, socially inept, threatening, condescending, volatile, uncommunicative, testy, and stubborn.

The Bitchy, Bossy Bully is a verbal terrorist, a loud, obnoxious, rude, demanding, stubborn know-it-all whose motto is "My way or the highway." Explosive and volatile, they fly off the handle in an instant. They are happy only when they are running the show.

Dr. Levack, a university professor, is the perfect example of the Bitchy, Bossy Bully. He orders his secretary and his students around, demanding that things be done "Now!" and be done his way. If someone makes a small mistake, he will yell, scream, and carry on. People cringe and shake whenever he walks into the room. He is definitely a type A+ personality, becoming nervous and agitated about everything. Always mean and hostile, he yells at people not only about what to do but about how to do it.

When Dr. Levack ended up in the hospital after a heart attack, everyone in the department was so happy that they threw a party to celebrate.

Bitchy, Bossy Bullies have a definite need to control, much like Control Freaks (see page 109), only nastier, as they have cruel and sadistic tendencies. In essence, Bitchy, Bossy Bullies get off on seeing people squirm. They enjoy torturing people and watching them cower like injured puppies while the Bullies bark out their inner hatred.

They are turned on by emotionally devouring you and spitting you out. These are people who give other people ulcers. They are the classic emotional abusers, and they win the prize for being most hated by the most people. Confucius's teachings confirm this: "Most often no one will obey the bully even if he gives orders." Feared and hated they may be, but nothing can make others respect them enough to do their bidding willingly.

THE JOKESTER

•

- **His wisecracks are often greeted with a tremendous burst of silence.**

- **When they leave a party where she is, guests finally know the meaning of comic relief.**

- **They have a repertoire of three jokes all told and told and told.**

The Jokester is annoying, insecure, weak, obnoxious, never serious, selfish, corny, offensive, sarcastic, socially inept, crass, crude, desperate for attention, superficial, disrespectful, loud, tenacious, offensive, and unaware of others.

Jokesters never take anything seriously. They start everything out with a joke. "Did you hear the latest one about such and such?"

Jokesters will often take potshots at you by using sarcastic humor and pretending that these verbal barbs are pleasantries. They react to your disdain by asking, "Don't you have a sense of humor? Everyone else laughs at this—what's wrong with you?" Their humor can be a weapon, implementing their underlying hostility.

At a breakfast meeting, they may say something like "Here, have another sweet roll—you wear it well," implying that you are fat. When you register surprise, they giggle and say, "Hey, can't you take a joke? I was only kidding." They are hostile indirectly because they are too cowardly to tell you outright what about you bothers them.

Whenever you want to discuss something seriously, they may giggle or joke about it because serious topics are too difficult for them to deal with.

Confucius found the same thing, commenting: "When I am with a group of people all day and the conversation never touches on matters of justice but inclines to the exercise of petty wit, I have a hard time." Like the sage, most of us have a hard time around Jokesters. Your anger is greeted with the inevitable laugh, as they cannot cope with honest emotions, which are too painful. If Jokesters are upset about something, they will never let you know it, disguising hurt feelings and even antagonism in wisecracks. In essence, Jokesters construct a protective shell of banter around themselves.

Jerry had a joke for every occasion. Though people may have enjoyed the occasional chuckle he inspired, for the most part Jerry was extremely annoying because he did not know when to quit. He could never take anything seriously, and he started every conversation with: "Hey, did you hear the latest one about . . ." and proceeded with his joke—occasionally funny but mostly rather stupid or silly. Any serious comment you might offer he would laugh at and relate to a silly story he had in his memory bank. When people saw Jerry coming, they tried to walk the other way.

One day his coworker Catherine was crying in her office. She had broken up with her boyfriend the night before, and everything had seemed to go wrong for her that day. Seeing her upset, Jerry barged into her office and started making light of everything she said. Instead of feeling better, Catherine ended up crying even harder. Finally, she yelled at Jerry to get out of her office. She told him she couldn't stand him because he was so insensitive to her.

In reality, Jokesters like Jerry are insecure and have very low self-esteem. They want so much to be liked and accepted that they feel they have to earn your acceptance by performing for you much like a clown.

As Arthur Miller once said, "Everybody likes a kidder, but nobody lends him money"—meaning nobody takes him seriously or respects him.

Jerry's desperate joking backfired on him. Instead of being won over, people ended up disliking him because they were annoyed by his never being able to take anything seriously.

THE UNCONSCIOUS SOCIAL KLUTZ

•

- **They always stop to think. The trouble is that they forget to start again.**

- **It's not that they don't have presence of mind; they have an absence of thought.**

- **She is a person of a few ill-chosen words.**

- **He has foot-in-the-mouth disease.**

The Unconscious Social Klutz is unaware of others, unreliable, rude, annoying, nerdy, offensive, unexpressive, unimaginative, untrustworthy, unkempt, blunt, bold, brazen, honest to a fault, sloppy, socially inept, selfish, slow, invasive, unaware, and unevolved.

Unconscious Social Klutzes have absolutely no clue. Dense clods who are totally unaware of themselves or their surroundings, they will often make rude comments without any regard for your feelings. They usually have poor eye contact, poor posture, poor handshakes, poor vocal intonation, and poor social graces.

In essence, they are unevolved creatures, who, like four-year-olds, are not conscious of your feelings as they blurt out whatever they are thinking. They say the wrong things and upset you. Even if they happen to be intelligent or good at their job, they are as devoid of common respect and courtesy toward others as they are careless and negligent.

Gordon attended a private school for the gifted through high school. Though intellectually gifted, he was definitely not gifted socially. When he got his first job as a computer programmer, he made faux pas after faux pas, alienating practically everyone he encountered. He bounced from job to job, because he inevitably offended someone and got fired. He seemed to be on another planet or at least in a dense fog. After being fired from five jobs in a row, he still had no idea what his problem was.

Often the Unconscious Social Klutz is a perfect stranger, who will come up to you and say something bizarre or out of line, leaving you wondering: How could he say something like that? Well, you had better believe it, Social Klutzes always say things like that.

THE MENTAL CASE

•

- **You can't tell Mental Cases they are crazy—they will think you are.**

- **No wonder they fly off the handle—they have a screw loose.**

- **They need a checkup from the neck up.**

The Mental Case may be unstable, overly emotional or emotionless, enigmatic, exhausting, frightening, unreliable, volatile, unpredictable, out of control, abusive, acrimonious, argumentative, harsh, reclusive, sad, paranoid, sabotaging, difficult, rigid, brash, brazen, hateful, hyperkinetic, infantile, insane, intimidating, irrational, shallow, depressive, sadistic, confrontational, desperate, selfish, testy, offensive or defensive, suspicious, stubborn, morose, mean, threatened or threatening, maniacal, ambivalent, and masochistic.

Being around Mental Cases is nerve-racking and downright frightening. They are mentally and/or emotionally disturbed. Mental Cases may have a psychosis like schizophrenia or manic depression and be out of touch with reality. They may have a borderline personality disorder, which can threaten their own life or the lives of others, or they may have a drug or alcohol problem, which makes them act strange and out of control.

I put drug and alcohol abusers in the Mental Case category because drugs and alcohol impair normal mental states. Abusers may generally be nice, sane people, but when alcohol or drugs are ingested, they transform into monsters, often acting violently.

Mental Cases can change from Dr. Jekyll to Mr. Hyde right before your eyes. They are the most difficult people to be around on any level, because, as with Silent but Deadly Volcanoes, you never know where they are coming from and when their outrageous behavior will emerge.

Bethany, an attractive thirty-three-year-old, put a singles ad in a magazine. She met Warren, who seemed to fit her requirements to a T—tall, successful, handsome, single, entrepreneurial, aged forty-two. On their first date, she noticed that he talked a little too fast and skipped from topic to topic. However, she attributed his loquacity to nervousness about the date and shrugged it off.

On their second date, he was weirder, babbling about things that didn't seem to make much sense. But he was so good-looking and so sexy that she ignored his strange behavior. Once again she chalked it up to his trying too hard to impress her.

On their third date, she finally realized that he was mentally disturbed, for he went off on her for no reason, calling her an "ugly slut" and a "pig" when they met in front of a restaurant. Luckily, she had driven there herself, so she ran to her car, locked the doors, and sped off. A friend of hers who had met Warren at a singles dance years earlier said that he was a manic-depressive and that she had had a similar experience with him.

Since statistics show that one percent of the population is schizophrenic and that the percentage of people with mental disorders, alcoholism, and drug use is growing exponentially (exacerbated by societal stresses such as joblessness, homelessness, and the destruction of the family unit), it is inevitable that we will be exposed to more and more toxic Mental Cases in the future.

THE BULLSHITTING LIAR

•

- **They are always selling themselves but misrepresenting the goods.**

- **They not only kiss and tell, they kiss and exaggerate.**

- **It's not so much that they exaggerate; they just remember big.**

- **You can believe half of what they tell you. The problem is which half.**

The Bullshitting Liar is untrustworthy, bold, fake, seductive, clandestine, dishonest, interfering, a know-it-all, shameless, effusive, enigmatic, fault-finding, manipulative, obnoxious, gossipy, unpredictable, unreliable, weak, unrealistic, backstabbing, double-crossing, selfish, and dishonest.

Bullshitting Liars don't know whether they are lying or telling the truth. These people have lied so much and spun so many yarns to build up low self-esteem that they usually end up believing their own lies. They can swear to you on a stack of Bibles that something is the truth and that they believe it wholeheartedly, when you in fact know that it is not true. They won't budge, as they are the ultimate manipulators.

What can be most confusing is that Bullshitting Liars sometimes say things that have a ray of truth in them. They often mix a little truth into their bullshit to confuse you. They may give you incomplete truths, insisting, when you call them on their bullshit, that they never lied to you.

Bullshitting Liars are very frustrating to deal with because you can never really trust them and never really communicate with them. Since trust is the key element of communication, it is virtually impossible to respect them or to relate to them honestly and openly.

Sharlene got involved with a man and discovered that he was married. Price insisted that he had never lied to her; he had told her he was not with his wife. Technically, Price did *not* lie. He merely gave her incomplete information.

There is an old cowboy saying: "If a man will lie to you, he will definitely steal from you." Sharlene found this to be true, as Price stole her precious time, her dignity, and her self-respect.

The Hollywood community is filled with a disproportionate number of Bullshitting Liars, telling you all kinds of stories about themselves and their projects. This is because they are in a business in which there is constant rejection, which creates low self-esteem. Many actors bullshit in order to pick themselves up and make themselves feel more important. They will usually embellish the positive and leave out the negative. Such Bullshitting Liars are usually harmless—bullshitting to impress or to enhance their self-worth—unlike Sharlene's married beau, who used bullshit to manipulate her. Bullshitting Liars such as Price often end up destroying the lives of the people they bullshit.

Bullshitting Liars may continue to stick to their story even if there is tons of evidence to show they are lying. Bullshitting Liars may be toxic enough to convince themselves the lies are true.

THE MEDDLER

•

- **They belong to the "meddle" class.**

- **Her plastic surgeon was able to do everything with her nose but keep it out of other people's business.**

- **Their business is what's none of their business.**

- **A good description of him would be fair to meddling.**

The Meddler is invasive, bold, judgmental, brazen, bulldozing, controlling, instigating, self-righteous, jealous, shameless, sharp-tongued, sneaky, gossipy, dogmatic, fault-finding, questioning, interfering, egotistical, sadistic, offensive, nosy, questioning, out of control, rude, annoying, conspiratorial, underhanded, offensive, and sabotaging.

Meddlers are a cross between the Gossip and the Instigator (see page 115), only more toxic. They get involved in your life (business and personal) by physically manipulating it with the aim of making it miserable. They don't just talk about you to others, like the Gossip, or incite you, like the Instigator. Instead they actually get involved in your life by phoning or setting up meetings with others to tell them about you.

Remember the popular 1960s TV show *Bewitched?* There was a nosy neighbor, Mrs. Kravitz, who was always calling the police or trying to get Samantha (the witch) and her husband, Darin, into some kind of trouble. Well, Mrs. Kravitz is a classic Meddler, a snitch and tattletale who can make your life a living hell.

Every daytime soap opera has its Meddler, who tries to seduce someone's husband, break up someone's marriage, or take away someone's child. The Meddler is always trying to get people in trouble or ruin their life.

Since Meddlers don't have much of a life of their own, they will often try to live vicariously through you as they attempt to manipulate your life. Meddlers get a thrill out of doing this.

Jerome, who lives in a condominium next door to Gloria, is a typical Meddler. If Gloria's door is cracked open, Jerome will stick his nose in and ask what she is doing, who is in there with her, and even what she is cooking. He will often come in uninvited and try to involve himself in her business.

One day Gloria was having a heated discussion with her girlfriend by the pool. Jerome swam over to where they were and put in his two cents, telling Gloria that she was wrong and sticking up for her friend's viewpoint. Another time, Gloria got a bill for a hundred dollars from her condominium association because a neighbor reported that her dog had peed on the grass in the courtyard. She was not surprised to learn that the neighbor was Jerome, just as she wasn't surprised to find out that Jerome was the one who called the police to her door to quiet down a "noisy" party she was having.

Jerome, an unemployed character actor who virtually had no life—other than sticking his nose in his neighbors' business—envied those who had active, exciting, and productive lives.

THE PENNY-PINCHING MISER

•

- **He loves to see a woman wearing expensive clothes, unless of course it's his wife.**

- **They are real carefree. They only care when it is free.**

- **They are people of rare gifts—it's rare that they give one.**

- **They are satisfied to let the rest of the world go "buy."**

- **Their pockets are low and their arms are short.**

The Penny-Pinching Miser is selfish, lacks generosity, is rigid, guilt-ridden, haggling, cheap, controlling, limited, unimaginative, narrow-minded, anxious, obstinate, repressed, stubborn, empty, fearful, petty, skeptical, unevolved, insecure, threatened, weak, wimpy, conniving, neurotic, and victim-like.

Penny-Pinching Misers have such low opinions of themselves that they don't think they deserve anything unless it is cheap or free. They are not only cheap with money but cheap with compliments and stingy with love and affection. Their conversations frequently focus on money, how much they paid for certain things, what kind of deal they got, how they bargained people down. They are impressed with their cleverness in haggling.

These very petty people think in such small terms that they often miss the big picture. They are so busy worrying about nickels and dimes that they end up with a nickel-and-dime life.

Penny-Pinching Misers will always be the last to reach for the check in a restaurant. If they do pay, they will scrutinize every figure on the bill and will haggle with the waiter even if it is a few cents over.

Penny-Pinching Misers end up alienating everyone around them, much as Jay did.

Jay assumed a prominent position in a new company and began to invite different people to lunch with him every day. After a while, he could never get anyone to join him at lunch. Mystified, Jay finally asked one of his associates why he always put him off. The man told him bluntly: "It's because you're too cheap and you never pick up the check."

His colleague's comment hit home. At last Jay was able to understand why Tina, his ex-girlfriend, had broken up with him. Though she never directly said, "You're stingy and cheap," she constantly hinted at wanting him to buy her flowers, a piece of jewelry, or a nice outfit. When I talked to Tina, she revealed to me that Jay was even stingy in his lovemaking. He "gave only so many kisses, so many hugs, and so many thrusts."

No matter how many good qualities a stingy person has, they are all canceled out, as Confucius asserts. Associating with a miserly person, he claims, "is not even worth considering."

THE FANATIC

•

- **This is the kind of person who is hard to find and harder to lose.**

- **They are like summer colds—you can't get rid of them.**

- **The real problem of having leisure time is to keep them from using it.**

The Fanatic is dogmatic, stubborn, irritating, controlling, brazen, clinging, attacking, narrow-minded, conniving, irrational, intimidating, shallow, self-righteous, socially inept, neurotic, demanding, fastidious, fearless, frightening, offensive, obnoxious, petty, unpredictable, pushy, pugnacious, unrealistic, threatening, rejecting, unreasonable, judgmental, disrespectful, and defensive.

The Fanatic is a zealot who believes all out in something or someone without any consideration for other points of view. As with the Bitchy, Bossy Bully and the Control Freak, it is "their way or the highway." They are passionate about whatever they say and reject anyone who doesn't follow their belief system. Fanatics are always trying to convert you to their way of thinking. If you should have an opinion of your own or disagree, however mildly, they get angry, tell you how wrong you are, and consider you a traitor. You can't have a decent, intelligent conversation with them because they are unwilling to listen to any points of view except their own. They seem to have all the answers and monopolize every discussion. They are inflexible and highly judgmental, which makes it virtually impossible to have a give-and-take dialogue with them.

Fanatics are like a dog with a bone. Once they get an idea in their head, Fanatics never let go.

Edith tried to live her life according to Christian doctrine, but she seldom went to church, rarely read the Bible, and never spoke in tongues. Maggie, who did all those things, told Edith that she was not a true Christian unless she did them as well. There was no use talking to Maggie, though Edith tried to explain her point of view. Maggie spoke louder and became more vehement as she expressed her beliefs, quoting Scripture liberally.

Perhaps the most devastating and powerful example of a Fanatic was that in the film *Fatal Attraction,* in which the woman portrayed by Glenn Close stalked her married lover, refusing to let go of her fantasy of him until it ended in her death.

THE ME, MYSELF, AND I NARCISSIST

•

- **He likes people who say what they think, as long as it agrees with what he thinks.**

- **She wants only one thing in life—herself.**

- **Every time he looks in the mirror, he takes a bow.**

The Me, Myself, and I Narcissist is selfish, egomaniacal, lacking in self-confidence, shallow, insecure, arrogant, boring, limited, socially inept, exhausting, obnoxious, flamboyant, self-centered, ostentatious, indiscreet, and a show-off.

Me, Myself, and I Narcissists have only one thing on their agenda: themselves. The most self-centered individuals you will ever encounter, they don't want to talk about or do anything unless it pertains to them. They want to hear about your issues only if they affect them. Their vocabularies are overabundantly supplied with the words "me" and "myself." "I" is the first word of every sentence they utter. Trying to have a conversation with a Narcissist can be the most frustrating experience you will ever have, because they speak a monologue instead of a give-and-take dialogue.

The gifts these people treasure most are a mirror and a tape recorder, for they love to look at themselves and hear themselves talk. It is difficult to have any kind of relationship with Me, Myself, and I Narcissists unless you cater to them on every level. Narcissists will only do things that pertain to them. If it's not their job, they won't do it.

Their behavior is perfectly reflected in the famous Hollywood joke about the actor who was at a dinner party, talking to a woman whom he just met. After realizing that he had spent two entire hours discussing his past projects, his current projects, his future projects, and telling her what a fantastic actor he was, he said, "Oh, I'm sorry, I've been so rude. I've only been talking about myself for the past two hours. Let's talk about *you* now. What do *you* think of me?" The epitome of the Me, Myself, and I Narcissist.

People cannot relate to you if you constantly chatter about *your* self, *your* child, *your* spouse, *your* career, *your* success. This can be unnerving, revolting, and even nauseating to someone who realizes that you feel the entire world revolves around you. Being so self-consumed makes you an uninteresting bore, as you have the same unevolved, egocentric view of the world that a two-year-old has. Such a view is definitely unacceptable for an adult.

THE EDDIE HASKELL

•

- **You can get diabetes or go into insulin shock if you are around them long enough.**

- **Their flattery makes you feel like a pancake that's just had the syrup poured over it.**

The Eddie Haskell is underhanded, lying, phony, bullshitting, bitchy, effusive, brown-nosing, conniving, double-crossing, hypocritical, shady, shameless, sneaky, annoying, ass-kissing, sugary, gregarious, duplicitous, nosy, fake, gossipy, pretentious, irritating, meddling, manipulative, superficial, two-faced, controlling, dishonest, disloyal, a turncoat, and a user.

Remember Eddie Haskell in *Leave It to Beaver*? This boy was sweet, polite, and gentlemanly to his teachers, his parents, and Mr. and Mrs. Cleaver, his best friend's parents. But when no one else was around, he was a mean and nasty jerk to his best friend's little brother, Beaver, and all *his* friends.

The Eddie Haskell is the ultimate manipulator—flattering you to death just to get what he wants. He lavishes you with excessive praise and acts as though you are his best friend and he would do anything for you.

Deep inside, Eddie Haskells may not really like you at all, but they will never let you know it to your face. They are effusive in their flattery and when you try to stop them or slough them off, they often get indignant, insisting you are the most beautiful, the smartest, and the best. You can't help but smile, as deep inside you'd love those things to be true and you love hearing them. When you do break into that smile, they know they have you. Watching them in action is disgusting, as you see how phony they are, kissing up to anyone who can do them any good.

THE SELF-RIGHTEOUS PRISS

•

- **The only time they are ever squeezed is when they are wearing tight shoes.**

- **They lack only a few more obnoxious traits to be perfect.**

The Self-Righteous Priss is stubborn, controlling, dogmatic, judgmental, rigid, hypocritical, condescending, uncommunicative, boring, fault-finding, selfish, old-fashioned, snobby, pretentious, un-evolved, unreasonable, negative, obstinate, critical, meticulous, su-perficial, offensive, petty, and a know-it-all.

Self-Righteous Prisses think they are perfect and can do no wrong as they sit on their high horse, looking down their nose in judgment of you. They are rigid, uptight, judgmental people, who expect oth-ers to live by their code of ethics. For example, they may look down on anyone who smokes, drinks, curses, has premarital sex, or isn't as well groomed or as tightly organized as they are. They are usu-ally filled with anger, disdain, and disgust, as they have very little tolerance toward others. These perfectionists are finicky and like only a limited number of things and people. Their attitude is much like that of the Fanatic, the Bitchy, Bossy Bully, and the Control Freak, in that it is "their way or the highway."

They are extremely difficult to be around and even more diffi-cult to live with, as very few people can come up to their expecta-tions. Living miserable existences, they can never let go and enjoy the world or stop, relax, and smell the roses.

Their rigidity is imposed in an attempt to hide the fact that they aren't perfect. Since they are, after all, human beings, subject to er-ror and to desires that threaten their brittle moral framework, they find themselves becoming hypocrites and in turn feel ambivalent about themselves, which diminishes their sense of self-worth.

THE SNOOTY SNOB

•

- **They like you only if you dislike the same people they dislike.**

- **They want to know only the people who don't want to know them.**

- **They are so class-conscious, they have no class and everyone is conscious of it.**

- **She needs a plastic surgeon to have her nose lowered.**

- **His head is so uplifted he has a double chin on the back of his neck.**

The Snooty Snob is pretentious, self-righteous, shallow, arrogant, belittling, fault-finding, aloof, insecure, weak, bitchy, uncommunicative, selfish, hostile, intimidating, egotistical, judgmental, nitpicking, unfriendly, rejecting, rigid, unreasonable, condescending, disrespectful, petty, rude, condescending, superficial, and holier than thou.

Snooty Snobs act as though they are superior to everyone else. Thus do they make themselves feel more important, for deep down inside they are trembling with insecurity. They have to drop names and go to the best, chicest "in" places in order to feel any sense of self-worth. If you are not part of the in crowd they won't even bother to say hello to you. They go around with their noses in the air, talking to you only if you are "cool" and "hip." They are condescending and talk down to you. Snooty Snobs are often found in Snooty Snob clubs, which let you in only if you look right, are popular, or have a lot of money to bribe the doorman with. These people desperately need the validation of such clubs to feel like functioning human beings.

Snooty Snobs are also temperamental and insist on getting special attention. They will butt in line to get ahead of you and act like spoiled children with very little regard for anyone but themselves. The "I'm better than you" attitude they exhibit masks their "I'm worse than you" inner conviction. They are riddled with insecurity and have very fragile egos.

Sometimes Snooty Snobs have no money at all but have positions that place them in contact with the rich and famous. This is most evident in places like Beverly Hills, where an assistant to a celebrity may assume a vicarious "I'm better than you" persona.

Snooty Snob behavior is evident in the movie *Pretty Woman* when Julia Roberts's character walks into a store on exclusive Rodeo Drive in Beverly Hills wearing shabby clothes. The Snooty Snob saleswomen treat her like dirt, as they think she has no money. Having experienced similar hostile treatment personally in Beverly Hills, I can say that this fictional scene is, alas, all too true.

Though these salespeople could never in their wildest dreams afford the clothing of the people they sell to, they are exemplary Snooty Snobs and endear themselves to no one.

T H E   C O M P E T I T O R

•

- **For years they have been racing for supremacy, but it's high time they settle down.**

- **They never hit a man when he's down—instead they kick him.**

- **They are interested only in the kind of friends whose inferiority they enjoy.**

- **He can't put his best foot forward without stepping on someone's toes.**

The Competitor is provocative, fearless, fanatical, obnoxious, paranoid, offensive, pushy, aggressive, resentful, sabotaging, conniving, intense, intimidated, defensive, confrontational, threatened, untrustworthy, negative, insecure, argumentative, and always looking for a fight.

• • •

Competitors see every occasion as an opportunity to outwit or sur-pass you. Everything is a competition, from getting a job to getting a boyfriend or girlfriend, husband or wife. Tell Competitors a story about how great your dog is, and they will tell you their dog is big-ger, better, and smarter. Tell them how hard you worked today, and they will surpass your story by telling you how hard they worked, despite the multitude of obstacles they had to overcome.

There is no relaxing around Competitors. You always feel they are ready to pounce. They generally have a negative attitude about people because they are so busy competing with them. Let's say that you make a comment that a mutual friend looks particularly attrac-tive today. The Competitor may retort, "I've seen her look better. Actually I think she's worn out. Look at those circles under her eyes."

Competitors tend to be show-offs and braggarts who gloat about their achievements past and present. They constantly try to impress you with how much better they are than you. The truth is that they have such low self-esteem that the only way they can re-late to you is by turning everything into a contest.

THE CONTROL FREAK

•

- **They call him Bus Driver—he tells everyone where to get off.**

- **He married his secretary, thinking he'd continue to dictate to her.**

- **She believes in law and order, just as long as she can lay down the law and give the orders.**

The Control Freak is invasive, sabotaging, rigid, manipulative, arrogant, aggressive, forceful, backstabbing, bulldozing, self-righteous, meddling, confrontational, dogmatic, egotistical, obstinate, pushy, unreasonable, stubborn, selfish, unaware, threatened, threatening, disrespectful, uncommunicative, stubborn, tenacious, and unevolved.

• • •

Control Freaks can never let go. Much like Bitchy, Bossy Bullies, they are immobilized if not in control. However, unlike Bullies, they don't always use anger or meanness to get what they want. Control Freaks often use sweet talk and manipulation.

Control Freaks are not team players and have difficulty delegating authority, as they try to do everything themselves. If things don't go their way, they get angry or lose interest, for they feel they *must* orchestrate every move. They set themselves up for lives filled with frustration and disappointment by *never* going with the flow. Instead they force things to happen, and when things don't go their rigid way they panic and become either angrier or more manipulative.

John was miserable on his trip to Indonesia with Jill. Nothing went right for him in this third world country. The more he tried to control things, the more they did not work out. Plane reservations, shops, hotels, the food, the weather, all made his life miserable because he did not have any control over what was happening to him at every minute. He refused even to consider that Indonesia was a different culture, with different values and different ways of doing things.

Control Freaks literally "freak out" if they can't control things, no matter how small. One of my clients, Anita, realized that her Control Freak husband was so out of control that she had to divorce him.

One day Anita and Phil took a two-hour drive to the desert, listening to the radio en route. The radio began to give off static, and Phil couldn't seem to fix it. He kept cursing a blue streak. Finally, he screeched to a halt, got out of the car, pulled a crowbar from the trunk, yanked the radio out of the socket, threw it on the side of the road, and began beating it with the crowbar.

Anita couldn't believe what he was doing. She was numb and didn't dare say a word, for fear she would be beaten up next.

The irony is that Control Freaks cannot control themselves. Unable to control a person, a situation, or even a thing—such as a radio—they lose control of themselves. These are the people who punch holes in walls with their fists when things don't go their way.

You can't hold others on such a tight rein that they cannot

move. If you do, they will break, emotionally or physically. Think of a butterfly: if you hold it too tightly its wings will break, so you end up destroying its beauty as well as its life.

THE ACCUSING CRITIC

•

- **She spends most of her time at the complaint counter.**

- **They stopped dating and started intimidating.**

- **He'll ask a question, answer it himself, and then tell you what's wrong with it.**

The Accusing Critic is complaining, intimidating, fault-finding, bitchy, attacking, blunt, whiny, uncommunicative, hateful, instigating, irrational, jealous, a know-it-all, sadistic, self-righteous, sharptongued, shameless, abusive, acrimonious, annoying, obnoxious, rejecting, rigid, dogmatic, overemotional, negative, unreasonable, questioning, pugnacious, unrealistic, petty, nitpicking, dissatisfied, testy, rebellious, condescending, controlling, disrespectful, offensive, meddling, threatened, threatening, suspicious, mean-spirited, and a perfectionist.

Accusing Critics have to make you feel wrong in order to make themselves feel right. In criticizing you directly to your face, they try to convince you you're less than a person. You can never do anything right around Accusing Critics, so you are always uncomfortable. They are like bad parents, always admonishing and accusing their children even when it isn't deserved.

Instead of *asking* you, they *accuse* you. They do this to gain power and control, much like the Control Freak. In essence, they feel it is their duty to find something wrong with you and to let you know it in a harsh, cynical, and attacking tone, reflecting their constant state of dissatisfaction. They make accusatory statements like:

"You are the reason we were late" or "You didn't get the job because you are so intense."

Here is a conversation I overheard at a restaurant one night.

He: You were the reason we were late.

She: No, it was you.

He: It was you and your makeup.

She: It was you and your phone calls.

He: You're always late; everyone in your family is always late. Didn't anyone ever teach you how to be on time?

These two were typical Accusing Critics. Though the man made the first accusation, each party tried to use the conversation to make the other wrong.

Accusing Critics are so demanding of perfection that they are never satisfied. Much like the Self-Righteous Priss, the Accusing Critic is constantly frustrated in trying to make an imperfect world perfect. Thus, the Critic lashes out at you by invalidating everything about you, taking joy out of a situation, and looking for the negative—even in something so insignificant as what you choose to eat for dinner.

If you are around these Accusing Critics for any length of time, you will doubtless end up getting physically ill, as they are a difficult type of Toxic Terror to "stomach."

Accusing Critics are petty people who often nitpick, finding fault with insignificant things that don't really matter. Unfortunately, Accusing Critical behavior happens in way too many marriages, which may account for the high divorce rate nationwide.

THE ARROGANT KNOW-IT-ALL

•

- **She's smart—a regular encyclopedia. One thing she doesn't know is that reference books are never taken out.**

- **They know all the answers, but nobody asks them the questions.**

- **If they can't boast about knowing something, they boast about not knowing it.**

The Arrogant Know-It-All is pretentious, confrontational, inse-cure, socially inept, exhausting, manipulative, pedantic, limited, noncommunicative, judgmental, selfish, self-righteous, pushy, reject-ing, annoying, rigid, unaware, stubborn, condescending, sarcastic, controlling, offensive, talkative, and critical.

Arrogant Know-It-Alls don't know anything at all when it comes to dealing with people. Though they may seem to know everything and have all the self-confidence in the world, they are really very in-secure people. Otherwise they wouldn't have to let everyone know how smart they are and how much information they have stored in their brain.

Arrogant Know-It-Alls usually talk *at* you, not with you. In fact, they often act as though by talking to you they are doing you a fa-vor. They enjoy using big words and are very quick to put down your ideas. Their condescending tone makes you feel like a dummy, while they in turn feel smarter.

Another tactic of Arrogant Know-It-Alls is to overwhelm you with data and information. You don't have a chance to even com-pete with them, much less talk about anything intelligently. Since they know it all, they can never be open-minded enough to learn more, especially if you are the one talking to them.

THE EMOTIONAL REFRIGERATOR

•

- **They have as much expression as a pickled herring.**

- **They have the personality of the back wall of a handball court.**

- **When they give a blood transfusion, the patient gets pneumonia from the ice water in his veins.**

The Emotional Refrigerator is cold, calm, aloof, emotionless, secretive, quiet, dishonest, indifferent, intimidated, limited, inse-

cure, unreliable, unexpressive, fearful, rejecting, unevolved, enigmatic, uncommunicative, cowardly, unpredictable, suspicious, and
depressed.

Emotional Refrigerators express only one thing—aloofness. They
use cold silence the way the Bitchy, Bossy Bully uses threats. They
are reserved and secretive, much like the Silent but Deadly Volcano,
except Emotional Refrigerators never erupt.

You don't know how they are really feeling, as you never get a
true reading from their voice or body language. You never know if
they are happy or sad. They usually have a vacant or dull look in
their eyes and rarely express what they feel.

Though they may be able to do their jobs well, anyone who
gets involved with an Emotional Refrigerator on a personal level is
headed for disappointment. They are so emotionally unresponsive
that it becomes terribly frustrating to deal with them. They refuse to
tell you what is wrong or why they are so quiet. Often they use
their silence as a form of manipulation, to intimidate you. They get
pleasure out of seeing how uncomfortable you are with the silence
that comforts them.

They may have the same emotions as you, but sharing them
with you would make them feel as though they lost their power
over you. In essence, they keep you wondering about what is going
on inside them.

THE SKEPTICAL PARANOID
•

- **You can never tell him he is skeptical or paranoid, because he
  will never believe you.**

- **She thought everyone against her was following her, but then
  she didn't believe it.**

- **He thinks the world is against him, and he is right.**

The Skeptical Paranoid is intimidated, spineless, negative, fearful, complaining, self-destructive, depressive, irrational, judgmental, limited, tentative, timid, questioning, resentful, dogmatic, egotistical, insecure, masochistic, victim-like, fault-finding, rejecting, rigid, scared, threatened, weak, unstable, unrealistic, nonbelieving, contradicting, always doubting, and unconfident.

Skeptical Paranoids never believe a word that anybody says without proof. Even if they see it or hear it, they *still* don't believe it. They often have doubting looks on their faces and usually seem to be hesitating as they throw cold water on every idea you have.

They are the ultimate pessimists and nonbelievers. Before anything happens, they are convinced that it will *never* work, much like the Gloom and Doom Victim. They are extremely difficult to be around, because they are so suspicious and feel that everyone is against them. Trust is not what they do best.

As a result, it is very difficult to get close to Skeptical Paranoids, because they doubt your intentions and your sincerity. In essence, they think that you are trying to plot against them in some way.

THE INSTIGATOR
•

- **They seldom repeat gossip the way they heard it.**

- **They can't leave bad enough alone.**

- **They suffer from acute indiscretion.**

The Instigator is sabotaging, meddling, controlling, interfering, indiscreet, sadistic, negative, angry, adversarial, backstabbing, judgmental, fault-finding, sneaky, hurtful, jealous, spineless, pushy, unreliable, untrustworthy, petty, lying, offensive, manipulative, disrespectful, confrontational, critical, troublemaking, and double-crossing.

Instigators are interferers who like to make trouble for other people. They want you to stick your neck out so that they can be entertained if it is chopped off. Unlike Meddlers, Instigators don't get greatly involved. Instead they egg people on, perhaps knowing full well that what they advise is the very wrong thing.

Perhaps their own lives are so miserable and so dull that the only way they can generate some excitement is by verbally stirring up the waters in other people's lives. Often they will communicate with innuendos, such as: "Oh, I'm sure your husband is completely devoted to you, even though he spent the afternoon with, um, his secretary the other day" or "I'm not one to pry, but isn't Robert supposed to be working exclusively for you? I saw him doing some work for three other people in the office."

Instigators have no regard for anyone but themselves or anything but their own entertainment. They are alarmists who get a thrill out of manipulating situations and making mountains out of molehills.

Sirvone, a hairdresser, laughed hysterically as he told me how he instigated a fight between one of his clients and her teenage daughter.

In an alarmed tone, he told his client that she had better keep an eye on her daughter. He had heard what was going on at the local junior high school, and her daughter could very well be doing drugs and getting pregnant if this client didn't watch her more closely. If it were his daughter, he said, he wouldn't even let her out of the house. The girl was probably already engaged in drugs and sex.

The woman was so upset that she got out of the chair to call her daughter and tell her she couldn't go out with her friends that night. A huge fight erupted between mother and daughter over the phone. Sirvone was practically clicking his heels in the air with glee as he related the story to me, which told me how dangerous and toxic the man was. He was thrilled with his cleverness in alarming the woman so.

Instigators instigate in order to gain control and achieve a sense of importance in their small lives. Manipulating the actions of others makes them feel powerful. Because they stir people up, trying to provoke negative actions, Instigators are among the worst troublemakers out there. They may twist the truth or goad people into doing things they would not ordinarily do. They ignite the fire and fan the flames, then enjoy watching the glow from a distance.

Instigators are also tattletales, who will spread stories about people in order to get them in trouble. Like Gossips, they can never keep a secret, but unlike true Gossips, they will make up a story in order to manipulate others. They seem to live for making trouble in other people's lives.

In essence, they are little devils trying to make the worst of every situation.

Sound Familiar?

Have you seen people you recognize in any of these thirty descriptions of Toxic Terrors? Have you identified anybody in particular whom perhaps you live with, or work with, or used to be friends or lovers with? Perhaps you have identified somebody you were married to. Maybe you have even seen yourself in many of these descriptions.

You may have noticed, too, that many of the Toxic Terrors share several traits with other Toxic Terrors, even though each Toxic Terror is unique and possesses their own specific characteristics. Often a particular toxic person you know may embody more than one toxic type. For example, they may be a Gossip and a Control Freak, or a Cut-You-Downer and a Smiling Two-Faced Backstabber.

After reading about the thirty Toxic Terrors, you should be equipped to understand exactly why you feel negative toward a person.

Dealing with a Toxic Terror is—as an attorney I recently met in Phoenix so eloquently put it—"like tasting a teaspoon of battery acid."

In the next chapter you will learn how to neutralize these battery-acid people, so they become less toxic to your system.

CHAPTER 6

TEN TECHNIQUES FOR HANDLING TOXIC PEOPLE

- **The Tension-Blowout Technique**

- **The Humor Technique**

- **The Stop-the-Thought Technique**

- **The Mirror Technique**

- **The Direct-Confront Technique**

- **The Calm Questioning Technique**

- **The Give-Them-Hell-and-Yell Technique**

- **The Give-Them-Love-and-Kindness Technique**

- **The Vicarious-Fantasy Technique**

- **The Unplug Technique**

Techniques *Never* to Use
Never Self-Destruct
Never Use Physical Violence

Other No-No's in Dealing with Toxic People

These Ten Techniques for dealing with toxic people have been utilized by countless clients of mine, who have found them effective in coping with the demons in their lives. After mastering the techniques, they have experienced dramatic improvements in their health, their attitudes, their business ventures, and their personal relationships.

THE TENSION-BLOWOUT TECHNIQUE

•

This technique underlies all the others, as it helps you to gain physical control over your emotions.

What happens when someone upsets you? When you are so angry you could "spit nails," your adrenaline starts to flow, your heart beats faster, your head begins to throb, and your face reddens and eyes begin to bulge as you hold on to your breath. Using the Tension-Blowout Technique helps you to oxygenate yourself immediately and serves as a vehicle for releasing your tension and regaining your body's homeostatic balance. It allows you to gain oxygen and release carbon dioxide in a controlled, systematic way. Here is the sequence to follow:

1. **Breathe in through your mouth for two seconds.**

2. **Hold on to that breath for three seconds, as you think of the toxic person.**

3. **Keep thinking of the person as you literally blow him or her out of your system with all your might, until you have run out of air.**

4. **Then *stop* for two seconds and do not breathe.**

5. **Repeat steps 1 through 4 until, by recalling the toxic actions and words and blowing out, you completely eject this person from your system.**

6. **Repeat the procedure once more, continuing to blow out the person's negativity. After the third time, immediately take a big breath in through your mouth, filling up your lungs, and exhale normally.**

You may feel a bit light-headed after you have done this technique. If so, don't worry about it. It is normal. If you become dizzy, you may want to sit down and start inhaling and exhaling slow and rhythmic breaths.

In any case, you should feel a lot less tense and angry. If not, repeat this procedure until the anger at the toxic person has left you.

The Tension-Blowout Technique is good to use when someone annoys you or is just plain irritating to be around. Releasing the air can often release you from excessive irritation.

The calming effect of this technique is also helpful in preventing your sticking your foot in your mouth and saying the wrong thing. That first held inhalation gives you an extra few seconds to think before you react.

As a professional who deals with myriad clients, I have personally found this technique to be a lifesaver when I face people who have severe emotional problems or may be out of control. It not only helps me to calm down but helps them do so as well. I also use it to gain composure when asked questions in front of a large audience after I have given a lecture or when I am on television. It aids me in controlling the rhythm of my speech so I don't talk too fast, stumble over my words, or end up putting my foot in my mouth. This technique can definitely help you to accomplish these things as well.

THE HUMOR TECHNIQUE

•

You can not only release tension but amuse yourself in the process. How often do you think of a clever response to a toxic comment hours later? How many times have you lain relaxed in bed at night and mulled over an incident, then mentally beat yourself up because you didn't say what you really wanted to at the time?

With the Humor Technique, you can respond at once and achieve the additional benefit of laughter.

Use the Tension-Blowout Technique, and when you hold in your breath, think of something amusing to say. It doesn't matter if it sounds stupid to them, as long as it's funny to you.

I used this technique at a dinner party where I was seated next to an obnoxious gentleman who bragged about himself nonstop. He told me that though he was a great singer, he had never made it "big time" in opera, so he made his living as a sing-ing teacher. Throughout dinner he kept trying to impress me with his knowledge of opera, which meant very little to me. The closest I'd come to opera was *L'italiana in Algeri* by Rossini, because I taught the infamous Rob and Fab of Milli Vanilli to lip-synch a bit of it for a Carefree gum commercial. Nevertheless, I smiled and listened graciously. Suddenly, as I reached over to get my second piece of delicious, cheese-laden garlic bread, he glared at me, and said, in a harsh, clipped tone, "You know, I just lost fifteen pounds, and you should do the same."

At first I was in shock, incredulous at what I'd heard. I started to feel a tinge of guilt as I thought: *Am* I eating too much? I immediately took a breath and held it in, as I thought to myself: No, the Tension-Blowout Technique won't work. I am livid, and what I really need to do is to have fun with him. Maybe I can play with his mind and have a good time.

I decided to goof on him with something related to opera. I looked him straight in the eye and, feigning surprise, exclaimed, "Lose weight! I want to gain seventy pounds. In fact, my aim is to look like one of those opera singers—you know, the ones that wear horns on their heads and have long braids," and I took a big bite of garlic bread.

The rest of the evening, he didn't say a word to me, which was my intention. I had had a giggle and I felt great. I had released the tension of having to deal with this toxic person through humor, poking fun at something he could relate to—opera.

The Humor Technique can also be used to save your self-esteem and enhance you in the eyes of others.

Juan, a new kid in school, had been born with a cleft lip and palate; his nose was flat, his upper lip scarred, and his speech very nasal. A rather unsightly boy, he was taunted unmercifully by the older boys in the schoolyard.

One day, an older boy pushed and shoved Juan and said, "Hey, what's that ugly scar on your face?" Juan looked the boy right in the eye and said, "Oh, that—that's the scar from when I cut myself shaving a while ago." The other boys started to laugh at the absurdity of a nine-year-old boy's shaving.

His humor endeared him to the other children. Early on, Juan had learned that laughter was his ticket out of hell, so he used the Humor Technique to make fun of himself and joke about others. Soon he became the most popular boy in his class, and the next semester he was voted class president.

Sometimes you can retort to a toxic comment by adding insult to insult. The toxic person may think that he or she is being cute, witty, and clever, but by making a more outrageous comment you shock the offender while amusing yourself.

The comedian David Brenner had a great comeback to anyone who disparaged his nose: "You think my nose is big—when I was a kid, I thought it was my third arm." Radio talk show king Howard Stern deprecates his penis size and his looks. It's hard to dislike anyone who laughs at himself.

If you can't think of anything to say, you may want to get a jokebook and memorize a few one-line comebacks that you think are particularly funny.

Comedians who have to deal with drunk hecklers or nasty clientele usually have an assortment of these retorts at their disposal. A major television comic responds to hecklers without missing a beat: "You know, this is what happens when cousins marry." The audience roars with laughter, the heckler shuts up, and the comedian continues his act.

Though I don't favor hostile sarcastic humor, in some cases it's called for. You may need to fight fire with fire. When someone is making toxic comments to you, the Humor Technique allows them to see how stupid they are acting and at the same time helps you release your tension and anger.

Often people want to use the Humor Technique but don't feel they have anything funny enough to come back with. I have listed some amusing comebacks that have been used by many comedians. Memorize them so that they will be available to you at a moment's notice. Because they are not too vicious or nasty, they will make you look good while you save face. Choose the ones you feel comfortable using.

1. **You've convinced me about reincarnation—now I know what part of a horse's anatomy you were in a previous life.**

2. **Are you the result of first cousins marrying?**

3. **Whatever is eating you must be suffering from indigestion.**

4. **You seem like the kind of person who always wants to save face, so why don't you stop shooting it off?**

5. **Look, I'm not going to engage in a battle of wits with you. I never attack anyone who is unarmed.**

6. **Why don't you leave here and go to the zoo? You'll be less conspicuous there.**

7. **I guess I can't ask you to act like a human being—you don't do imitations.**

8. **The last time I met you was in a nightmare.**

9. **You have a fine personality but not for a human being.**

10. **I don't know what makes you tick, but I hope it's a time bomb.**

11. **I don't know what I'd do without you, but I'd rather.**

12. **Don't you ever get tired of having yourself around?**

13. **The more I see of you, the less I like you.**

14. **I can't remember your name, but your nasty manners are familiar.**

15. **I never forget a face, but in your case I'm willing to make an exception.**

16. **Why don't you sue your brain for nonsupport?**

17. **Just keep on talking so I'll know that you're not thinking.**

18. **Your manners aren't half bad. They're all bad.**

19. **For a minute I didn't recognize you, and it was one of the most enjoyable minutes I've ever had.**

20. **You certainly have class—low class.**

THE STOP-THE-THOUGHT TECHNIQUE

•

Sometimes you may be so angry at a person that you feel as though you are going to explode. Every time you think of the individual, or of his or her actions, you are overwhelmed with negative emotion. In this case, not only do you need to do the Tension-Blowout Technique, but when you blow out you need to yell, *"Stop the Thought!"* Every time you think of the person or the situation, you have to hear yourself saying, "Stop the Thought," either out loud or quietly to yourself.

This technique can be a lifesaver: you won't drive yourself crazy rehashing a toxic situation over and over again in your mind.

You may wake up feeling great. Your day is going along just fine, until all of a sudden that ugly thought comes into your head, and your spunky mood turns sour as you relive the toxic moment. Soon you find yourself becoming even more irate as you beat yourself up for not saying what you should have said and for getting involved with the toxic individual in the first place. Your head feels like a volcano that is about to explode as visions of the toxic person and scenes of the toxic situation replay again and again in your mind's eye.

This is what happened to Glenda. After a tumultuous breakup with Mario, she still couldn't shake the nightmare of their toxic relationship. Because she thought about it so often during the day, her nightmare could recur at any hour during the twenty-four. They had broken up well over six months earlier, but she couldn't seem to shake the negative thoughts that put her deeper and deeper into a depressed state. When I taught her the Stop-the-Thought Technique, it literally turned her life around. At last she was able to gain some control over her life. Whenever Mario entered her mind, she screamed out, *"Stop the Thought!"* As her moods greatly improved, she was able to get on with her new Mario-less life and not dwell on the past.

The Stop-the-Thought Technique can be amplified with a positive affirmation. For example, you can say, "Stop the thought! Nobody is better than I am!" or "Stop the thought! I love myself. I am important. I am worthy." You can add anything that helps you feel positive about yourself.

THE MIRROR TECHNIQUE

•

The Mirror Technique forces toxic people to see their behavior reflected back to them.

My client Debora, an attorney, found this technique to be invaluable during her negotiations with a verbally hostile and abusive male attorney. Apparently he wouldn't allow her to get a word in edgewise, as he yelled, spoke over her speech, and shouted obscenities. One day, during a telephone encounter, she held the receiver away from her ear and began to bark like a dog as he spoke.

Abruptly the man stopped and asked, "What did you say?" Debora returned the phone to her ear and answered, "I said . . ." and she continued to imitate a dog. Then she stopped and said, "That is exactly what you sound like—a barking dog. Now, Mr. Jones, you and I are both well-trained, highly qualified, civilized professionals. Let's act that way and speak intelligently and quietly so that we can each listen to what the other is trying to say and come to an amicable resolution."

Mr. Jones was embarrassed, as he had had no idea that he barked. After Debora used the Mirror Technique, he became a completely different person—a gentleman who listened and was willing to negotiate in a civilized manner.

When you employ the Mirror Technique, you don't have to beat someone over the head with their ugly behavior. Instead you just need to give a glimpse of how ugly the person is being so that an immediate change for the better can be made.

This happened to me when I went into a small shoe store in Beverly Hills. Three times I called out, "Is anybody here?" Finally, I heard a hostile voice yelling, "What do you want?" A woman appeared from the back and headed in my direction. I was appalled. This was Beverly Hills, California—home of the posh, chic, and elite.

As the woman approached me, I calmly and quietly said, "You know, I came to this store because I know that your shoes are of the finest quality. When I entered the store, I didn't see a salesperson, so I called out three times, 'Is anybody here?' At last, I heard you scream, 'What do you want?'" I yelled in the same ugly, harsh, shrill tone she had used on me. The woman turned bright red, apologized profusely, and couldn't have been more helpful in trying to find the right shoe for me.

I didn't have to mention the incident again. I didn't have to beat her over the head with it. She clearly got it. She heard her own ugly tone from me and didn't like how it sounded.

Perhaps she will be nicer to the next customer who comes into the store. Perhaps she will never yell "What do you want?" in such an ugly tone to anyone for the rest of her life.

Sometimes people need to know how obnoxious they really are—and they need to know it immediately by seeing a reflection of the way they acted toward you. You are not only letting them know that what they said to you was unacceptable; you are causing them to realize what it feels like to have nasty things said to you—as Amanda did to Corinne.

Corinne spotted Amanda in the hallway outside the reception

room for their mutual friend's wedding. Approaching, Corinne oohed at how terrific Amanda looked and how wonderful she was. After fifteen minutes of positive chitchat, everyone began to meander over to the table where the wedding cake was being cut. Suddenly, out of earshot of everyone else, Corinne smiled smugly at Amanda and said, "No cake for you—you really put on some weight since I last saw you." She then turned on her heel to catch up with the others, leaving a shocked, stunned, and hurt Amanda behind.

When Amanda managed to regain her composure after this verbal slap in the face, she caught up to Corinne, grabbed her shoulder, looked directly in her face, and said, "That was a very mean and ugly thing to say to me. You know how sensitive I am about my weight. If you have negative thoughts about me, you should keep them to yourself, just as I have with my negative thoughts about you. Before this, I would never have thought of saying anything about your ugly yellow-stained teeth, your thin hair with the dark roots, your high forehead and sick-looking skin."

Now Corinne definitely had a taste of her own medicine. Her previous smirk turned into a pale, shocked expression as she digested what Amanda had dished out. In essence, she was now able to feel what Amanda had felt, through Amanda's using the language and communication pattern that Corinne herself had initiated. She started it, but Amanda clearly finished it!

Sometimes the Mirror Technique works well on children. I've had a child client come into my office and put his feet on a chair, then stand on it. I promptly mirrored the behavior, and the child said, "Dr. Glass, you're the doctor. You can't stand on your chair." I answered, "OK, I guess you're right," and then we both sat down and had a nice session.

The Mirror Technique enables children as well as adults to see the consequences of their toxic behavior clearly and to perceive how they come across to others.

THE DIRECT-CONFRONT TECHNIQUE

•

The Direct-Confront Technique is excellent to use when someone makes a nasty, biting comment to you. If you can't think of a funny or clever retort or can't recall a comeback from the Humor Technique section, then you may want to tell the person boldly how you feel about what he or she said or did.

The Direct-Confront Technique prevents you from becoming a victim. Others will usually respect you for speaking up and saying what is on your mind. In directly confronting someone, it is essential that you project your voice so that you can be heard and speak in a well-modulated tone. You can use emotion in your voice to make an impression of conviction and confidence.

Senator Dianne Feinstein of California expertly used the Direct-Confront Technique to respond to a condescending comment by Senator Larry Craig of Idaho. Speaking in opposition to Feinstein's proposal to outlaw semiautomatic assault weapons, Craig ended his argument on the Senate floor with: "So the gentle lady from California needs to become a little bit more familiar with firearms and their deadly characteristics."

Senator Feinstein replied as follows: "I'm quite familiar with firearms. I became mayor as a product of an assassination. I found my assassinated colleague and put a finger through a bullet hole, trying to get a pulse. I proposed gun control legislation in San Francisco. I went through a recall on the basis of it. I was trained in the shooting of a firearm when I had terrorists attack me with a bomb at my house, when my husband was dying, when I had windows shot out. So, Senator, *I know something about what firearms can do.*"

Using the Direct-Confront Technique not only causes others to respect you but allows you to gain more self-respect as you say what you mean.

Another perfect example of the Direct-Confront Technique was described by actress Meryl Streep in *Cosmopolitan* magazine. Early in her career, she was invited by Dino De Laurentiis's son to meet the famous movie producer. He spoke to her kindly in English, then turned to his son and said in Italian, "What is she? She's not pretty.

She's not beautiful enough, why do you waste my time?" Streep, who understood Italian, looked at the father and directly confronted him, saying in Italian, "I don't like that very much." This must have left a much embarrassed producer with one or both of his chins from each of his two faces fallen, as Streep walked out of the room. Of course, she went on to become one of the most beautiful and sought-after actresses in Hollywood, despite De Laurentiis.

In essence, the Direct-Confront Technique lets others know that you are onto their games, so they can't be sneaky and stab you in the back. Now they have to stab you in the front and confront you directly.

THE CALM QUESTIONING TECHNIQUE

•

The Calm Questioning Technique lets toxic people see how absurd, ridiculous, or stupid their ideas or comments are. As you take someone through a series of questions that require *yes* or *no* answers in a logical progression, you become like a courtroom lawyer who is trying to make an important point by having a witness respond to a succession of queries.

When using this technique, it is imperative that you speak calmly and sound as though you are in control, not allowing your emotions to take over.

Let's say someone makes the ignorant comment that he or she "hates blacks." You may want to ask the following questions to show up the stupidity of the statement. For example:

Do you hate every single black person in the entire world?

Do you know of a black person you like?

Do you like sports?

Are there any black sports figures whom you respect?

How about politics or music?

Is there any one black person who you ever thought was intelligent or talented?

Have black people ever done anything to hurt you?

Do you think there are some black people who work hard and care for their families?

Do you know a lot of black people?

Have you lived in the same neighborhood as black people?

Have you ever had anyone hate you because you are who you are?

Have you ever felt that if fewer people hated one another and got to know each other better as individuals, this would be a better world?

In essence, you are leading an ignorant fool through a line of questioning in which the person is forced to think about the implications of his or her stupidity and explore the feelings that underlie the statement that was made.

I often use the Calm Questioning Technique when I am a guest expert on talk shows, addressing people who are clearly missing the point of issues. On a Sally Jessy Raphael show about "Mothers and Daughter Who Party Together," one woman told how she and her twenty-year-old daughter had a great time together, getting gifts from the men they dated and then taking their money when they got drunk. Apparently the daughter was a virgin and didn't actually have sex with the men, though the mother did.

Needless to say, I, along with the entire audience, was appalled at the mother's lifestyle, and I used the Calm Questioning Technique to show her how inappropriate her behavior was:

Dr. Glass (to mother): Did you party with your own mother?
Mother: No, but I would have liked to.
Dr. Glass: What about your dad—did you get along with your dad?
Mother: No.
Dr. Glass: What about men in general—do you like men?
Mother: Sometimes.

Dr. Glass: I get that you really don't like men.
Mother: Well, you wouldn't either if they tried to use you.
Dr. Glass: Do you think men are to be used, to be taken advantage of, to take care of you, to buy you things?
Mother: Well, why not? They use women.
Dr. Glass: Do you think you are a good mother?
Mother: Yes, I think I'm an excellent mother.
Dr. Glass (to daughter): Do you think she's been a good mother?
Daughter (defensive): Yes, I do.
Dr. Glass (to mother): Are you proud of the fact that your daughter is a virgin?
Mother: Yes, I am.
Dr. Glass (to daughter): Are you proud that you're a virgin?
Daughter: Yes, I am.
Dr. Glass: What is a virgin?
Daughter: Someone who hasn't had sex.
Dr. Glass: Is a virgin someone who just hasn't had sexual intercourse?
Daughter: Yes.
Dr. Glass: Does a virgin take the upper half of a man's body while the mother takes the lower half? Is that a virgin?

The audience roared and applauded wildly as the mother and daughter shouted in an attempt to defend themselves.

Glass (to mother): Do you think you are being a good role model for your daughter, teaching her to use men and to get whatever she can from men?
Mother: Well, that's the real world.
Glass: So you feel comfortable in teaching your daughter, in essence, to be a prostitute?

By now the audience went completely wild, oohing, aahing, and clapping.

This technique is so powerful that, if you do it well, you can not only get your point across but often even change other people's way of thinking by presenting another viewpoint, based

131

on questions they have to answer and be accountable for. You are not talking to them but, rather, working out answers with them. By speaking and commenting, they become active parts of the communication process.

The Calm Questioning Technique can also help you acquire more information about a person or situation. You then know where you stand or what the real story is.

After I taught one of my clients this technique, she found that her dating life improved. She was less stressed because she asked a series of direct questions of her potential suitors and found out exactly where she stood in her relationships.

After meeting Claudia at a party, Dean pursued her, calling her up and taking her out to dinner several times. They communicated very well and had a lot in common. The four dates they had lasted into the wee hours of the morning, as they had so many experiences to talk about and so many viewpoints to share. Despite their excellent rapport, Dean never made a move on Claudia. She was dying to kiss him, as she was tremendously attracted to him.

At first she thought he was just shy, so on the fourth date she played "kneesies" with him—pressing her knee against his and leaving it there and touching his arm quite frequently during the conversation, making sure to leave her hand in position for a few seconds. Whenever she did this he would recoil. After touching him half a dozen times, she got the message that he probably wasn't interested in her. She then started talking about gays, thinking this might lead to an explanation for his behavior. The conversation indicated that he was an avowed heterosexual and could not stand it when gay men hit on him.

Dean's good-night peck on the lips, similar to those she might give her mother or sister, left her feeling sad and rejected when she walked into her apartment. She wondered whether she had bad breath or body odor, was too fat or not pretty enough for him. Maybe she talked too much. At any rate, she spent the entire night agonizing over why he wasn't attracted to her. When she woke up the next morning, she sadly wrote him off.

Later that morning, a chirpy, happy Dean called to ask her out for the following night. She then said, "Dean, I need to ask you something."

Dean: Sure.

Claudia: Would you be perfectly honest with me?

Dean: Sure.

Claudia: Even if you thought it would hurt my feelings?

Dean: Yes, of course. What are you getting at?

Claudia: I have to know, are you attracted to me?

Dean: Yes, I am. I know that you thought that I probably am not, but I am.

Claudia: Do you mean you are attracted to me as a friend?

Dean: No.

Claudia: Do you mean you are attracted to me as a person?

Dean: No. I mean I'm attracted to you in every way—physically, mentally, and emotionally—and that's the problem.

Claudia: Why is it a problem?

Dean: Well, I look at where you are in your life—you're established, you've got money, you've got a good career. I'm just starting out, and I can't afford to take you many places. Also, my head is a mess because I'm getting over a divorce and I don't want to get into another relationship.

Now Claudia knew for sure. Though she wasn't thrilled with his answer, she nevertheless found out what the true situation was instead of beating herself up, wondering if it was her breath, body, or looks that turned him off.

The famous maxim "Seek and ye shall find" applies to the Calm Questioning Technique: "Ask and ye shall know."

THE GIVE-THEM-HELL-AND-YELL
TECHNIQUE

•

We have all been taught that it is not "ladylike" or "gentlemanly" to get angry, scream or yell, or lose your temper. I say this is nonsense.

Sometimes you have to scream and yell, because this is the only way you can be heard. Sometimes you get so enraged that the only thing you can possibly do to let off steam so you don't end up with a cerebral hemorrhage is to yell and really let a person have it. Sometimes you use profanity or curse because that is the only way you can release your anger. As Mark Twain once said, "Under certain circumstances profanity provides a relief denied even to prayer."

Although I wouldn't recommend a steady diet of it—because that would turn you into a toxic person yourself—sometimes you need profanity to get your point across. Four-letter words may not be socially acceptable, but they may be the only words that toxic people will actually hear as you shock them into listening to you.

American tennis champion Pete Sampras used the Give-Them-Hell-and-Yell Technique to release his anger at toxic English fans during a Wimbledon match against a British player. Every time Sampras scored a winning point, members of the audience would boo and hiss. As soon as it was apparent that he had won, Sampras turned to the crowd and, as loudly and angrily as possible, screamed, *"Take that, you motherfuckers."* Many Americans were proud of this young man for standing up to the English, who pride themselves on politeness, manners, and class.

Another utilization of the Give-Them-Hell-and-Yell Technique relieved the inner pain a client had suffered for years. Forty-year-old Sandra was haunted by an incident that occurred when she was an innocent eighteen-year-old. As a dental assistant, she administered nitrous oxide to patients in order to sedate them. One day her employer told Sandra that he wanted to administer nitrous oxide to her, so she could feel what it was like and "be more sensitive to patients." She agreed, and as he turned the gas higher and higher, she giggled and felt open, free as a bird. The next thing she knew, her panties were off and the dentist was having sexual intercourse with her in the chair. She was in shock. After the dentist/rapist turned the gas off, she ran to the bathroom and vomited her guts out. Afterward the dentist acted as if nothing had happened and told her to clean all the equipment, to wash out the waste receptacle from the dental suction machine, and then to come into his office. Numbly she obliged, and when she went to his office, he fired her.

For years she felt awful about this incident and was too embarrassed to tell anyone. Eventually she blocked it out as though it had never happened, until one day she saw a tabloid TV show on which they had used a hidden camera to videotape a dentist fondling a client. She heard the reporter ask, "Could your dentist be doing this to you while you are under?" and all of a sudden her memory resurfaced. This time she not only felt nauseous but was enraged. She wanted to go there and knock all his teeth out. Picturing herself doing this, via the Vicarious-Fantasy Technique (see page 137) still wasn't enough to quell her anger. A lawsuit was out of the question, as she didn't want to put her husband, her children, or, for that matter, herself through such an ordeal. She knew she had to directly confront her attacker. She made an appointment under her married name.

When the assistant led her to the treatment room, Sandra said that she had a dental problem that was too embarrassing to talk about in front of anyone else and needed to see the dentist alone. Her heart was beating a mile a minute, and she used the Tension-Blowout Technique I had taught her to gain more control over the situation until he arrived. Finally, he came in, looking the same but older. She asked, "Do you remember me?" "No, I'm sorry, I don't," said the dentist. "I am the same person who was your dental assistant twenty-two years ago and whom you raped in this chair after giving me nitrous oxide." The dentist turned ghost-white and was visibly shaken. She then stood up, blocking the door, as she continued: "You humiliated me by making me clean up the grossest garbage in your office, and then you fired me." She reached for the waste can near the door, and then she shouted, "Well, you rapist, now you can clean this garbage," as she hurled the entire contents of the can, including gross dental debris, at him. She then went out to her car and laughed the entire way home as she recalled his wimpy little shaking body and thought of him tossing and turning all night, worrying about whether she would sue him and ruin his life. The Give-Them-Hell-and-Yell Technique was just the medicine Sandra needed to put an end to her feelings of rage and hatred toward an abuser.

The Give-Them-Hell-and-Yell Technique gives you permission

to act like a wild tiger, to contort your face, to have the veins in your neck pop out and the veins in your head pulsate, as you discharge your anger. You can yell, scream, curse, rant, and rave. You can say anything, but you must *not hit.* You can hit below the belt verbally, but you must *never* raise a hand or a fist or use *any* form of physical violence whatsoever.

THE GIVE-THEM-LOVE-AND-KINDNESS TECHNIQUE

•

We've all heard the Christian precept to "turn the other cheek" when someone does us wrong. It may be one of the most difficult things to do, especially if you subscribe to the "eye for an eye and a tooth for a tooth" philosophy.

Earlier in this book, the root of all toxicity was identified as jealousy due to insecurity and a lack of self-esteem. It is often the case that toxic people have received insufficient love in their life, or perhaps they were abused. The only way to handle such people may be through understanding, love, and kindness.

It takes a lot of inner strength and much compassion to turn your anger into love and kindness. Your first instinct may be to hit the person back, even harder than you were hit. Remember the saying "Kill them with kindness"? By means of the Give-Them-Love-and-Kindness Technique, you can instead love them with kindness and help them to improve their self-esteem.

In using this technique, it is important to keep in mind that no matter how ugly, nasty, or hateful-sounding a person is toward you, you must never lose your cool. You must be calm, use soothing and friendly loving tones, and you must smile. How can you do this in the face of so much negativity? Just keep remembering how much pain that person must be in—how empty and unloved they must be feeling inside and how much self-loathing underlies such actions.

As you put out love and kindness, it is amazing what behavioral changes you will see. The person's tone will often soften, the body language will loosen up, and they may even end up smiling and saying nice things back to you.

One of my clients, Vera, who worked as a bank teller, used the Give-Them-Love-and-Kindness Technique every time she encountered a hostile customer. In fact, Vera was always called upon to appease difficult customers. She was successful at defusing toxic people because she didn't take their anger as a personal affront but instead looked at hostile actions as an expression of unhappiness. She would calm people by agreeing with them, smiling and soothing them with her loving tone of voice. When these customers realized that she was on their side, their actions changed, becoming more positive.

Just as Vera did, you need to let toxic people know that you are not an enemy—that you are on their side. You need to do this with softness, tenderness, and love. After all, a pat on the back is only a few vertebrae from a kick in the pants and may be more effective in getting the results you want.

THE VICARIOUS-FANTASY TECHNIQUE

•

The Vicarious-Fantasy Technique can help you release tension by giving you a giggle or a laugh as you use your imagination.

One of my clients took his girlfriend to an expensive Chinese restaurant. The service was horrible, the food was disgusting, and everyone was rude and mean. He insisted that they take back some food, which was clearly uncooked, and they ended up charging him for it. As he relived the story by telling me about it, his face got redder and redder as he got increasingly angry.

Suddenly there was a booming burst of laughter, and a mischievous grin appeared on his face. His eyes sparkled. "You know what my fantasy is?" he asked. "It is to go into that restaurant when it's jam-packed with all these hoity-toity, snobby customers and release bagfuls of puppies, kittens, little white mice, and rats. Wow, I would die laughing at all these customers' faces as they see a kitten strolling by them and they're wondering what they are really eating as they chomp into their food. Ha ha." He got himself so revved up with laughter that he could barely finish telling me his fantasy. "Can you imagine the employees running back and forth after these little animals? I can guarantee you that you'd see them hopping. There wouldn't be any slow service then. I can just see that nasty owner's face scrunched up and hear him screaming and yelling."

When he left my office, my client felt great. He was no longer furious at the restaurant, as justice had been served vicariously. He would never carry out his fantasy in real life, but it allowed him to release his anger toward his toxic experience.

The Vicarious-Fantasy Technique has gotten a lot of play recently with the media frenzy over the John and Lorena Bobbitt case, in which the wife cut off her husband's penis and flung it out the window of her car. The police recovered the organ, and it was reattached in a ten-hour surgical procedure.

Personally, I think that this was the unconscionable action of a mentally deranged woman. Whether her husband came home drunk and raped her or not, she could have left, gone to a shelter, gotten a divorce, or gone home to Venezuela. Nothing excuses her heinous crime.

However, the case sparked a major war between the sexes, as evidenced by people phoning radio call-in shows across the country. Some women hailed her as a folk hero who stuck up for her rights. Men retorted, "How would she feel if someone cut her breasts off and threw them in a trash can?" The debate continued for weeks, until John Bobbitt was found not guilty by a jury that included nine women. Apparently this woman's motive in cutting off her husband's penis was that he was a selfish lover. As she acknowledged in court, "He always has an orgasm and he doesn't wait for me to have an orgasm. He's selfish. I don't think it's fair, so I pulled back the sheets and then I did it."

Many women reacted by vicariously living out what Lorena did to her husband. Feminist attorney Gloria Allred confirmed this on her radio show, as she told listeners that Lorena Bobbitt's actions represent a lot of women's fantasies of what they would love to have done to their abusers.

The operative word in using this technique is "fantasy." This means that it is *not reality*. You do *not* actually put these thoughts into action. Perhaps you visualize your boss's head being pummeled as you watch a heavyweight boxing fight. You release a lot of your anger and the horrible feelings you harbor toward a toxic person.

The Vicarious-Fantasy Technique can involve drawing ugly pictures of toxic people and mutilating them on paper. You can take their photo and draw horns or vampire teeth on them, or make them cross-eyed. You can rip up the drawing or photo, burn it, spit on it, or stamp on it, all the time fantasizing what you would like to do to the person in the picture.

There are people who are so toxic to you that you wish physical harm or even death on them. Though this is not a politically correct thing to think, much less a socially or legally acceptable thing to do, and definitely not a very Judeo-Christian way to live, the reality is that we do have these thoughts from time to time and that they are normal. They cease to be normal when we no longer engage in fantasy, but cross the appropriate boundaries. We must *never* physically harm another person. You can save your life by releasing anger against another person and save that person's life as well, because you don't have to act out your fantasies. The sheer fantasy is *enough* to satisfy your revenge.

At one time or another we have all used the Vicarious-Fantasy Technique unknowingly. How often have we laughed with glee as a pugilistic on-screen hero, be it Sylvester Stallone, Jean-Claude Van Damme, Chuck Norris, or Steven Seagal, kicked the enemy's ass? Deep down it gave most of us a thrill as we pictured, for even a split second, our own toxic enemy's ass being kicked.

Watching our heroes or athletes beat someone up in a fantasy or in a controlled environment is a safe and healthy release for our aggression. There are no negative repercussions, such as going to jail, getting maimed, or even getting killed.

The next time you want to let your anger out on someone in a safe way, you may want to use the Vicarious-Fantasy Technique to picture the toxic person's face being pummeled by your favorite superstar in a video or on the big screen.

It may sound sadistic, but it is definitely safer than doing it yourself, and it is an excellent way to release the hurt and anger you hold inside, which could eventually destroy you.

Once again, I must make it clear, the Vicarious-Fantasy Technique is *only a fantasy*. You may fantasize about punching the person out, you may fantasize about slapping his face, pulling a chair out from under her, even seeing his penis thrown out the window, as in the Bobbitt case. The key word is "fantasy." *You must never carry out this fantasy or cross the line over into reality.* Otherwise the consequences will be disastrous! You may have released your anger, but you will have definitely destroyed your life. *Never use violence. Never take the law into your own hands.*

THE UNPLUG TECHNIQUE

•

The Unplug Technique should be reserved for the most severely toxic people, those with whom you can no longer deal. When you have tried every other technique, to no avail, there is nothing you can do but let them go. Visualize yourself unplugging from them, as if from an electric socket. You need to become devoid of emotion regarding them. You completely let go and no longer care what happens to them. You don't care if they live or die. You don't wish them evil, and you don't wish them well either. You just let them out of your life for good and never look back.

I once had a friend with whom I had grown up and attended college. Samantha was always nasty, critical, and competitive with everyone, but we remained friends because of our shared history, and I accepted her, "warts and all." One day she came to visit me on her way to the Orient. Although I was very busy, I had canceled some clients just to spend time with her. She arrived, making a snide comment about the decor in my office, which I ignored. Before I left, I said to my assistant, "Now, remember that we have to call Singapore today, so it is important that we get that letter out as a priority. Also, don't forget to call Mr. Jones, and we need to order some supplies."

My assistant, professional, respectful, and yet warm and

friendly, said with a smile, "Dr. Glass, don't worry about a thing. Have a great lunch, and everything will be done when you return."

As we sat down in the restaurant, my "best friend" asked me what I wanted to do with my life. Since we had such a long history together, I was completely open with my innermost thoughts, as I shared at length and in detail my mission to promote global peace through communication.

Now, most people would think that after such a goal is revealed, a longtime best friend would smile and say, "What an admirable goal! I know how hard you have worked in your life, and how much you deserve these things. I'm *so* proud of you."

Well, *my* old friend looked at me and said, "You know, Lillian, global peace begins at home. The way you treat your secretary is atrocious. How dare you order him around that way?"

I was stunned. The Tension-Blowout Technique did not work for me this time. There was nothing about this situation that I could ever find humorous. As I mentally ran through each of the other techniques, I found that there was nothing left for me except the Unplug Technique. I had to get her out of my life—for good.

I looked directly at her and, in a calm tone, said, "You know, Samantha, all my life you have managed to rain on my parade or pop my balloon—always saying something negative to me. Well, I've had enough! I don't want to be friends with you anymore, and I don't want you in my life." Then I got up from the table, turned on my heel, and never looked back.

Though Samantha has made attempts to contact me since, there is no use. She is out of my life and will never get back in, ever. You may say to yourself, "How cold, how cruel. How can you let this person whom you've known forever go just like that?" I reply, How can I *not* let this person go? How can I allow this person, who keeps cutting me down, being nonsupportive, and looking at me with crooked eyes, even remain in my life, when there are so many beautiful people in my life—people who want the best for me, who *want* me to succeed, who *believe* in me, who do not say negative things to me?

There was absolutely no way I could continue to deal with Samantha. It was too frustrating and too upsetting. I don't hate

Samantha; in fact, I have no emotion toward her, as I have released her from my life completely.

With the Unplug Technique, you often have to unplug not because you don't like the person but because you *do*. You may need to unplug as a form of "tough love," where you set limits and let the person handle the situation. Then you won't end up becoming a codependent and contributing to toxic behavior.

Techniques *Never* to Use

NEVER SELF-DESTRUCT

Never turn your anger at another person inward. Alcohol, tranquilizers, amphetamines, marijuana, cocaine, crack, heroin, or any of the new "designer" drugs are definitely not appropriate ways of handling toxic people. The same is true for overeating and/or bulimia. Though these may provide quick relief or a temporary high, they are likely to shorten your life.

Taking your life because you think there is no hope is unconscionable. When I read about fifteen-year-old Megan Pauley, who killed herself because she could no longer stand the torments of her toxic peers, I was deeply saddened. Even sadder is the fact that teenage suicide has gone up over 40 percent in the past few years. Why? Primarily because of peer pressure and the desperation to be accepted.

There are ways to deal with toxic people, and taking your life is *not* one of them. If you ever have thoughts of ending it all, call the suicide hot line in your community or get professional help—*immediately*. Nobody should drive you to the point where you are considering killing yourself.

NEVER USE PHYSICAL VIOLENCE

It has been said repeatedly throughout this chapter that you must *never* use physical violence as a technique to handle a toxic person.

The consequences are not worth it. Ellie Nesler must now face such consequences after killing the man being tried for molesting her son. Although any parent can relate to Ms. Nesler's anger and devastation and can perhaps even get a vicarious thrill out of what she did, the consequences are that she is now locked up in a prison, away from the son whom she loved so much and tried to defend.

There are alternatives in dealing with the toxic people in your life, using *verbal fists,* not *actual fists.*

Nobody on this planet ever has the right to hurt another person physically, and if it should happen to us, we need to leave that person and/or seek appropriate legal channels for protection. Nobody ever needs to be a victim again!

There is no excuse for any kind of physical violence whatsoever. Even though the headlines have sensationalized a genetic cause for violence, the results were based on the findings from only one family. It is obvious that further work is needed to determine how prevalent the flawed gene is in the general population before we give up taking responsibility for our hostile actions and blame it on our genes. No matter how hostile your genes may be, you need to *control* your violent behavior. Get professional help, or suffer the consequences of your actions.

Other No-No's in Dealing with Toxic People

NEVER TAKE HOSTAGES.

Never use a child or any other person to get back at someone who is toxic to you. Unfortunately, this is all too common in divorce. The results are devastating. Too many children have been emotionally destroyed, not because the parents have gotten divorced but because they have taken the children as mental hostages. In this situation, one parent says bad things about the other parent, putting the child in the middle to play one side against the other. This is cruel and indefensible. You cannot destroy an innocent person's life by using him or her to deal with your own anger against a toxic person.

DON'T STICK AROUND AND TRY TO GET A PERSON TO LIKE YOU

You cannot convince anyone to like you, so stop driving someone crazy by trying to win his or her affections. If a relationship is over, let go. Don't be obsessive, and never stalk someone in a Fatal Attraction relationship. If you have trouble letting go, seek professional help immediately; there are wonderful psychologists out there who can help you.

CHAPTER 7

TECHNIQUES TO USE WITH SPECIFIC TOXIC TERRORS

- The Cut-You-Downer

- The Chatterbox

- The Self-Destroyer

- The Runner

- The Silent but Deadly Volcano

- The Gossip

- The Angry Pugilist

- The Gloom and Doom Victim

- The Smiling Two-Faced Backstabber

- The Wishy-Washy Wimp

- **The Opportunistic User**

- **The Bitchy, Bossy Bully**

- **The Jokester**

- **The Unconscious Social Klutz**

- **The Mental Case**

- **The Bullshitting Liar**

- **The Meddler**

- **The Penny-Pinching Miser**

- **The Fanatic**

- **The Me, Myself, and I Narcissist**

- **The Eddie Haskell**

- **The Self-Righteous Priss**

- **The Snooty Snob**

- **The Competitor**

- **The Control Freak**

- **The Accusing Critic**

- **The Arrogant Know-It-All**

- **The Emotional Refrigerator**

- **The Skeptical Paranoid**

- **The Instigator**

- **Choosing Specific Techniques**

The common thread that runs through each of the thirty types of Toxic Terrors is very low self-esteem and insecurity. Research has shown that people who have low self-esteem will either act out in ways to sabotage relationships or do whatever it takes to feel more important. In addition, each of these Toxic Terrors has horrible communication skills, which reflect true weaknesses.

In this chapter you will learn how best to communicate with each of these toxic individuals and which of the Ten Techniques from the last chapter are most likely to produce a change in toxic behavior. When choosing the best techniques to use to communicate and cope with a toxic person, you should consider two things: first you must identify the individual's specific Toxic Terror type, as certain techniques are more effective with certain terrors than others. The second concern is what role the Toxic Terror plays in your life.

In the next chapter you will learn the best techniques to use according to a toxic person's position in your life, but here the focus is on specific techniques that are most effective for particular types of toxic terrorists.

THE CUT-YOU-DOWNER

•

Because Cut-You-Downers are among the most insecure of all the Toxic Terrors, they are best handled with the Calm Questioning Technique or the Give-Them-Love-and-Kindness Technique.

In using the Calm Questioning Technique, you must take care not to use a whiny or an argumentative tone; it makes people more defensive and their actions even more obnoxious. Here is a possible scenario applying the Calm Questioning Technique with a Cut-You-Downer.

Cut-You-Downer: Look at the way that man's eating over there—what a pig.
You: What is it about the way he's eating that makes him look like a pig?
Cut-You-Downer: He's gross. He's eating so fast and slurping his food down. He's got no manners.

You: Why does that bother you?

Cut-You-Downer: Because it's disgusting to look at.

You: Are you more bothered by the fact that you're sitting here waiting and waiting with no food in front of you and you're forced to look at this man slurping his food because he's so hungry?

Cut-You-Downer: Well, yes.

You: Are you really disgusted because you're hungry and you want your food to come and you don't want to be forced to watch someone else enjoy his food, even if he is enjoying it like a pig in a trough?

Cut-You-Downer: Yes, I guess that's it. (He smiles.)

With this technique you are literally cross-examining someone to get to what is really bothering the person. As you pursue your line of logical, nonaccusatory questioning, you will notice how the Cut-You-Downer's toxic behavior completely changes for the better, as he or she gets calmer and less hostile, and even begins to smile when the truth is reached.

An alternative is to ask just one question, such as: "Now, why would you make a comment like that?" or "Why would you say something so rude?" This cuts to the bone. Now the Cut-You-Downer has to account for the toxic behavior, since you have not let him or her get away with a toxic action or statement.

When people have to cut you down, it is often because you have something they want or you represent something they can't face. In most cases, they feel inadequate around you. So an alternative method is the Give-Them-Love-and-Kindness Technique, whose focus on compassion makes it easier for you to deal with them.

THE CHATTERBOX

•

The first method to use with the Chatterbox is the Tension-Blowout Technique. It will allow you to keep your cool so that you don't end up covering your ears and yelling, *"Shut up, shut up, shut up!"* as loud as you can. You may end up doing this anyway—with the Vicarious-Fantasy Technique.

Chatterboxes need to be told that their constant talking is inappropriate, so the Direct-Confront Technique may be effective. It is best to use this technique when you are not in the presence of others, because Chatterboxes need to be able to save face and preserve their dignity. After all, the reason they are chattering away is so they can feel accepted, loved, and important. Therefore tactile reassurance is important: touch them to assure them of your concern. You also should incorporate the Give-Them-Love-and-Kindness Technique.

You may want to start out by telling Chatterboxes kindly and politely how much you like them (if you do) but that sometimes they talk too much and talk about things that may not interest everyone. Encourage Chatterboxes to read others' facial and body language cues in order to determine if people are interested in hearing what they have to say. At first Chatterboxes may be shocked and go on the defensive. If they do this you need to be more direct, using specific examples of their inappropriate chatterboxing. You may have to keep reassuring them that you are on their side.

Offer to give them a gesture—a raised eyebrow or a touch—as a cue that they should stop talking. Often their defensiveness and fear come out because they have not developed good enough communication skills to read other people's body and facial language.

If Chatterboxes still don't get it, or continue to monopolize your time and energy, you need to become more straightforward, using the Direct-Confront Technique as you firmly set limits so that you won't be manipulated.

THE SELF-DESTROYER

•

These people, filled with so much self-loathing and self-hate, are best approached via the Give-Them-Love-and-Kindness Technique. Self-Destroyers need to be spoken to with love and kindness because they probably got little of it while growing up. Otherwise they would not have ended up being the way they are. Self-Destroyers aren't just hungry for food, alcohol, cigarettes, or sex. They are starved for attention and acceptance.

Sometimes you have to use "tough love" with the Self-Destroyer. Put your foot down and set limits via the Direct-Confront Technique, just as Bernadette did. She told Theodore that she would marry him only on condition that he get counseling, stop smoking and drinking, and lose weight. Otherwise, she knew, she would be walking into a nightmare that could drag her down as well.

There are times when you can no longer sit by and watch people destroy themselves, as it is just too painful to see. In that case, the Unplug Technique may be your only choice for survival. When you have loved someone and been brutally honest, letting the person know that you are aware of the problem, and have offered your help—all in vain—you *have* to unplug and let the individual deal with the problem alone and in their own way. You can never help Self-Destroyers unless they are willing to help themselves.

"If you hang out with dogs you'll get fleas," says the old adage. If you hang out with a Self-Destroyer, you can be destroyed. Therefore give them love and kindness and, if that fails, unplug.

THE RUNNER

•

To communicate with Runners, you first have to catch them, preferably *before* they run away. The first thing to try with Runners is the Direct-Confront Technique. Don't think of how uncomfortable it may seem for them; that is not your concern. Instead you must let them know that you are onto their weakness of running away from the problems at hand, that you will have none of it, and that they have to deal with their problems.

Usually Runners are not used to being confronted, so when you confront, they will often listen and begin to act. Of course, they may end up running away anyway, as the issue may be just too difficult to handle.

When Bree directly confronted Dick about marriage, it was too much for him to take, so he left. After two weeks she confronted him again, letting him know that she was glad she had brought the subject up and found he couldn't cope, because she didn't want a man like that. Bree was by now completely turned off by Dick's lack of communication skills and his running away, so she used the Unplug Technique. Now she was the one who could run the other way and leave any thoughts of Dick behind.

If you confront the Runner and he or she still runs, you should never regret confronting, because at least now you will know whose behavior is wrong. Just remember that when this person runs, it has very little to do with you.

THE SILENT BUT DEADLY VOLCANO

•

The only method to use with this scary type of Toxic Terror is the Calm Questioning Technique. You need to question them because they certainly will never volunteer to tell you what is going on in their mind. You need to keep calm and get feedback from them periodically. Ask if they are OK with doing something you asked them to do. Ask open-ended questions that require more than yes or no responses. This way you force them to interact with you so you can monitor their thoughts and feelings.

Every time you get a Silent but Deadly Volcano to talk, you are defusing a walking time bomb.

For example, you may ask, "Did you feel overworked today?" or "What was your reaction to that call?" or "What was your opinion about what the boss said today?" or "What's your reaction to the problems we're having at work?"

THE GOSSIP

•

Gossips are extremely dangerous, because they can make your life a living nightmare. Gossips need to know right away that you are well aware of who they are and what they are trying to do. Use the Direct-Confront Technique and tell them that their behavior is unacceptable—especially if they have gossiped about *you*. If they gossip about someone you know or like, cut them off by saying, "I'm not going to listen to this" or "I don't believe a word of this" or "I'm not interested."

You may want to use the Humor Technique, with a comeback such as: "Do you know what they did to people who gossiped in medieval times? They would put iron masks on their head and lock them with a key. Come to think of it, you might look pretty good in one of those masks. Maybe I can find one for you."

Like the Instigator, Gossips are so insecure and have such low self-esteem that they dish up the latest dirt to feel important, powerful, and in control. Therefore saying something blunt, like "I'm sure it makes you feel important to have the inside information, but frankly, gossiping doesn't put you in the best light," will most likely hurt them, perhaps to the point where they may never want to speak to you again. So be it! Good riddance to bad gossipers!

There is absolutely no room whatsoever for Gossips in your professional life, as they can ruin your life's work. A Gossip can destroy your business as fast as an arsonist destroys a forest with fire. Unplug!

I experienced the repercussions of working with a Gossip before I was fortunate enough to unplug him from my life. Even after I warned him not to get too chummy with my clients and never to discuss my celebrity clients with anybody, he continued to do so. On one occasion, a tabloid called to ask if I was treating a certain celebrity for a vocal condition. Instead of referring the call to me, as he had been instructed, this assistant acknowledged that the celebrity was working with me. As a result of his indiscretion, the information ended up in the tabloids, and I never heard from that client again. After a concert once, this toxic Gossip had the audacity to go up to a celebrity I had worked with and tell the person I said hello. When I heard about this, I used the Direct-Confront Technique and finally fired him, telling him that my business could no longer afford to have someone like him trying to ruin it with his gossiping. I have spent too many years building my reputation and professional integrity, and I pride myself on discretion.

THE ANGRY PUGILIST

•

What Angry Pugilists need most is TLC (tender loving care). It is amazing how the Give-Them-Love-and-Kindness Technique can knock the wind out of their sails and even begin to turn them around. It may not happen immediately, but eventually a kinder and more docile person will emerge.

If the Angry Pugilist becomes physically violent, taking out hostility on you, your only recourse is the Unplug Technique: say "Good-bye," "Adios," and "Sayonara," and never look back.

The Unplug Technique may also be necessary when such a person becomes impossible to deal with. This is what happened with a once popular television actress. Besides her personal problems, which ranged from lawsuits and evictions to chronic lateness and absences from the show, her fellow performers and staff members found her behavior so mercurial, demanding, and detrimental to the show's reputation that she was unplugged and let go.

When an Angry Pugilist fails to respond to any of the other techniques, you have no recourse but to unplug.

THE GLOOM AND DOOM VICTIM

•

The best technique to use around the Gloom and Doom Victim is Tension-Blowout. You need to blow out their energy repeatedly, as it can be debilitating to be around them for a length of time. These people are like living negative mood contagions, and it may be very easy to catch their bad moods.

It may also be advisable to unplug from them, since they will rarely accept your help or suggestions or listen to your advice without a "Yeah, but." Even if you use the Give-Them-Love-and-Kindness Technique and tell them how terrific they are, they will never believe you because of their feelings of total inadequacy. Therefore, if you value your sanity and you don't want to live a life of constant frustration, you have no choice: unplug.

THE SMILING TWO-FACED BACKSTABBER

•

You must first use the Direct-Confront Technique with Smiling Back-stabbers, letting them know that you are hip to their two-faced ways. You should never let these people off the hook.

After being confronted, Backstabbers may try denial, even though you may have caught them in the act. In this case, you can employ the Give-Them-Hell-and-Yell Technique to let your anger out. Once again, *never use any form of physical violence,* no matter how badly you want to. Often your emotional, highly charged reaction will linger in the minds of Backstabbers, causing torment for the rest of their life.

It had been some twenty years since Todd had taken advantage of Susan, the girlfriend of his best friend, Bob. But Bob's reaction to seeing Todd and Susan kissing in a restaurant had left an indelible impression on Todd's mind. He had nightmares of Bob's contorted face and his shocked, screaming mouth when he discovered his "best friend" 's betrayal. Now, as part of his Alcoholics Anonymous twelve-step program, Todd called Bob to apologize and to make amends for what he had done. However, it was too late. Bob told him to "fuck off" and hung up, which left Todd even more disturbed and with more guilt to deal with for another twenty years.

Bob had unplugged. He had no hate, no love, no time, and no room for a stupid apology that came twenty years too late. Like Bob, after an encounter with the Smiling Two-Faced Backstabber you have to unplug and never, ever deal with them again. You should never waste your time on trusting a person with this character trait.

THE WISHY-WASHY WIMP

•

Wishy-Washy Wimps are so insecure and so fragile that they need to be handled gingerly. Therefore the Give-Them-Love-and-Kindness Technique is most helpful in letting them know that you are being supportive through a decision-making crisis.

You also may want to use the Calm Questioning Technique to help these people make decisions. Ask questions that will clarify the issues and help the Wimp reach a logical conclusion.

If the Wishy-Washy Wimp drives you crazy and doesn't respond to the Give-Them-Love-and-Kindness or the Calm Questioning Technique, you have to unplug and leave the individual sitting on the fence all alone.

THE OPPORTUNISTIC USER

•

The Beverly Hills doctor and the rich socialite were peas in a pod— two Opportunistic Users who tried to use each other, only to learn that neither had what the other wanted. These two obviously could never use the Direct-Confront Technique, because each was trying to use the other. However, in most cases there will be just one Opportunistic User taking advantage of an innocent victim to get what he or she wants, and the Direct-Confront Technique is the method of choice.

This technique lets people know that you feel used and hurt by their actions. In some cases, confronting them will make people feel bad or guilty about what they did. If your friendship or relationship had any meaning, users may take a second look at their behavior and how they have treated you. As long as it is done calmly, the Direct-Confront Technique allows two people to begin to establish an open line of dialogue that could help in resolving any disturbed feelings.

Sometimes you may use the Direct-Confront Technique and the Opportunistic User will deny or just not get it. When you know that the person is trying to use you or manipulate you in a situation, you have to say directly and bluntly, "No, there's no way I'm going to do that. I'm not going to let anyone take advantage of me, because I won't feel very good if I do."

Your alternative may be to unplug and never allow the Opportunistic User to use you again.

THE BITCHY, BOSSY BULLY

•

The Mirror Technique is the best approach to use with Bitchy, Bossy Bullies, who hate to be bullied, bossed, or bitched at. Having their ugly actions thrown right back into their faces will usually put a damper on their toxic behavior.

One of my clients was a waitress in an exclusive restaurant. Her Bitchy, Bossy Bully boss yelled at her nastily in reprimand for not doing something correctly. Immediately my client responded to her boss's accusations, mimicking the screeching, bitchy tone. Her boss stopped dead in her tracks. "Is that how I sound?" she asked sheepishly. "Yes, it is," replied my client, who had resumed speaking in a calmer, more pleasant tone.

Often these little Hitlers, given a taste of their own medicine, will be both shocked and disgusted by their behavior. In essence, bullying or bitching back stops any further negative behavior toward you. What you have done is regained your power by barking louder than they did.

In addition, the Give-Them-Hell-and-Yell Technique is often appropriate for the Bitchy, Bossy Bullies in your life. You cannot allow them to get their cheap thrills by tormenting you and watching you squirm. Instead you have to act fearless and in control. If you give them hell and yell, they will gain respect for you as you put them in their place. You must never give them the satisfaction of seeing you cower.

A Bitchy, Bossy Bully who is your boss may either respect you or fire you when you bully back. You win in either case; if you are fired, at least you will have left with your self-respect intact.

Another option in dealing with Bitchy, Bossy Bullies is to un-plug and get as far away from them as possible.

You may also use the Humor Technique. Many times, good-natured humor will make your point, and the Bitchy, Bossy Bully will lighten up.

On a flight from L.A. to Boston, I met a store owner who used the Humor Technique on bitchy, bossy customers. When someone would be nasty or order him around, he would stop what he was doing, look up, and ask himself out loud, "Was it John? No, it couldn't be. No, no, I'm sure it was Mike. No, I'm certain it was Suzy. Definitely." By now the toxic customer would be puzzled, wondering what in the world he was talking about. Then the store owner would look directly at the customer and say, "I was just won-dering who sent you in here to make me miserable today." He would then smile, forcing the Bitchy, Bossy Bully to give an embar-rassed smile in return and begin to act a lot kinder and more ac-commodating. This man told me that through the years, his humor technique worked like a charm every time.

THE JOKESTER

•

The Direct-Confront Technique lets Jokesters know right up front that you don't think they are funny and that you won't be subjected to their stupid jokes or stories.

You need to use a firm voice to cut Jokesters off at the pass. It's OK to talk over these people if they don't get the message. When Jokesters make a sarcastic comment at your expense and claim to be "only kidding" or they try to get you on the defensive by saying, "Can't you take a joke?" you need to put them in their place imme-diately. Tell them that you *can* take a joke, but you find what they said to be nowhere near funny or humorous. Don't worry about speaking up or hurting Jokesters' feelings. After all, these people don't give your feelings too much thought.

Because Jokesters have put up a wall to shield their extreme insecurity, you may not be able to penetrate their obnoxious joking demeanor. Jokesters may ignore you and continue with their jokes. If that is the case, you need to resort to the Give-Them-Hell-and-Yell Technique, just as Jerry's coworker did when he didn't get the point to stop joking and stop trying to cheer her up. She let him have it verbally!

Also, reminding Jokesters through the Direct-Confront Technique that in today's world there are such things as harassment suits will often put an immediate end to their jokes, especially if they are ethnic or sexually provocative.

THE UNCONSCIOUS SOCIAL KLUTZ

•

With the Unconscious Social Klutz you can try a variety of techniques to get your point across. Your choice depends on how thick-skulled or socially backward the Klutz is. Begin with the Tension-Blowout Technique, as you will find these people so exasperating that it is best to handle your anger and tension immediately by taking that breath in, holding it, and blowing them out.

Usually, this will not be sufficient to release your anger at Klutzes. Therefore you must engage them with the Direct-Confront Technique, letting them know, just as you would let a little child know, that their actions are *completely* unacceptable.

Social Klutzes often approach me when I'm walking with my little Lhasa apso and begin to tell me about their dogs. Somehow, in most cases, they are *dead* dogs. I never let them get anywhere with their dog stories. I immediately use the Direct-Confront Technique and interrupt them midsentence to say, "If this is about a dead dog, I don't want to hear it," and then I go about my business, refusing to be victimized.

All too often, Unconscious Social Klutzes will say vulgar, rude, socially unacceptable things that you cannot believe you heard. If they do, reflect their comments right back to them via the Mirror Technique. Suppose a Social Klutz says, "Boy, you're fat!" You respond, "I may be fat, but that can be changed. You're stupid and uncouth, and you're stuck with that."

Sometimes this technique won't work, especially on dense people. If they are not getting it, often the Give-Them-Hell-and-Yell Technique will shock some sense into the Klutzes.

There are Unconscious Social Klutzes who are so clueless that nothing will work. In cases where the person makes the same mistake repeatedly and refuses to listen to anything you say or do, you must unplug in order to preserve your sanity.

THE MENTAL CASE

•

The best methods to use with the Mental Case are the Tension-Blowout and the Calm Questioning Techniques. The calmer you are, the less you will agitate the Mental Case and the easier it will be to communicate.

Smelling something very strange in my waiting room one evening, I went to see what it was and was startled by a man who looked as if he hadn't taken a bath in years. His hair was dirty and matted, and his face and clothing were tattered. He had long and dirty fingernails, wild eyes, and a long beard, and was missing numerous teeth.

He started raving and shouting at me: "Where's the moon phone? I need to call the moon." I asked, "The moon phone?" in a soft and soothing voice. He said agitatedly, "Yes, the moon phone—where is it? I have to call the moon." I calmly replied, "Oh, the moon phone—it's outside. Let's go find it." I escorted him out the office door, immediately locked it behind him, and phoned the security guard to escort him from the building.

Ultimately, with the Mental Case, you will probably have to unplug and go your merry way, because unless they get professional help they can *never* change their sick behavior patterns. Do whatever you can to help get them into professional care, and if that fails, detach yourself.

Sometimes these people are too far gone for professional care. A man who appeared on a television talk show had physically and emotionally abused his twelve children since they were small, and now, as adults, they had no recourse but to unplug and have nothing more to do with this dangerous monster who continued to abuse them as adults.

Though you may be devastated and feel like strangling a person who does horrible things to you, you must *never* act on your violent impulses or do anything that could put your future or your life in jeopardy.

I am sure that the ten sets of parents who were conned by twenty-year-old Angela Andrews, a single mother-to-be who offered her baby to each couple after collecting a large sum of money, all felt like pounding some sense into her. Although Angela is obviously a very sick and mentally disturbed girl, she nevertheless left twenty people emotionally devastated and is now deservedly behind bars, where she will stay for a very long time.

In dealing with such dangerous Mental Cases, *never* take the law into your own hands but use appropriate legal channels to see that justice is served. Then, painful though it may be, use the Unplug and the Stop-the-Thought Techniques to help you cope with the pain created by the toxic Mental Case.

THE BULLSHITTING LIAR

•

Bullshitting Liars are best handled with the Calm Questioning Technique. If, suspecting they are lying, you ask more and more questions, eventually the Liars will paint themselves into a corner and reveal their true colors.

Next employ the Direct-Confront Technique to let liars know you are onto them, as Sharlene did. When the Calm Questioning Technique elicited that her lover was married, his lame response was: "Well, if you knew I was married, you would never have spent time with me." He was absolutely right! She was not only hurt but very angry, especially after he suggested continuing their illicit relationship. She hung up on him, unplugging not only their telephone conversation but her emotions as well, leaving him to deal with his own bullshit.

Some Bullshitting Liars stretch the truth primarily to impress you. You may want to let them save face even though you know they are bullshitting. Utilize the Tension-Blowout Technique and let it go, or if they are trying to impress you with little white lies that aren't going to hurt anybody, employ the Humor Technique. Smirking at them often will let them know that you are onto their bullshit but saves them from humiliation.

You can *never* believe anything these people say to you, because they are *not* trustworthy. If people lie or exaggerate casually before you do business with them, they will most likely lie while you do business with them. I see so many people in my office who have been screwed by Bullshitting Liars in business or in their personal lives. When I ask if the people lied before they got involved with them, nine times out of ten the answer is yes. So there are clues. Look for signs of tale-telling *before* it is too late.

THE MEDDLER

•

Meddlers need to be told in no uncertain terms that their meddling is not appreciated and is completely unacceptable. The Give-Them-Hell-and-Yell Technique, followed by the Unplug Technique, works best, informing Meddlers that you mean business.

Gloria was victimized by her neighbor Jerome's meddling because she was much too nice to him. She would respond to him gently, saying, "Oh, Jerome, you don't have to say that," or she would remain silent. Meanwhile she built up a reservoir of anger and disdain toward him, which he obviously sensed, for he became even more meddlesome, interfering in her life. One day she wised up and screamed at him at the top of her lungs. She threatened to contact a lawyer and sue Jerome for harassment if he didn't bug off and leave her alone. That obviously did the trick: Jerome has never bothered her since.

You must never be nice or polite to Meddlers, because they usually won't "get it." They are too manipulative and too dangerous to deal with, so after you give them hell and yell, you *must* unplug! Get the Meddler out of your life for good.

THE PENNY-PINCHING MISER

•

Penny-Pinching Misers constitute a pathetic type of Toxic Terror, because they have such low self-esteem. The Calm Questioning Technique can really help you deal with them. By asking numerous questions, you can help Penny-Pinching Misers understand just how stingy they are being. They will probably be embarrassed into getting your point. And their answers will give you more insight into their fears, thereby enabling you to understand and tolerate them, even though you may not like their actions.

One of my clients used the Calm Questioning Technique with her gentleman friend and discovered that as a Depression child, he had had only one pair of shoes and hardly enough food. As an adult, he couldn't shake his memories of poverty. Though now a millionaire, he never felt as if he had enough money. Having learned this, she tried to help him work through his problem logically and systematically.

Another method to use is the Direct-Confront Technique. Instead of abandoning Jay for avoiding the lunch checks, his colleagues should have confronted him by saying, "Hey, Jay, it's your turn to pay." It's important to be direct and open with these miserly people so that you don't harbor hard feelings and end up hating them. It's terribly difficult for Penny-Pinching Misers to change, but when they are aware of their actions, they will often be more receptive to changing their behavior and loosen their tight-fisted grip on money.

Compassion and understanding are necessary, so a caring tone of voice is essential in dealing with the Penny-Pinching Miser. The Give-Them-Love-and-Kindness Technique facilitates your compassion toward them.

THE FANATIC

•

Once, in London, I had a date for dinner with a friend who was starring in a play. After the performance, I met her backstage. At the stage door, a fan came up and became very manipulative with my friend's time, not letting her go and asking question after dumb question. My friend, polite and gracious, stood there listening to the barrage of weirdness. After ten minutes of this, I finally said, "Come on, let's go," and we left. My friend, who had always had a problem with fanatical fans, was clearly too nice.

Certainly you want to be pleasant to people who like you and appreciate you, as you don't want to offend them—especially if you happen to be in the public eye. However, when they get out of hand and try to manipulate you, you have to set limits firmly, using the Direct-Confront Technique in a strongly projected voice so they get the message loud and clear. If they don't respond, you must put your foot down and use the Give-Them-Hell-and-Yell Technique.

All too often, Fanatics do not get the message. They may have received encouraging vibes initially, so they continue to infiltrate the life of their object of desire.

You do not have to be a celebrity to have a Fanatic in your life. Fanatics are single-minded about their desires or their belief systems, as was Maggie, who tried to tell Edith that she was not a true Christian unless she went to church regularly, read the Bible twice a day, and even spoke in tongues. These discussions went on for months, until Edith finally let Maggie know, through the Give-Them-Hell-and-Yell Technique, that the way she prayed was *her* business, and no one had the right to judge her degree of Christianity. Maggie got the point and backed off on her preaching.

In some cases when you can't reason with Fanatics, especially after letting them have it verbally, you have to unplug and allow no further contact whatsoever.

If the Fanatic is a Mental Case, a common situation, protect yourself by going through appropriate legal channels. Also, make sure that your home and your business are secured, so that the person does not have easy access to you.

The Me, Myself, and I Narcissist

•

Me, Myself, and I Narcissists cannot speak any language unless it has to do with themselves. Thus the Give-Them-Love-and-Kindness Technique is the best way to get through to them, as the reason they are narcissistic and self-absorbed is that deep down they are frightened, insecure, and underdeveloped human beings.

Understanding this may help you to become more sensitive to their needs and better able to deal with them. They are not necessarily *trying* to be selfish, they just are, because they lack self-esteem. They can't give to others because they are depleted and empty as human beings, with nothing there to give.

If their self-absorption neutralizes your patience, the Tension-Blowout Technique is effective in releasing your frustration while still allowing you to deal with them.

When their selfish ways and insensitivity become hurtful to you, you *must* speak up, using the Direct-Confront Technique. However, employ a calm, controlled tone, otherwise they won't hear you. If you sound accusing or whiny, they will go on the defensive and either attack you verbally or deny that they are being selfish. Their egos are usually as fragile as eggshells.

If you find that the Narcissist makes time for you only when convenient, ignores what you say, and relates everything back to him- or herself, you may want to question why you are around this person in the first place. You may want to unplug and be done with the Narcissist. Most people who deal with Narcissists for any length of time will use the Unplug Technique eventually, their patience exhausted. After you have let these people go, you may benefit not only from the Stop-the-Thought Technique whenever you think of them but from the Humor Technique, focusing on the absurdity of the Me, Myself, and I Narcissist.

THE EDDIE HASKELL

•

Although Eddie Haskell types are obviously manipulative phonies, you can't totally dislike them because deep inside you hope that at least some of what they have said about you was true. When their sweetness becomes too sugary, the Tension-Blowout Technique can help you deal with your emerging negative feelings. If this is not enough to release your negativity, you can call upon the Humor Technique to help you deal with this person's ingratiating comments.

You may want to smile and say lightheartedly, "Oh, come on now, I can't be all those nice things you say; you must be buttering me up for something." This combination of the Humor and the Direct-Confront Techniques may induce an adamant denial, whereupon you can add more humorous comments, such as: "If you keep saying all those sweet things about me I might end up a diabetic" or "Are you pouring on all that sugary syrup because you want to watch a bunch of ants crawl all over me?" or "Boy, your nose is getting browner by the minute." Let them know that you are onto their Eddie Haskell "kiss-ass" games.

If they have any sense at all, they will back off with laughter, a denial, or protests that they really mean it, you *are* terrific.

If you can't tolerate them or their "Haskelling" anymore, try the Mirror Technique. Reflect back to them exactly what they said to you, in the same sickeningly sweet tone. They will usually get the message and cease and desist their kissing up.

THE SELF-RIGHTEOUS PRISS

•

With Self-Righteous Prisses you may first want to try using the Calm Questioning Technique to let them see how imperfect and rigid they are.

On a *Donahue* show that featured a panel of prostitutes, a Self-Righteous Priss from the audience admonished the women that they were "going to go to hell." Hearing this, a caller to the show asked her, "Ma'am, what kind of God do you believe in? Who is your God?" The Priss replied, "My God is the God in heaven." The caller then asked, "Who put you in charge to be God and to make these judgments against these women?" The Priss was at a loss for words, and the audience, made aware of her self-righteous, hypocritical behavior, applauded wildly in agreement with the caller.

When the Self-Righteous Priss starts attacking you, you need to attack back through the Mirror Technique and the Give-Them-Hell-and-Yell Technique.

One of my clients really shocked a Self-Righteous Priss into shape. After mirroring the woman's finicky behavior right back to her, which almost gave the Priss a heart attack, she gave her hell, telling the Priss to clean up her own "uptight, lockjawed, rigid, orgasmless self" before she judged others.

That master of doling out judgments and critical remarks was devastated when it was done back to her. Shaken up, she was also shaken into having greater tolerance for others and undertaking self-examination. For the first time in her life, she saw how rigid she was, how toxic to others. Perhaps the tears she shed as a result of my client's confrontation washed away some of her nearsightedness in judging others and thereby allowed her not to take herself so seriously.

If on the other hand the Self-Righteous Priss is in a position of authority and you find it too big a risk to mirror or give the person hell, you may want to use the Vicarious-Fantasy Technique to help you get through the time you have to spend together.

THE SNOOTY SNOB

•

When Snooty Snobs give you the "I'm better than you" routine, the Calm Questioning Technique works quite well. Ask Snobs enough questions to make them see how absurd they are for treating others without respect. Questions such as "What makes you feel you're better than everyone else?" or "Why wouldn't you talk to this type of person?" often throw them off guard, as they have no clue to how they should respond.

The Direct-Confront Technique also tends to leave the Snooty Snob's mouth agape. In *Pretty Woman*, after Julia Roberts's character is dressed up like a princess, she goes back into the Beverly Hills store where the saleswomen snubbed her and confronts them, saying, "Remember how you treated me when I came in here?" Then she displays all her shopping bags and adds, "Well, you shouldn't have done that." Smirking, she turns on her heel and leaves the saleswomen, who earn their living on commissions, to kick themselves for being Snooty Snobs.

Directly confronting Snooty Snobs is very pleasurable, as they never expect it and are quite shocked by your audacity.

If you find you have had enough of the Snooty Snob's shallow values and shallow friends, you need to dump them and unplug in order to keep your nerves intact. People who think they are better than you and want to associate only with those who can raise their self-esteem are not worth knowing.

THE COMPETITOR

•

In this day and age, women are often more successful than their male counterparts, and many insecure men cannot cope with a woman's success. Though a lot of these men think they are evolved and progressive human beings, they are really dinosaurs who have not shaken their preadolescent assumption that boys should be bigger, better, stronger, and smarter than girls.

A client of mine who was an attorney got fixed up on a date with a moderately successful orthopedic surgeon. They had a lovely evening and began dating—until one night when the surgeon phoned the lawyer and asked her how her day had gone. The lawyer told him what she did that day and then asked if he did good in the operating room. "Did good?" He squealed in joy. Confused, she asked, "What are you talking about?" "Good! You said 'good' instead of 'well'—I got you!" Suddenly every ounce of her attraction to this man evaporated. He was obviously trying to compete with her. She realized how often he had tried to one-up her.

Using the Calm Questioning Technique, she asked, "So do you feel better about yourself now that you know you have better grammar than I do?" That put him in his place while putting her in hers—out of his life.

The Direct-Confront Technique is also of value in telling the Competitor that you are not about to compete with him or her. If the Competitor tries to top you, you might say, "I'm glad you feel so good about yourself, but it isn't necessary to show off to let me know how much better you are. I'm only trying to make conversation." Confronting the Competitor directly often defuses the situation and lets the person see him- or herself more clearly.

Augmenting this with the Mirror Technique, you could use an outrageous response to reflect back the Competitor's silliness. If you say, "My muscles are so sore—I bench-pressed two hundred pounds yesterday," and the Competitor comes back with, "Well, I benched three hundred pounds, and I have no muscular pain," you can reply, "I'm surprised, because the first two hundred pounds really get to you, so maybe I should have bench-pressed four hundred—then I wouldn't have felt the pain either." Then you can smile, hoping the person will get the message. Here mirroring was combined with the Humor Technique.

Competitiveness is a sign of jealousy. As we now know, jealousy seeks to destroy everything and everyone. There's no way that you can have a meaningful relationship with anyone who is overcome with jealousy of you. It is in your best interest to unplug a personal relationship with anyone who persists in being competitive.

THE CONTROL FREAK

•

The Control Freak—a baby Hitler—cannot function unless he or she is running the show. Children have a certain need to be controlled, but to adults with minds and values of their own, it is downright insulting and humiliating to be controlled by anyone.

You *have* to set limits with Control Freaks. Let them know that it is their business if they are trying to control everything around them, but it is your business when they try to exert control over you. At the first inkling of controlling behavior, you must speak up, using the Direct-Confront Technique. The Mirror Technique can also work wonders, inducing Control Freaks to "freak out" as they immediately rebel against your attempts to control them. Apparently they really cannot abide what they do to others. Be aware that if you persist in your mirroring, they will probably lash out at you verbally, with extreme vehemence. Eventually, however, experiencing what it feels like to be told what to do and when and how to do it will usually deter their further attempts to control you.

Joshua had always tried to control Wendy's life. Not only did he order meals for her in restaurants, but he would pick out her clothes, her hairstyles, her makeup. One morning, having decided to give him a taste of his own medicine, she went into his closet and set out his clothing for the day, even his shoes and socks. Seeing what Wendy had done, he went nuts, yelling, "You're not my mother. You can't pick out what I'm gonna wear. I don't want to wear this today. Stop trying to control me." She looked at him and said, "This is exactly what it feels like when you try to control me and what I wear."

Joshua never again tried to control Wendy's appearance. Now she plans to use the Mirror Technique when Joshua tries to order for her in restaurants.

Relentless Control Freaks call for the Give-Them-Hell-and-Yell Technique. Dig in your heels, push out your abdominal muscles, and bellow that you will not be controlled or told what to do, as you are a responsible adult who can make your own decisions. Interspersing a bit of profanity may convince them of how angry you really are.

If nothing works and the Control Freak continues to try to control you, leaving you upset and frustrated, you need to unplug. Otherwise you will be assured of losing your identity and your ability to think for yourself.

THE ACCUSING CRITIC

•

Since Accusing Critics are so insecure and so intent on being right, you must approach them with the Give-Them-Love-and-Kindness Technique. This may be reflected in your tone of voice and in the gentle words you choose.

You can also detoxify the Accusing Critic by means of the Calm Questioning Technique:

He: You were the reason we were late.
She: Honey, how did you come to that conclusion?
He: Well, it takes you forever to put on your makeup.
She: Sweetheart, don't you think that the last three calls you made right before we left had anything to do with our being late?
He: You're right. I guess we're both guilty.

The terms of endearment "honey" and "sweetheart" incorporate the Give-Them-Love-and-Kindness Technique, diluting any potential challenge.

The Mirror Technique may be useful in alerting Accusing Critics to their obnoxious behavior. Let's say you ordered the steak dinner and an Accusing Critic commented that it would make her sick, that she would never eat red meat, that you should feel guilty for ordering red meat. To make her conscious of how she sounds, you might attack what she is eating, using the same words and identical disgusted tones.

The Direct-Confront Technique is also applicable. Tell your dinner companion that her comments are rude and you would appreciate her allowing you to enjoy your meal. You must make Accusing Critics accountable for their actions and not let them get away with anything.

If the Critic persists, you may just want to unplug. In the restaurant situation, you could get up from the table, dramatically throw down your napkin, and make a dramatic exit. You will definitely have made your point.

The Unplug Technique, in which you just walk away, leaving

the Critic no one to accuse and criticize but him- or herself, can be used whenever the Critic persists in attacking you verbally.

THE ARROGANT KNOW-IT-ALL

•

Since Arrogant Know-It-Alls use their knowledge as a defense mechanism in order to overcome insecurity and feel accepted, intelligent, and admired, you have to let them know that you accept and appreciate their erudition. Use the Stop-the-Thought Technique and the Give-Them-Love-and-Kindness Technique to defuse your own negative feelings.

Whenever you find these people exasperating, you may want to release some of your pent-up frustration with the Tension-Blowout Technique. Just remember that by showing off their knowledge, they are trying to build themselves up so that you will accept and appreciate them. Therefore the more love and kindness you give them, the less they will feel that they have to show off.

If they aren't receptive to your point of view, because they know it all, you need to use the Direct-Confront Technique and tell them that you appreciate their knowledge and insight but would appreciate their letting you contribute some information. Make the point that intelligent people like them listen to what others say. This way you have not only flattered their ego by complimenting them on their knowledge and intelligence but also reduced their insecurity and opened the door to give-and-take communication.

I once had a client whose brother was an Arrogant Know-It-All. She fought and argued with him repeatedly. In reality, he was very insecure and convinced that their mother had favored her over him while they were growing up. His attempts to impress with his knowledge only caused arguments and further alienated him from his family's love and acceptance.

When my client came in and complained about him, I explained the reasons for his actions and recommended the Give-Them-Love-and-Kindness Technique and, whenever she got really upset, the Tension-Blowout Technique. After utilizing these, she found herself becoming more relaxed around him, and their relationship improved tremendously. Eventually her brother felt that he didn't *have* to know it all, didn't *have* to lecture her all the time, and he started to ask her questions. The moment he felt sure of her acceptance, he stopped playing the Know-It-All all the time. The moment she stopped blaming and dismissing him and instead started respecting and appreciating what he knew, their relationship took a complete turn for the better. Today they are not only the best of brothers and sisters but the best of friends.

THE EMOTIONAL REFRIGERATOR

•

For the most part, Emotional Refrigerators are a lost cause. You may want to shake some feelings into these people, but screaming and yelling won't help. Instead it will further alienate them, causing them to freeze you out even more. The approaches that work best are the Tension-Blowout and the Give-Them-Love-and-Kindness Techniques. Through these the Emotional Refrigerator will often come around, feeling safer and more accepted. Frequently, deep down, these icebergs don't want to be the way they are, but they can't help themselves because they have never learned how to communicate and express their feelings. They are afraid to make fools of themselves by looking and acting emotional.

The Humor Technique can be very effective with such people. You may not get them to share their feelings with you, but if you can at least get them to laugh, some connection may be made.

There are Emotional Refrigerators who may not be held back emotionally at all but merely have poor vocal skills and tend to speak in a monotone. Using the Calm Questioning Technique can help you discover what they think and how they feel about a situation, a person, or an event.

THE SKEPTICAL PARANOID

•

I have encountered many Skeptical Paranoids in the Hollywood community, people who've endured years and years of disappointment. In essence, they have heard and seen it all. As well, many are afraid for their jobs. If their projects fail or if they make a wrong decision, they can be immediately discarded. Therefore the paranoia, fear, and skepticism.

I've found that both the Direct-Confront and the Calm Questioning Techniques can help alleviate the fears of Skeptical Paranoids, by enabling them to see logically that the decisions they have made are the right ones. When you assure them and reassure them through these techniques, they gain more confidence not only in you but in themselves as well.

Because the main motivator for Skeptical Paranoids is fear, you have to do whatever you can to assure them of your trustworthiness, so they can feel safe around you, knowing you are not out to hurt or take advantage of them.

You need to have a lot of patience with Skeptical Paranoids. The Tension-Blowout Technique can help with this, as you blow out your frustrations. If you just hang in there and offer support with the Give-Them-Love-and-Kindness Technique, you may well see them come around and maybe even become your close friends and allies.

If, on the other hand, they tax your nerves too greatly, you must unplug, just as you must with other Toxic Terrors who deplete too much of your energy. Leave them for the psychologists to deal with!

THE INSTIGATOR

•

There are two fundamental approaches to take with Instigators. The Calm Questioning Technique usually stops them in their tracks, as they quickly realize that you are onto their game. Questioned, an

Instigator will squirm, become uncomfortable, or even say, "I was only kidding" or "I was just curious." When the hairdresser Sirvone was trying to stir up trouble by telling his client that her junior high school daughter was probably having sex and taking drugs, the mother should have questioned Sirvone extensively.

Mother: What makes you think my daughter is having sex and taking drugs?

Sirvone: Oh, I know how kids are at that age. I hear things, you know?

Mother: Have you spent time talking to my daughter?

Sirvone: No.

Mother: Are you a friend of hers?

Sirvone: No.

Mother: Do you follow her and her friends around, so you know what she's doing?

Sirvone: No.

Mother: Do you have children of your own?

Sirvone: No.

Mother: Do you know what goes on in our home and how we have educated our daughter?

Sirvone: No, but I was just trying to warn you so you can be aware in case there would be a problem.

Mother: Thank you, Sirvone, but I think everything concerning my daughter is under control.

Through the Calm Questioning Technique, Sirvone would have gotten the point that he could not play his little game with this mother.

The Direct-Confront Technique can also be used to defuse Instigators. In this case, you let them know that you know what they are up to. For example:

Sirvone: You'd better watch your daughter. I'm sure she's taking drugs and having sex.

Mother: Sirvone, if you spent as much time trying to create positive excitement in your business as you do trying to create negative excitement in your clients' lives, you'd be a lot busier in the salon.

The Humor Technique also works well on Instigators. As they try to rile you, you could use a humorous comeback such as: "Just keep on talking so I'll know you're not thinking."

Say whatever humorous thing comes to your mind, as long as you let Instigators know that you are definitely onto them and are not taking anything they say seriously. In essence, you need to make light of all provocative comments they make. Eventually they will surely get the message.

Choosing Specific Techniques

Based on my own research and on client feedback, the techniques listed for each Toxic Terror have proved to be the most effective ones. However, that doesn't mean you have to stick to the specific technique or techniques listed under each of the thirty types of terrors.

You can use one, any combination, or every one of the Ten Techniques when you are dealing with a Toxic Terror. It all depends on your preference and what you feel comfortable doing. No matter what technique you choose, the main thing is to release your anger and your frustration effectively so that you don't end up with cancer, heart disease, or any of the other stress-induced illnesses.

CHAPTER 8

CHOOSING A TECHNIQUE BASED ON THE TOXIC PERSON'S ROLE IN YOUR LIFE

- Toxic Mothers and Fathers
- Toxic Siblings
- Toxic Spouses
- Toxic Children
- Toxic Friends
- Toxic Lovers
- Toxic Neighbors
- Toxic People at Work
- Toxic Bosses
- Toxic Coworkers

- **Toxic Subordinates**

- **Toxic Authority Figures**

- **Toxic Professionals**

- **Toxic Service People**

- **We Have Options**

The role a Toxic Terror plays in your life affects your choice of technique. Certain techniques may be more effective with family members, while other techniques may be more successful with coworkers, and still others prove to be more useful with authority figures or subordinates.

People act different ways with different individuals, depending on each person's effect on their life, their well-being, and their livelihood.

Consider your family. The television families that we grew up watching—*Ozzie and Harriet, Leave It to Beaver*—are fantasy families. They do not exist in the real world. No family gets along that well all the time.

We have all been taught that we have to love our families simply because they *are* our families. Unfortunately, there is toxicity in every family. Some families are not worthy of love, and you do not *have* to love any member of your family who has been horrible to you.

TOXIC MOTHERS AND FATHERS

·

Clearly, some parents had no business ever becoming parents—those who physically or sexually abuse, torture, or neglect their children, thereby inflicting severe and irreparable damage. Often harassment, mental abuse, and even physical abuse continue into a child's teen or adult years. I wholeheartedly agree with the many psychologists who believe that the Unplug Technique is the only way out in these cases. Here it is in the victim's best interest *never* to deal with his or her parents again—to have no communication whatsoever with them—for a happier and more productive life.

Of course, most parents are not vicious, premeditating abusers. Instead toxic mothers and fathers may be poor souls with bad self-images, who have tried to do the best they could for their children. Because of their ignorance, low self-esteem, or own familial history, they became toxic to their children. With them, techniques other than unplugging should be utilized.

Some parents who are unknowingly toxic discover the consequences of their behavior when it is too late. Surely actor Hervé Villechaize's mother searched her soul after Hervé killed himself. Notwithstanding the pain and agony of being a little person, according to Hervé, his father and his mother didn't make matters easier for him. His father, a prominent physician, could never accept Hervé's dwarfed stature, so he took Hervé around the world in search of a cure, a vain pursuit that involved much physical anguish. Finally, as a teenager, Hervé refused to be carted around and begged his father to accept him as he was, but apparently the man could not.

His mother was not much help either. Hervé told me, as he told many people who interviewed him about his life, that he never felt as though his mother really loved him or wanted him; whatever he did never seemed good enough for her. At his elaborate wedding, Hervé excitedly introduced me to his mother, saying, "Mother, Mother, this is my speech doctor. She's teaching me how to improve my speech." Without a smile, his mother looked at me and coldly replied, "Well, I still can't understand him." I remember thinking: No wonder this poor man has had so much trouble all his life. His own mother doesn't seem supportive of his efforts to better himself. After Hervé died, *People* magazine recounted an incident that further demonstrated his mother's unacceptance. Apparently, Hervé, an accomplished artist, painted a lovely portrait of his mother, to which her response was: "Well, it doesn't look like me."

Unfortunately, Accusing Critic or Cut-You-Downer toxic mothers are all too prevalent and need to be treated with the Direct-Confront or Calm Questioning Technique. They must be told bluntly and directly that their words and behavior are hurtful.

Some parental behavior—especially that of Mental Cases, Angry Pugilists, Control Freaks, Competitors, and Bitchy, Bossy Bullies—can not only hurt but embarrass a child. The child wants desperately to love the parent and "fix" him or her, but it will never work unless the parent takes action. In these cases, the Unplug Technique is appropriate.

Tennis pro Mary Pierce has an abusive father who was a Control Freak. After a match, Jim Pierce would swear at her, berate her in front of other players and officials, even beat her. Tennis officials unplugged him from all games, and Mary followed through, letting go and unplugging him from her personal and professional life. She went on to win international tennis championships.

In cases like this, there is no alternative but to let go in order to preserve your own life. There have been headlines about cases in which young children have legally divorced toxic mothers and/or fathers who have been negligent or abusive.

Other parents are embarrassing because they are Gossips, Jokesters, Unconscious Social Klutzes, or Chatterboxes. Though not vicious, they can be a handful to deal with. Actor Sylvester Stallone has repeatedly mentioned his mother in interviews. Apparently Jackie Stallone always seeks the limelight and speaks embarrassingly about her son's ex-wife or his girlfriends. Sly has doubtless let out many a deep breath to cope with his mother at these times. He seems to love Jackie, and good-naturedly accepting her behavior as "just being her," makes jokes about it.

Along with the Humor Technique and the Tension-Blowout Technique, parents who have these less lethal toxic traits are best approached with the Calm Questioning, Direct-Confront, and Give-Them-Love-and-Kindness Techniques. For a resistant parent to hear your annoyance and start to listen to you, the Give-Them-Hell-and-Yell and the Mirror Techniques can be employed.

Parents who are Runners, Wishy-Washy Wimps, Smiling Two-Faced Backstabbers, Bullshitting Liars, or Silent but Deadly Volcanoes are scary to be around, because you can never really trust them. You wanted so much from them, but they gave you so little and caused you so much pain and anger and disappointment. Your main concern now should be self-preservation.

In dealing with parents who have abandoned you, the Stop-the-Thought Technique and even the Vicarious-Fantasy Technique can help restore your sanity and repair your shattered feelings about them. As Miss U.S.A., Kenya Moore seemed to have it all. In fact, she had suffered tremendous pain because her mother left her as a child, and when finally contact was renewed, the mother treated her daughter as if she were invisible. Kenya made a vow at the age of twelve never to let her mother hurt her again, a not unusual strategy with children whose parents have abandoned them. The Stop-the-Thought and Vicarious-Fantasy Techniques might help Kenya further deal with her anger toward her mother.

Finally, there are parents who are really sad children and have created a relationship whereby you have switched roles. The Self-Destroyer and the Mental Case, the Wishy-Washy Wimp, Gloom and Doom Victim, and Bullshitting Liar all fall into this category. The child ends up trying to rescue these pathetic people because they are so fragile. I would prescribe the Give-Them-Love-and-Kindness Technique, but often you will have to incorporate "tough love." To avoid becoming a codependent, you must unplug—not because you hate them, but for the sake of your love for them. You must set limits and not allow them to drag you down in their pain and sickness. Often this technique forces them to grow up and face their problems directly.

We need to break the toxic legacy of passing down to our children behaviors we learned from our own parents. By applying these techniques, we can finally end the vicious cycle.

TOXIC SIBLINGS

•

Brothers and sisters can cause one another more grief than anyone else in the world.

We may have laughed when, in the popular Smothers Brothers show back in the sixties, Tommy said to Dickie, "Mom always liked you best," but jealousy and sibling rivalry are no laughing matter. Many a child's self-esteem has been destroyed by feelings that one or both parents like a brother or sister more.

Sometimes one sibling is clearly more successful than the other, and the unsuccessful one will often act out the role of "bad seed" or "black sheep." As a result, either the sibling and the entire family feel pain and embarrassment or the less successful sibling turns into a child and expects the successful one to take on the role of parent and bail him or her out of trouble.

One of my clients had to use the Unplug Technique because he was constantly being dragged down by his heroin addict brother. When my client, now a prominent physician, was in medical school, there were times when he could barely function because of late-night calls to get his brother out of jail or out of some drug-related mess. Because they were brothers and he felt guilt, Marty always felt obligated to help. As Marty became a successful physician, he found himself spending half his income to support his brother and bail him out of nightmare situations. No technique worked with his brother: not Mirroring, Give-Them-Hell-and-Yell, Humor, or Give-Them-Love-and-Kindness. To preserve his own life—mentally, financially, and emotionally—he cut his brother out of his life and totally unplugged. Unfortunately, his brother died of a heroin overdose, but Marty rarely feels guilt because he feels he did his best for him. If he ever does feel a tinge of guilt, he overcomes it with the Stop-the-Thought and Vicarious-Fantasy Techniques. His fantasy is that his brother would have appreciated his help, gotten straight, and lived a happy and productive life.

Because of the complex family dynamics, most people feel guilt and shame, anger and disappointment, regarding a sibling—even more than they may feel for a parent or child. Since you shared the same parents, you may believe you should think, feel, and act the same way. When this doesn't happen, people are often furious and feel betrayed.

In dealing with a sibling, you have to realize that even though you share similar genes, you are completely different. You can never expect your siblings to be the way you want them to be. This is where communication is essential. The Humor, Direct-Confront, Mirror, and Calm Questioning Techniques, even Give-Them-Hell-and-Yell (a very popular technique with siblings), can radically improve your relationship with your sibling.

In my practice, I have seen brother sue brother, sister hate sister, brother want to kill sister—and why? Because over the course of a shared lifetime, one sibling *never* learned how to talk to the other.

These techniques afford you the opportunity to forge a meaningful relationship with your brothers and sisters.

TOXIC SPOUSES

•

Having written a book titled *He Says, She Says: Closing the Communication Gap Between the Sexes,* traveled around the world lecturing about the topic, and read countless letters from people who have been helped by my books and seminars, I am *convinced* that the reason the divorce rate is so high is the lack of knowledge of how to communicate. We don't give one another a chance, and we are willing to discard our partners after a few years simply because they upset us.

Instead of using humor, calm questioning, direct confrontation, and even the Give-Them-Hell-and-Yell Technique (a necessity in *any* marriage or love relationship), we are all too quick to run away.

Now you have options. Even if you are head-over-heels crazy in love with someone, there are times when your beloved will drive you crazy and make you terribly sad and horribly angry. When tense times arise, you cannot run away, and you cannot stuff your feelings until they build up beyond repair. Instead you must deal with what is bothering you. You must communicate! That is the only way you can ever expect to remain together.

Sometimes, however, people have grown so far apart and created such different lifestyles that they have nothing left in common. Others won't ever be able to forgive the person they once loved for doing something like cheating on or betraying them and feel they can never trust that individual again. Those people need to unplug and let go, no matter how painful it may be. The Stop-the-Thought and Vicarious-Fantasy Techniques aid in coping with anger against a toxic spouse. Use your anger to remove yourself from the toxic relationship, leaving with your dignity and self-respect intact.

You don't have to try to destroy your mate by seeking revenge for the rest of your life, the way a midwestern woman did. After a decade of marriage, a multimillion-dollar settlement, and a remarriage years later, which afforded her the opportunity for a fresh start, she persistently harassed and intimidated her husband, keeping their children from him, defacing his car, and taunting his girlfriends.

TOXIC CHILDREN

In the "tough love" movement of several years ago, parents put their incorrigible children through a special disciplinary program in order to teach them to be accountable for their actions. In many cases, the children recovered and were able to change their toxic ways.

These days, it is easy to blame a parent for a child's toxic behavior or toxic nature. Critics may say that a child was given too much or too little love. I personally believe that a child can't be given too much love, and it is apparent that whether or not children become toxic may have very little to do with how their parents raised them. Today there are many influences that parents have very little control over—the media, peer pressure, the pressure to achieve, drugs, gangs, violence in the schools, and random violence. I know many model parents whose children have ended up as drug addicts, single mothers, or gang members.

Although many parents feel hopeless when their children are out of control, they must *never* give up. There are options available to you. Begin with the Direct-Confront Technique—talk to your child as an adult, not condescendingly. Because of the strong influence the media have on their lives, children are well aware of what is happening around them, so don't be afraid to talk to them person-to-person, as adults. Let them come up to your level, don't go down to theirs.

Use the Give-Them-Love-and-Kindness, the Calm Questioning, and the Mirror Techniques. Don't be afraid of Give-Them-Hell-and-Yell—but don't use the technique too often, or it will lose its effectiveness. *Never* hit a child—no matter how much you think the child deserves it. Studies show that violence never works as a deterrent to negative behavior. It only fuels more hate and anger toward the person who is hitting and may leave lifelong emotional scars.

When children will not cooperate or listen to reason, you have to let them suffer the consequences of their actions through "tough love." Unplug and get them the appropriate help, even if it means putting them in a mental institution or a juvenile hall.

Although you cannot be completely responsible for your children's actions at all times as they grow up, you can be responsible for starting them out right by teaching them good values and moral principles.

You must establish open lines of communication with your children early on so that they will *always* know that no matter how awful things are, you are available to talk. You need to teach children ways to communicate with you through example.

Teaching them the Calm Questioning and Direct-Confront Techniques early in life will be not only the best gift you can give them but the best gift you can give to your relationship, to assure clear understanding. If children see their parents talking openly and honestly with each other, they will learn to do the same thing.

TOXIC FRIENDS

•

We have all heard the expression "With friends like these, you don't need enemies." There is nothing so disheartening or emotionally devastating as when someone whom you trusted, whom you believed, whom you loved, betrays you. Sometimes we tolerate people and call them friends when they are anything but. Perhaps we feel sorry for them because their lives didn't turn out as well as ours; perhaps we grew up with them and went to school with them, and we stick by them because they have been part of our lives for so long. No matter how we rationalize it, these people who cause us grief, pain, and severe disappointment by disrespecting us, not supporting us, and betraying us can never be our "friends."

A friend is not just a person whom you have known for a long time. A friend is someone who helps you through crises, who is elated at your happiness and is not jealous of you. A friend is someone who will never break a confidence and will defend you. Friends do not try to compete with you. They are respectful, generous, sensitive, and accepting.

A true friend openly and honestly shares thoughts and feelings with you and doesn't judge you.

Anyone who has less than these characteristics is *not* a friend. Certainly nobody is perfect, and friends may slip from time to time, but that is where communication comes in. Communicating through the Direct-Confront Technique, the Calm Questioning Technique, and the Give-Them-Love-and-Kindness Technique is what allows you to maintain that intimate bond between friends so that you can continue respecting and appreciating one another.

TOXIC LOVERS

•

The most intimate of friends are, of course, lovers. If we can be open and naked with someone in the bedroom, engaging in the most private acts, why is it sometimes so difficult to communicate with that person? Perhaps it has a lot to do with our own sense of self-worth. Often we don't know how to talk to a lover. Since this special person is capable of making us feel so good, what we do and what we say when a lover disappoints us or hurts our feelings may seem awkward. We feel vulnerable and unprotected. As a result, we may overreact and not put his or her actions in perspective. Intimate relationships quickly become "toxic" when there is no communication.

A person you have been intimate with should be treated with the greatest respect. Use a positive, loving tone and work out any disagreements through the Give-Them-Love-and-Kindness Technique, the primary means to prevent your becoming toxic to each other. The Calm Questioning and the Humor Techniques are also essential to help quell hurt feelings and to establish more open lines of communication.

Toni and David, honeymooning in Barbados, failed to express their fears and uncertainties about being married. Instead David became withdrawn and turned into a Runner, both figuratively and literally, as he spent hours on the roads. Meanwhile Toni turned into a cross between a Gloom and Doom Victim and a Bitchy, Bossy Bully. By the end of their week together they were hardly speaking. Finally, things exploded, and they used the Give-Them-Hell-and-Yell Technique. It turned out to be a great tension release, and the couple were finally able to talk to each other and get their feelings on the table. Although the harsh words they exchanged didn't make for the greatest of honeymoon experiences, it got them communicating.

TOXIC NEIGHBORS

•

You can pick your friends, spouse, and lovers, but neighbors are a different story. Having heard enough "neighbors from hell" stories to last me a lifetime, I have come to appreciate the good fortune of a person who has a warm and friendly, non-petty, non-meddling, non-gossiping, non-angry, non-fanatical, non-opportunistic, non-competitive, non-accusing neighbor. Living in close quarters, as in an apartment building, especially brings out people's toxic traits.

Your best defenses are the Give-Them-Hell-and-Yell, Tension-Blowout, Stop-the-Thought, and Vicarious-Fantasy Techniques.

Humor, Direct-Confront, Calm Questioning, and Give-Them-Love-and-Kindness don't work with neighbors who are attacking you. When you employ the Give-Them-Hell-and-Yell Technique from the start, the neighbors usually won't bother you again. Like the barking of an aggressive dog, this method will establish your power and strength in sticking up for yourself.

If the toxic neighbors don't back down, just breathe in, hold it, and let them go as you use the Tension-Blowout Technique. If that isn't effective enough, utilize the Stop-the-Thought Technique, so you don't get an ulcer. To further relieve your anxiety and anger, employ the Vicarious-Fantasy Technique and imagine their house burning down, their condo flooding, or, better yet, their moving out.

Never take your fantasy to the reality stage. If you have insoluble neighbor problems, let the courts—not your fists—handle your disputes. Acts of violence can only get you in trouble.

If things become unbearable, you can use the Unplug Technique and move out. It may be a hassle, but it can save your life. Before you move, be sure to check out the neighbors at your new home!

TOXIC PEOPLE AT WORK

•

As with your neighbors, you have no control over whom you encounter in the workplace—unless, of course, you run the company. Today's financial climate does not allow even most bosses to pick and choose their clients or customers freely.

An employee in these tight times must learn to get along with all kinds of toxic people merely to keep his or her job. In the work environment, learning to handle toxic people is literally a matter of survival. The Tension-Blowout, Stop-the-Thought, and Vicarious-Fantasy Techniques may be your best workplace bets.

TOXIC BOSSES

•

Bosses are bosses, and *they* are in charge, so whether you like or respect them doesn't really matter if your intention is to keep your job and earn a living. What matters is that you learn how to get along with them as best you can and cope with any anger you may feel.

High-powered toxic people tend to be Bitchy, Bossy Bullies; Accusing Critics; Control Freaks; Opportunistic Users; Competitors; Smiling Two-Faced Backstabbers; Arrogant Know-It-Alls; Penny-Pinching Misers—often in combination.

I have heard countless stories from my clients about toxic bosses who fall into one or more of these categories. After they apply techniques I have recommended, their work lives often change for the better as they are no longer victimized in the workplace. If they want to keep their jobs and ascend the corporate ladder, methods found effective in releasing ill feelings are Tension-Blowout Technique, repeated every twenty minutes, the Stop-the-Thought Technique—especially if they keep dwelling on something negative their toxic boss said to them—the Give-Them-Love-and-Kindness Technique, in which they make every effort to say nice things and treat their boss with respect, and the Vicarious-Fantasy Technique, which involves thinking evil thoughts and fantasizing about things they would like to do to their toxic boss.

If you value your job, other techniques may be too risky. Bosses should never be put on the defensive or made to look wrong, because they are in charge and there is nothing you can do about it—except release your anger appropriately.

If you don't care about your job, you can take a risk and use the Direct-Confront, Calm Questioning, Mirror, or Give-Them-Hell-and-Yell Technique. Should your workplace be so toxic that the anxiety and stress you feel threaten your health, unplug if you can.

We no longer have to be victims. We now have the option to speak up, leave, or go through legal channels to help us deal with unfair or toxic bosses. If toxic bosses keep up their toxic behavior, they may end up with a toxic lawsuit for their toxic harassment.

TOXIC COWORKERS

•

I have heard countless stories of coworkers trying to sabotage their fellow employees. Their actions have caused my clients great pain and despair. When a toxic coworker has taken successful covert action, it has often cost clients not only their health but even their jobs.

A toxic coworker may take the form of a Competitor, a Cut-

You-Downer, a Smiling Two-Faced Backstabber, a Gossip, a Meddler, or an Instigator.

Although the work environment is vastly different from that at home, some people look at the boss as a parental or authority figure and at their coworkers as siblings. As a result, the dynamics that exist in families often cross over into the work situation.

Most effective in dealing with toxic coworkers are the Tension-Blowout, Direct-Confront, and Calm Questioning Techniques. *Never* lose your cool at work or use the Give-Them-Hell-and-Yell Technique. Any type of verbal violence in the workplace is unacceptable! Whatever your job description, you need to act in a civilized and professional manner. If you are clearly being sabotaged, use the Direct-Confront Technique with the toxic coworker *and* the boss, openly telling the boss what has gone on. Let the toxic coworker know you are onto their game, that you will have no part of it, and that you will go to a higher authority—the boss—to achieve honesty and justice.

TOXIC SUBORDINATES

•

Some subordinates feel so resentful or jealous of their superiors that they enact the role of Gossip, Silent but Deadly Volcano, Instigator, Eddie Haskell, Self-Righteous Priss, or Skeptical Paranoid.

Subordinates must always treat their bosses with respect simply because of their position, just as bosses need to respect their subordinates yet maintain a position of authority.

A boss who is upset at a subordinate must keep a calm professional demeanor at all times, never getting angry or using the Give-Them-Hell-and-Yell Technique.

It is the Direct-Confront and the Calm Questioning Techniques that are essential in dealing with a toxic subordinate. When a subordinate doesn't "get it" after being talked to repeatedly, the boss needs to document the incidents of toxic behavior in writing, complete with dates and times. If problems are documented, there is less chance of the subordinate taking legal action.

Next the toxic subordinate needs to be unplugged, as soon as possible. After telling my subordinate repeatedly that gossiping and meddling would not be tolerated, I finally unplugged him, because his toxic behavior threatened my business and my reputation. If a toxic employee could potentially ruin your business, don't even consider giving two weeks notice.

When reprimanding subordinates or letting them go, you must allow them to retain their dignity. You never know: yesterday's mailroom lackey can end up as tomorrow's studio head. Watch where you kick them, or how you kick them out.

TOXIC AUTHORITY FIGURES

•

Just as your boss has control over your livelihood and financial status, there are individuals who may have control over your life—to the extent that they can destroy it. Their being in positions of authority is no guarantee that they cannot be toxic. Look at the toxic politicians who have been accused of stealing and having illicit affairs with members of both sexes.

These toxic individuals—whether law enforcement officers, teachers, or even clergy—may be powerless people outside their positions and will often use their authority as a means to feel more powerful. They will usually manifest themselves as Control Freaks, Arrogant Know-It-Alls, Accusing Critics, Self-Righteous Prisses, Emotional Refrigerators, Cut-You-Downers, Angry Pugilists, or Bitchy, Bossy Bullies.

If they hold the power of your life in their hands, do not attempt to upset them. However angry and violent you feel, do not give them hell and yell, because they won't hear you. They'll only get angrier and angrier, and you will suffer more negative consequences. Instead keep breathing, and force yourself to do the Tension-Blowout and the Stop-the-Thought Techniques. Think up the most heinous Vicarious-Fantasy and picture yourself torturing them in order to release your rage. Don't speak—just breathe!

After the dust has settled, you can make the lives of these toxic authority figures miserable, expressing your rage through legal recourse. You no longer have to feel victimized by their actions and keep your anger deep within you, thus becoming scarred for life.

TOXIC PROFESSIONALS

•

Just as there are toxic authority figures, there are toxic professionals: doctors, lawyers, business managers, CPAs, even therapists.

Just because people were intellectually capable and did well in school, completed a medical residency, or passed the bar or other professional examination does not mean they are superior to you or free of toxicity.

All too often professionals who may be losers as people hide behind their degrees as a means of feeling powerful and important. All too often they may manifest toxic behavior as Bitchy, Bossy Bullies, Angry Pugilists, Competitors, Smiling Two-Faced Backstabbers, Cut-You-Downers, Narcissists, Snooty Snobs, Arrogant Know-It-Alls, Control Freaks, Accusing Critics, or Skeptical Paranoids.

They may treat you condescendingly, acting as though they are doing you a favor by even talking to you.

These toxic professionals need to be put in their place. Their place is to help you and support you. It doesn't matter how famous doctors or lawyers are or how many articles have been written about them—they must first and foremost be of service to you.

You are the one paying the bill, the one who has sought out their services, so never feel intimidated by them. You have every right to ask questions and every right to be treated with respect. The Calm Questioning Technique is best used with a toxic professional. The key word is "calm." Professionals are after all sensitive human beings and will often get offended if you ask them questions in a way that sounds like an attack. They may react defensively and start talking down to you or acting abrupt. Therefore it is imperative that you be conscious of your voice when talking to professionals.

Maintain a calm and respectful tone that can be heard yet is not too harsh or too loud.

If, having asked your questions in this manner, you still find that you are treated disrespectfully, then you should use the Direct-Confront Technique and let them know in a calm but firm tone that you would prefer to be treated with respect and not talked down to.

A client of mine used this technique with an incredibly chauvinistic dermatologist, who ignored her questions and spoke to other doctors in the room as though she were an object on display. She immediately spoke up, saying calmly, "Doctor, I am not a child and I am not ignorant, so please speak to me directly if you want me to be your patient." He apologized, then obliged, and she became one of his favorite patients.

In a situation where the doctor does not oblige and continues to treat the patient insensitively, the patient needs to unplug and leave. Some excellent doctors are tremendously lacking in acceptable bedside manners. The key point is to speak up. Express your dissatisfaction, then unplug if your wishes are not granted. This holds true for attorneys, CPAs, and anyone else whose job it is to help you.

TOXIC SERVICE PEOPLE

•

In contrast to professionals who are toxic because they feel superior to you, service people will often be toxic because they are jealous of you or insecure in your presence. Maybe they detest being salespeople or doing home improvements or repairing cars or waitressing. But they shouldn't take their unhappiness out on you.

Toxic service people may manifest themselves as Snooty Snobs, Self-Righteous Prisses, Opportunistic Users, Bitchy, Bossy Bullies, Chatterboxes, Competitors, Smiling Two-Faced Backstabbers, or Eddie Haskells.

The reason so many salespeople are rude and unhelpful these days may be that they are envious of you for being able to buy what they cannot afford. They would rather be you—buying, not selling.

Many male auto mechanics have been known to treat female customers as if they are stupid, abruptly dismissing women's questions or requests. Perhaps they wish they were driving the Jaguar or Lexus instead of repairing it. Perhaps they are still of the childish mind-set that girls aren't supposed to know anything about cars or that they aren't as smart as boys.

You don't have to be victimized by whatever contributes to such people's toxicity. Now you have options for handling these negative entities in your life.

The toxic service person can best be controlled through the Direct-Confront Technique. If that doesn't work, you may want to try mirroring, and if that fails too, don't take their crap. Instead use the Give-Them-Hell-and-Yell and Unplug Techniques—leave and don't pay for services not rendered. For example, if a waiter has been rude and awful, you don't have to leave a tip. You shouldn't feel obligated to pay anyone who has abused you or treated you shabbily.

One of my clients, a very kind professional woman, was traveling with her cat, for whom she had purchased a pet ticket. As my client placed her cat, in an airline-regulation Sherpa Bag, under the seat in front of her, the stewardess yelled out, "Is that an animal? Let me see your ticket." My client was holding her ticket, and the flight attendant snatched it out of her hand, then shouted that the ticket was for the wrong day. She scurried out of the plane to get a supervisor.

By now my client was humiliated. Everyone seemed to be looking at her as though she were a criminal. The stewardess marched back down the aisle, with the ticket agent, a supervisor, and a security guard in tow, and said to my client in a harsh, cold tone, "That is not a regulation travel bag." My client, using the Direct-Confront Technique, calmly explained that it was a regulation bag, to which the stewardess hastily replied, "It's not a Sherpa Bag." My client, switching to the Give-Them-Hell-and-Yell Technique, displayed the bag and said in her loudest voice, "Yes it is, and I just purchased this ticket for the ninth, which is today."

The stewardess grinned sheepishly and said in a meek voice, "Oh, I'm sorry. Here's your ticket. I thought today was the eighth."

Before the stewardess's entourage could leave, my client, still in her Give-Them-Hell-and-Yell mode, yelled, "Look, this is *not* how you treat passengers. You have humiliated me in front of all these passengers and accused me of doing something wrong. This is completely unfair."

By now the pilot got involved and, smelling possible legal action, offered my client a first-class seat, which she gladly took. Throughout the flight she kept doing the Tension-Blowout and the Stop-the-Thought Techniques, as she averted the idea of getting thrown off the plane and missing her big meeting the following morning. She used the Vicarious-Fantasy Technique to visualize the toxic stewardess being sucked out of the plane as she flushed the toilet.

When my client hit the ground, she continued using the Direct-Confront Technique and wrote to the proper airline authorities, who bent over backward with apologies and provided her with several first-class tickets and a lifetime travel voucher for her cat. It was only then—when justice had been served—that she could finally unplug.

We Have Options

We are bombarded on a regular basis by toxic people. They infiltrate every aspect of our daily lives. We can no longer run and hide. Instead we have access to specific techniques for dealing with them. We don't have to be victimized by toxic people any longer.

CHAPTER 9

DEALING WITH THE ANGER AND HURT OF A TOXIC RELATIONSHIP

- Being Brutally Honest with Yourself

- Acknowledging Whom You Are Really Angry At

- Accepting the Roller Coaster of Emotions

- Ending It in a Letter

- Ending It over the Telephone

- Ending It in Person

- Using a Third Party

- Handling the Residual Effects of Anger

  Never Use Violence

  Letting It Out Physically

Talking It Out

Keeping a Written or Verbal Record

Photo-Ripping Ceremony

Cleansing by Candlelight

Returning Gifts

- **The Solace of Knowing That What Goes Around Comes Around**

- **Success Is the Best Revenge**

- **Forgiving Means Giving Up and Getting On with Your Life**

BEING BRUTALLY HONEST WITH YOURSELF

•

Even though I believe that people are generally good and can change if they want to, I know there are those who will never change.

They consider it to be their nature to act in a certain way. A parable that reflects this was popularized in the movie *The Crying Game*. A scorpion wanted to get to the other side of the river, and the only way he could get across was by hitching a ride on the back of a turtle. The turtle said to the scorpion, "I can't let you ride on my back. You could sting me, and then I would drown."

"Now, why would I sting you?" said the scorpion. "If you drowned, so would I. Why would I do something that stupid?"

The turtle thought that what the scorpion said made sense, so he let it climb on his back. In the middle of the river, the scorpion stung the turtle on the neck. As the turtle drowned, he asked, "Why did you sting me? Now you have destroyed us both."

The scorpion lifted his claws and replied, "That's my nature."

Sometimes people do things because they feel sure they can't help it. You might give them chance after chance, until you become thoroughly disappointed and disgusted with them.

One of my clients, Patsy, repeatedly broke up and reconciled with her boyfriend of two years. Every time she went back to him, I asked, "Are you sure you know what you're doing?" Patsy would reply, "Well, I am giving him one more chance. That's it." Sure enough, he would disappoint her, and sure enough, she would break up, and sure enough, she would return to him.

Patsy's boyfriend was like the scorpion in the story; he could never change his womanizing ways. The repeated chances she gave him served only to confirm this. Relationships like theirs are irreparable. When there's nothing more you can do, you have to be brutally honest, not only with the other person but with yourself as well.

Some relationships will never work. There are people who have character traits that are so toxic to you that it is virtually impossible for you to be around them. In such cases you have no choice but to leave the relationship behind in order to save yourself. You don't need to salvage anything. Leave it all behind, with the exception of your dignity.

ACKNOWLEDGING WHOM YOU ARE REALLY ANGRY AT

So many of us spend our entire lives feeling angry, depressed, unloved, or empty. Often we can't put our finger on anything specific, but we know that something isn't right.

It is only when we search our lives, looking deep into our hearts and honestly examining our past and present, that we can clearly see how we have internalized our hostile responses to certain toxic people. Perhaps we're angry at our mothers for not acting as we wanted, or we are upset by all men because we can't find the right mate after going from disappointment to disappointment.

You mustn't ever take your anger out at anyone—especially yourself—other than the source. That way, you would end up a toxic person yourself.

The next time you want to overload on chocolate cake, snort a line of cocaine, smoke crack, finish a whole bottle of Scotch, or chain-smoke pack after pack of cigarettes, ask yourself whom you are really angry at. You will usually discover that it is not yourself. And you will be able to stop doing horrible things to yourself.

Marianne made the discovery that it was her toxic Control Freak husband she was really angry at. She directly confronted him and unplugged—unplugging, too, the eighty pounds she had gained over the previous ten years.

Margie felt no more need for plastic surgery when she discovered that she kept trying to change her looks out of deep anger toward her parents, who had told her in childhood that she was "goofy-looking." She had transferred that anger to herself for not being perfect. When she unplugged from her toxic parents, she became, for the first time in her life, a happy person.

Getting to the root of the matter and finding out whom you are really angry at can positively change the course of your life, as you never have to take your negative feelings out on yourself again. Instead you will begin to love yourself. As Oscar Wilde put it, "To love oneself is the beginning of a lifelong romance."

Accepting the Roller Coaster
of Emotions

•

After you have identified the person who has caused your problems, remember that to make the decision to end this toxic relationship is to do the best thing possible for your self-esteem. If you have tinges of remorse or guilt, just remind yourself of how horribly you were treated. Remaining around the individual will only restimulate your anger and poor self-esteem.

Despite the hatred you may feel and your excitement to be free, you may be sad to have separated yourself from a parent, lifelong friend, husband, wife, or family member, someone who has been part of your life for so long. The absence may be traumatic for you. These emotions are perfectly natural as you mourn the toxic relationship, no matter how bad it was. It is normal to feel remorse and guilt, even though you know you have done the right thing.

As you achieve closure in the relationship, do not be surprised by your myriad emotions. You may cry, you may scream, you may get quiet, you may dance, you may sing. Your reactions will be unpredictable. Don't worry about it; just go with the flow. Feel what you're feeling, for doing so can definitely help the healing process as you let go of the toxic person.

ENDING IT IN A LETTER

•

One of the best ways to end a toxic relationship is to write a letter. Here you have the time to analyze exactly what you want to say. You may write and rewrite and edit.

In the beginning of the letter, review the positive things you felt for the toxic person. Then go on to describe the effects the toxic behavior had on you—how it made you feel. Cite specific incidents in detail as you discuss why it is necessary to bail out of the relationship.

Vent all your feelings, leaving nothing out. It is a great way to release your anger toward the person. Many psychologists suggest that you write a letter expressing all your thoughts but not send it. If you want to end the toxic relationship, though, I think people need to know how you honestly feel about them, no matter how painful it is. So I say send the letter. Sometimes, through reading about how toxic they have been, people learn that their actions do have consequences and that others will not always put up with their antics. They may accept that if they want to have other meaningful relationships, they need to examine their toxic ways.

When you decide to end a toxic relationship through a letter, you must consider that when something is in writing, it becomes evidence. In addition, it may not be as private as you might think. Therefore, be prepared for possible negative consequences. Your letter may be read by others, it may be ridiculed, it may be dismissed.

Here are two letters written by clients of mine who ended the toxic relationships in their lives. The first letter is from a daughter to her father.

Dear Dad,

I am writing you this letter to let you know that you are not welcome in my life anymore. When I was a child you abandoned me. Now that I am an adult, I am abandoning you!

Never under any circumstances call me, write me, or talk to me. You have never been a part of my life and never will be in the future.

I can go on and on and chronicle all the hurts—the pain and misery you have created in my life—but I spare us both. You know what you did. Only God can forgive you, because I can't.

To refresh your memory, here are eight reasons why I find you despicable.

1. You never call me on my birthday or Christmas.

2. You didn't tell me you remarried and let me find out on my own.

3. You are a stingy, cheap miser, who looked in the refrigerator at what I ate when I came to visit and made me pay for the food I ate.

4. You woke me up at 2 a.m., hitting me for no reason at all.

5. You stole money I worked hard for from my wallet to pay for your drug habit.

6. You yell at me and hit me instead of talking to me.

7. You didn't put me on your insurance policy and are stubborn and cheap.

8. You treat me as less than human by minimizing everything I say.

I hate your guts. To me, you have died. So never contact me again.

You are a complete loser—a cheap, selfish, uncaring bastard and a dreg of society.

So live your life in the hell that it is and stop contaminating mine with your ugly voice and ugly words. If you call, you will be hung up on, and any letter will be ripped up.

Goodbye forever.

This letter clearly shows how abusive and toxic her father was to her all her life. Obviously, no door was left open, as she wanted complete closure.

The next letter is from a boyfriend to a now ex-girlfriend:

Dear Donna,

I am writing you to let you know that I no longer want you in my life. Throughout the years you have consistently hurt me, and I refuse to allow you to be in my life to hurt me anymore, as I find you to be completely toxic to me. This last disappointment I experienced with you clearly illustrates how irresponsible and unreliable a person you have been.

I could go on and on, but I have lost respect for you and I no longer want you in my life.

I want your actions, your insensitive words, and your constant putting me down to be something I never have to experience again, as I release you completely from my life.

I think too much of myself to put up with you any longer.

Do not call me, do not write to me or attempt to contact me in any way. Your letters will be returned unopened, your calls will not be taken. In fact, when I hear your voice, I will hang up on you, and I will never allow you in my physical presence. So leave me alone. Get on with your life as I will get on with mine without you.

Gary

Gary's letter is honest and to the point, and it clearly lets Donna know that under no circumstances is she welcome in his life.

Both of these letters are excellent examples to follow if you want someone out of your life for good.

ENDING IT OVER THE TELEPHONE

•

For some, it is preferable to end a toxic relationship over the telephone, because it puts a mechanical and physical distance between people. Since you are not looking at the other person directly, you may be able to express yourself better.

Remember to keep your voice low, because the telephone is a microphone, which picks up and carries your voice. Speak slowly and distinctly. Be prepared for the toxic person to yell and scream at you. Be prepared to be hung up on or, on the other hand, to be called back repeatedly because the person cannot believe what you said.

Have a notepad before you, listing the important things you plan to say, so that you won't forget anything you want the toxic party to hear.

ENDING IT IN PERSON

•

Many people feel that no matter how painful it may be, confronting in person is the right way to end a toxic relationship.

When you end the relationship in person you have to be prepared for tears, agony, screaming, and crying.

You may want to have your confrontation at the person's home or at a quiet restaurant that will allow you some privacy.

However difficult, it is important to keep your voice calm and modulated and try to maintain your composure.

USING A THIRD PARTY

•

It may seem a bit cowardly, but in this age of legal intervention it may be in your best interest to hire an attorney, especially in the case of a toxic business situation.

If it is a personal relationship, you may want to terminate it via someone the two of you have in common. However, in this scenario the third party needs to know that the messenger is often beheaded.

On the other hand, an intermediary can help to defuse the hatred and the venom by providing an objective, non-emotional viewpoint.

HANDLING THE RESIDUAL EFFECTS

OF ANGER

•

Never Use Violence

Even after you have used all the appropriate methods for helping you deal with the pain of a toxic person in your life, you may still be angry and want to seek revenge.

Whatever you do, *never* seek physical revenge. *Never* use violence to settle a score.

Though you may be so livid that you want to take matters into your own hands, use the Vicarious-Fantasy Technique instead. Do *not* make it a reality.

Never let your anger blind you so that you do something you will have to pay for.

Letting It Out Physically

As you confront your feelings toward the toxic person, you may be so angry that the Vicarious-Fantasy Technique doesn't work. To release your anger, use the pillow-screaming technique: put your head in a pillow and scream at the top of your lungs. Or: punch a pillow while fantasizing that it is the person you are livid at. You could even get a punching bag. You may even want to do aerobics or work out with weights. Whatever the means, you need to confront the anger.

Talking It Out

Talking it out can also be a great way to release anger. It is often a good idea to do this with a professional. If you talk indiscriminately, it may restimulate your hostility and negative feelings. Be selective about whom you talk to. People who are not professionals or who lack sufficient wisdom may give you advice that may not be right for you.

So share your most intimate thoughts only with friends and family members who truly understand or with a professional who can serve as a positive support system and reinforce your beliefs and your actions.

Keeping a Written or Verbal Record

Should you want to express feelings but have no one to talk to, consider recording your thoughts. Some people feel comfortable writing in a journal, while others are most at ease talking out their emotions and feelings into a tape recorder.

Either technique will help you express yourself and release your pain and anger. You can go back later on and relive your feelings or see if they have changed over time.

It is crucial to point out that diaries, audiotapes, and videotapes should be kept under lock and key. They are yours and yours alone. No other eyes or ears should have access to them unless you wish to share your intimate feelings. If you do want your husband, wife, or loved one to feel what you have been going through or to be aware of the situation in which you are involved, it is fine to show them what you have written or to let them hear what you have said.

Photo-Ripping Ceremony

Sometimes a person has made you so angry that you never want to see even a likeness again—especially in photographs. It may prove gratifying to rip up all your photographs of the individual and throw them in the garbage or even burn them. Whatever it takes for you to release the person from your life is what you must do.

One of my clients purged herself of an old boyfriend by tearing photos of him in half and burning them, then watching his face crumble. He had caused her so much pain that she took pleasure in visualizing his being reduced to ashes, through the offices of the Vicarious-Fantasy Technique.

Cleansing by Candlelight

Soaking in a bubble bath surrounded by candles may be spiritually uplifting as well as symbolically cleansing when a relationship has ended. As your bathwater drains out, so does the pollution of your toxic memories.

Returning Gifts

Just as you don't want to see the person or a likeness, you may not want any objects around that might serve as reminders, such as gifts or articles of clothing. You may send the things back, give them away, or even throw them into the garbage.

THE SOLACE OF KNOWING THAT WHAT GOES AROUND COMES AROUND

•

You may want to find solace in the principle that is called different things in different circles. "Reap what you sow"; "Do unto others as you would have them do unto you"; "What goes around comes around"—however it is expressed and whatever its civilization of origin, the truth is that eventually justice will be served. Not immediately, perhaps, but it will be served over time. In every belief system, it is universally agreed that good begets good, while evil begets evil.

If you treat people well, it will return to you tenfold; and if you treat people poorly, it will likewise come back to you tenfold. In essence, nobody gets away with murder in the big picture.

One of my clients experienced the results of her bad "karma" rather quickly in her attempts to seduce a seemingly wealthy man whom she wasn't at all attracted to. This young woman would come into my office all decked out in beautiful clothes and brag to me about an older gentleman who was totally in love with her and showered her with gifts. Volunteering that she didn't even have to sleep with him—she thought he was gross—she continued to mock him for being a fool and catering to her every whim.

Then she learned that he was definitely not a fool. In fact, he was just as manipulative as she was. This seemingly smitten man offered her a trip to New York; he asked to use her credit card, promising immediate reimbursement with a check. She obliged. Upon their return, he did indeed give her a check—from a closed bank account. She now had to pay for thousands of dollars in expensive meals, travel, theater tickets, and gifts she had in essence bought herself.

This young lady learned that nothing is free and that you can't take advantage of someone and expect things to work out in your favor.

SUCCESS IS THE BEST REVENGE

•

There's a wonderful French film, *Coup de Tête* (*Hothead*), that serves as a great example of living well and sticking it in your enemy's face. A second-rate soccer player on a small-town team is ignored as a loser while the community celebrates the team's success. Through a misunderstanding, he gets convicted of a crime he did not commit and ends up in prison.

Meanwhile the team, on its way to a match in a neighboring city, is in a bus accident. Major players are injured, and an alternate is needed to play a key position in the game. Team officials manage to get our man released from prison, just to play the game. He scores point after point and becomes an instant hero. Although he is eager to return to prison, where the jailers and inmates respect him because he is a soccer player, the officials insist on obtaining his permanent release. They put him up in the best hotel. Everyone wants to be his friend. He is given gifts, and women come on to him. People wine and dine him, catering to his every whim, which disgusts him.

Finally, he throws a dinner party, purportedly to thank all the important people who are treating him so nicely. His real intention is to show them what hypocrites they are, and he individually embarrasses them in front of the others. Using various methods of confrontation, he allows each of them to self-destruct. By letting the truth be known, he ends up as the most decent man in town and walks away with his self-respect.

A gorgeous client of mine experienced the sweet revenge of success when she was crowned "Most Beautiful" at her twenty-year school reunion. Throughout her high school years, she had been treated like a pariah and tormented by her peers because she was fat, wore thick glasses, and had acne. Her proudest moment at the reunion occurred when the best-looking, coolest guy, who gave her the most hell when they were students, asked her to dance and she had the pleasure of telling him to "get lost."

Remember, success is the best revenge on those who've been toxic to you.

FORGIVING MEANS GIVING UP
AND GETTING ON WITH YOUR LIFE

•

Whether you have been toxic to another person, or he or she has been toxic to you, you need to forgive. To forgive does not mean to forget. Forgiving means giving up: letting things go. That is not to say you should completely and forever block out all the toxic things done to you; but you should give up the self-abuse or the pain you have suffered. You need to let go of the negative feelings and the hate, because *hate consumes the hater.*

When you hate, you continue to perpetuate negativity and ill feeling, not only in the lives of others but in your own life as well. Hate makes nasty lines on your face, so that you have an angry expression on your face and in your heart.

If you find that you need professional help to cope with the person who has literally ruined your life, I urge you to get that help immediately. There are many wonderful qualified professionals who can help you to improve your life so that you won't have to hang on to the hate, guilt, or self-pity. Let it go. *Forgive,* as this is the first step toward living a toxic-free life.

CHAPTER 10

The Importance of the Outward Self: The Toxic Image Inventory

- **Your Own Mood and the Toxic Effect It May Have on Others**

- **Toxic First Impressions**

- **Toxic Image Inventory**

- **Applying the Toxic Image Inventory**

Your Own Mood and the Toxic Effect It May Have on Others

•

Just as other people's moods can have an effect on you, you can affect the moods of others.

It is easy to point the finger at others in explaining your

bad mood, but you must never hesitate to look at yourself as well. Remember, when you point at someone else, three fingers point back at you.

If you walk around with a chip on your shoulder, people will react to your hostility or your bad moods. If you have a persistent frown on your face, exhibiting your inner turmoil to the world, you can be sure that most people will be put off by you and will want to keep their distance.

There's truth to the old saying "Laugh and the whole world laughs with you; cry and you cry alone." It is not that you will never be in a bad mood or never be depressed. But realize that when you feel that way and happen to be around other people, you should be prepared for their negative or hostile reactions.

Luck was definitely not on Marlene's side. She was laid off from a job of seven years. She was going through a divorce. Then she found out her youngest son had a learning disability.

Marlene was depressed, and rightfully so. However, she could not shake her constant negative mood. Months and finally years passed, and Marlene's unhappiness continued to show on her face. In three years, not much had changed in her life. She still had no love life and could not find a job. She'd had to enroll her child in a special class. She was living with her parents to save on rent.

One day her brother, who was home from college for the holidays, decided to have a heart-to-heart talk with her. He said, "I've been watching you mope around here like a zombie every time I come home, and frankly, I'm sick of your bad moods. Look, Marlene, nobody owes you anything. Yes, Martin's got a learning problem, but at least he's in a school where he's getting help. Mom and Dad are nice enough to help you out so you're not homeless. The reason you haven't gotten a job yet is that, first of all, you really haven't tried, and second, you are so negative that who would want to hire you anyway? Sure, you can blame everything on John's leaving you. Get over it! Put on some makeup. Wear something sexy. Go out with your girlfriends. Go meet some guys, and for heaven's sake, *smile.* No one will ever go near you if you're frowning all the time, looking like you're pissed off at the world."

Marlene was stunned. Nobody had ever spoken to her like

that. Instead everyone had pitied and coddled her. Her younger brother was the first person who was totally honest with her. He told it like it was—that her constant negative mood was keeping good things from happening to her. She knew he was right. After hearing her brother's words resounding in her brain all week, she decided to take his advice and go out to a club with a girlfriend. She kept forcing herself to smile, even though she didn't feel like it. Although she didn't meet a guy, she did meet a woman, sitting at the next table, who happened to be looking for someone to manage the front office of her company. She liked Marlene's sense of humor when they chatted together that evening, so she told her to come in for an interview. The woman hired Marlene.

Each day, Marlene forced herself to be in a better mood. While driving to work, she reminded herself to be enthusiastic, upbeat, and not dwell on negative things. Her newfound attitude began to be reflected in how she answered the phone when customers called. She developed a good rapport with one particular customer—Robert. He told her how much he liked her bubbly personality over the phone. His compliment encouraged her to continue being bubbly. Whenever Robert called, they joked over the phone, and one day he asked her to have lunch with him. When they finally met in person, they continued to hit it off. In fact, they are continuing to hit it off, because they are engaged to be married—all because Marlene consciously changed her attitude and forced herself to cheer up.

I have seen the same thing in my own life. If things are hectic or not going the way I want them to, I try desperately never to take it out on other people. I remain friendly and positive, and suddenly good things start happening to me, because people in turn begin to treat me more positively.

Though you may not realize it, your bad mood can definitely affect others, putting them in bad moods that in turn can reinforce your own. The result is known as "circular contagion."

My dear friend Rabbi Joseph Telushkin, author of a new book called *Words That Hurt and Words That Heal,* asks people at his lectures, "How many of you think that you are a good person?" The entire audience usually raise their hands. He goes on to say that most people think they are good. But you ask your enemies if you are a good person, and they would definitely counter your impression of yourself.

What Rabbi Telushkin is illustrating is that just as others can be toxic to you, you may be toxic to others. Perhaps you possess characteristics that rub certain people the wrong way. There is nothing wrong with this, because nobody is perfect. You, like everyone, may be driving other people crazy unknowingly or making them miserable, because of certain personality traits you possess, or because you are who you are.

The old maxims "You can't please everybody all the time" and "Not everybody is going to like you" are quite true. Just knowing these truths, and remembering them from time to time, can make living your life a whole lot easier.

TOXIC FIRST IMPRESSIONS

•

First impressions affect how others relate to you. People will often dislike you for reasons that are not justifiable. It may be because of who you are, or because they are jealous of you. Perhaps you remind them of a person whom they can't stand. You cannot do anything about this. However, there are things that are in your control, things you can change if you wish to encourage a more positive perception of yourself.

These elements relate to the way you dress and keep yourself, how you talk to other people, your posture and body language, the way you touch a person or shake hands, your facial expressions, the way you sound, the kind of words you use, and even what kind of listener you are.

Each of these factors can make a huge difference in how people perceive you, relate to you, and, finally, treat you.

Remember the person in grade school who was disliked the most? Often his or her lack of popularity had little to do with personality traits. It usually had a lot to do with the individual's appearance. Maybe that person dressed a little oddly or had hand-me-down clothes from older brothers or sisters that were out of style and too big. Perhaps the person smelled bad and came to school with dirty clothes, a dirty face, matted hair.

There was nothing the child could do about these things, which were a parental responsibility. Unfortunately, some parents are more responsible than others.

My client Ivy Lynn was the poorest child in her school. She lived in a trailer and had three dresses and one pair of shoes to her name. Her father was absent and her mother, an alcoholic, was on welfare. Ivy told me that because of how her mother sent her to school, the kids hated her and teased her cruelly throughout grade school.

By high school, Ivy got a job and earned enough money to dress nicely and to groom herself, but the kids never forgot her early reputation. She was never accepted, no matter how she looked or how sweet a person she was. She left town as soon as she graduated so she could start a new life, free from the toxic image of her past.

Even as children we make superficial judgments about others. We decide whether or not we will be their friends based solely on how they look and what they wear.

As we become adults, we continue to make judgments about others based on appearance, whether we admit it or not. Physical traits and external factors can make us perceive someone as toxic.

Research shows that a person who looks good and speaks well is perceived as being more physically attractive, more intelligent, more successful, more energetic, more likable, more sexually exciting, and more credible.

Attorneys are well aware of the effect of image in the courtroom. This is why they coach clients or witnesses on what to wear and how to speak.

My own research has demonstrated that even if people are not physically attractive, if they have good speaking skills they are perceived as more attractive, as well as more intelligent, and others want to be around them.

Even nice people may present themselves in such a way as to turn people off. They may not even know why.

Taking the Toxic Image Inventory will enable you to identify potentially toxic traits.

TOXIC IMAGE INVENTORY

•

The Toxic Image Inventory is designed to help you isolate exactly what it is about a person's image that turns you off. It can also be used for a self-check. For example, perhaps you never think about what message your rounded, hunched-over shoulders convey to others. Perhaps you never pay any attention to your fingernails—whether dirty or bitten off. Whether you like it or not, such traits may influence how people will perceive you. Your first instinct may be to say, "Who cares? I don't give a damn how I come across." Well, you had better care how you come across if you want to compete and win in today's extremely difficult job market and in this unstable business climate.

Using the Toxic Image Inventory, you can analyze every aspect of a personal image. You can determine if you or another person is presenting a toxic image in any of ten areas: dress, hair, nails, skin, hygiene, mouth, body language, facial expressions, speaking and vocal skills, and communication skills.

To see if you or anyone you know possesses any of these toxic elements, complete this inventory by answering *yes* or *no* to the following questions.

Toxic Dressing

1. **Do they wear the wrong type of clothes socially?**

2. **Do they wear the wrong clothes to work?**

3. **Are their clothes usually dirty?**

4. **Are their clothes usually unpressed or wrinkled?**

5. **Do their clothes smell from perspiration or smoke?**

6. Do they usually wear polyester?

7. Are their clothes unstylish or out of date?

8. Do they wear clothes that are too tight?

9. Do they wear clothes that are too big?

10. Do they wear clothes that are uncomfortable?

11. Do they wear too much makeup?

12. Does their makeup look outdated?

Toxic Hair

1. Do they wear an appropriate hairstyle for work?

2. Do they wear an appropriate hairstyle socially?

3. Is their hair greasy?

4. Is their hair often dirty?

5. Is their hair very dry, broken off, or matted?

6. Is their hair uncontrollable or unmanageable?

7. Is their hair ungroomed, hardly ever brushed or combed?

8. Is the color of their hair anything other than blond, brown, black, gray, red, or auburn?

9. Is their hair stringy?

10. Do they wear a wig or toupee that doesn't fit well?

11. Do they wear a toupee or wig that doesn't match the color or texture of their natural hair?

12. Is their wig or toupee obvious to others?

13. Is his mustache and/or beard dirty or flaky?

14. Does he need a shave?

15. Does she have a dark mustache?

16. Does she have stray facial or chin hairs?

17. Do they have long hairs growing out of their nose?

18. Do they have hairs growing on top of their nose?

19. Do they have hairs growing on top of or in their ears?

20. Are their eyebrows unkempt?

Toxic Nails

1. Are their nails dirty?

2. Are their nails too long?

3. Are their nails bitten?

4. Is their nail polish chipped and untidy?

5. Are their nails discolored?

6. Are their nails misshapen?

Toxic Skin

1. Do they have unsightly pimples?

2. Do they have large pockmarks?

3. Is their skin peeling, flaky, scaly, or too dry?

4. Is their skin greasy, oily, or shiny?

5. Is their skin red and raw?

6. Is their skin blotchy?

7. Is their skin filled with blackheads?

8. Is their skin filled with whiteheads?

9. Do they have unsightly brown moles?

10. Do they have a melanoma?

11. Do they have warts?

12. Do they have rashes?

13. Is their skin discolored?

14. Is their skin too pale?

15. Is their skin too wrinkled, baggy, and loose?

16. Is their skin tone yellow?

17. Is their skin tone green?

18. Is their skin tone ashen?

Toxic Hygiene

1. Do they take a bath or a shower less frequently than every day?

2. Does their body smell bad?

3. Do their underarms smell bad?

4. Do their private parts smell offensive?

5. Does their breath smell offensive?

6. Do they wear too much cologne or perfume?

7. Do they have visible wax around their ears?

8. Do they have a dirty face?

9. Do they have a dirty neck with black rings of dirt in the folds?

10. Do they perspire a lot?

Toxic Mouth

1. Do their lips have sores?

2. Are their lips dry and peeling?

3. Do they often accumulate white spittle in the corners of their mouth?

4. Do they drool when they are listening, speaking, or eating?

5. Are their teeth dirty?

6. Are their teeth discolored or stained?

7. Are their teeth broken or badly chipped?

8. Are their teeth crooked, misshapen, or jumbled?

9. Do they spit when they speak?

10. Do their gums look puffy, swollen, and red?

11. Do their front teeth protrude badly?

12. Does their lower jaw jut forward?

13. Do they have large jowls?

Toxic Body Language

1. Do they stand too close for comfort?

2. Do they stand too far away?

3. Do they stand off to the side when they talk to people?

4. Are their hands all over the person they are speaking with, constantly touching that person?

5. Do they constantly touch themselves?

6. Do they slouch?

7. Do they have a stiff, rigid, robot-like posture?

8. Do they have a sloppy, too loose posture and stance?

9. Do they hang their head down when they talk or listen?

10. Do they flail their arms around when they talk?

11. Do they recoil every time someone touches them?

12. Do they have a clammy, sweaty handshake?

13. Do they have a can-crushing handshake?

14. Do they have a "dead fish" handshake?

15. Do they continue to shake hands too long (over three seconds)?

16. Do they rock back and forth when standing and talking?

17. Do they rock back and forth in their chair when talking?

Toxic Facial Expressions

1. Do they look off to the side when they talk to someone?

2. Do their eyes dart around the room when they talk to someone?

3. Do they squint their eyes, furrow their forehead, or knit their eyebrows when they speak or listen?

4. Do they not look at the person they are talking to?

5. Do they look people up and down when they first meet them?

6. Do they jut their jaw forward, creating an angry look?

7. Is their usual facial expression a sad-looking frown?

8. Are their lips tense?

9. Do they have a tense, strained, pinched smile?

10. Do they have a phony mask-like smile?

11. Does their upper lip curl when they smile, indicating that they're not really happy?

12. Are their eyes dead and lifeless when they listen to someone?

13. Do they usually have a dull or bored expression on their face?

14. Do they raise their eyebrows and open their eyes wide when they speak, giving the impression of doubt or fear?

15. Do they stare?

16. Do they blink too much?

17. Do they squint too much?

18. Is their normal facial expression tense?

19. Does their mouth hang open when they are listening?

20. Is their normal facial expression angry?

21. Is their normal facial expression sad?

22. Do they clench their jaws when they talk, or do they talk through their teeth without opening their jaws?

Toxic Speaking and Vocal Skills

1. Do they have an offensive, loud, booming voice?

2. Do they have a soft, weak voice that is difficult to hear?

3. Does their voice fade at the end of sentences so that it is difficult to hear them?

4. Are they often asked to repeat what they said?

5. Do they often say "I don't know" when they are asked questions?

6. Are they silent during conversations, as if they don't know what to say?

7. Do they sound bored and speak in a monotone?

8. Do they put people to sleep or bore them when they tell a story?

9. Is the pitch of their voice too high?

10. Does their voice sound squeaky?

11. Does their voice sound creaky and crackling, especially at the end of a sentence?

12. Do they mumble?

13. Do they have a loud and disturbing laugh?

14. Do they talk too fast?

15. Is their voice often hoarse?

16. Do they use words in the wrong context?

17. Do they use improper grammar?

18. Do their tones sound choppy or staccato?

19. Do they sound breathy?

20. Do they take in a lot of little breaths when they speak so their speech pattern sounds labored?

21. Do they let all the air out before they speak, so that their voice is strained?

22. Do they clear their throat during conversations?

23. Do they smack their lips before they start talking?

24. Does their voice sound gruff and gravelly?

25. Do they have a nasal whine?

26. Do they often mispronounce words?

27. Are there certain sounds they mispronounce?

28. Do they talk so fast that they are asked to repeat what they said?

29. Do they talk so slowly that they often forget what they were talking about?

30. Do they often repeat themselves?

31. Do they tell the same story over and over again?

32. Do they often hesitate on words or sound tentative?

33. Do they stutter or stammer?

34. Do they sound nasal and whiny?

35. Do they lisp?

36. Do they use a lot of slang words?

37. Do they often say "like," "um," "uh," and "you know"?

38. Do they have an accent or a dialect that makes it difficult for them to be understood?

Toxic Communication Skills

1. Do they enjoy gossiping about others?

2. Do they "diss" people, cutting them down or saying negative things about them?

3. Do they order people around?

4. Do they yell at others?

5. Are they cordial to people, only to talk about them behind their back?

6. Do they often fight or argue?

7. Do they often play "devil's advocate," taking the other side just to be argumentative?

8. Are they stingy with compliments?

9. Do they fawn and gush over people and really not mean it?

10. Do they often say nice things about people just so they can get what they want?

11. When angry, do they hold it in until they've had enough, then lash out verbally?

12. Do they tell too many jokes or try to be clever, making light of everything?

13. Do they enjoy cutting people down or making fun of them?

14. Do they often brag about their possessions and accomplishments?

15. Do they often stretch the truth?

16. Do they make up stories and bullshit?

17. Do they have trouble keeping a secret?

18. Do they tell too much?

19. Do they have difficulty getting to the point of what they're saying?

20. Do they have to be the center of attention?

21. Do they elicit information from others but divulge nothing about themselves?

22. Do they usually take charge of the conversation?

23. Do they change the topic of conversation midstream?

24. Do they often ignore a question and continue talking about what they want to talk about?

25. Do they interrupt a lot?

26. Do they often answer questions that are not addressed to them?

27. Do they think that what they say is usually more important than what anyone else says?

28. Do they have difficulty listening to others' points of view?

29. When something is sad or serious, do they often laugh inappropriately?

30. Do they seem tense and nervous when meeting others?

31. Do they sound dumb or stupid?

32. Do they name-drop?

33. Is what they mostly talk about negative?

34. Do they complain a lot?

35. Do they use a lot of curse words or profanity?

36. Do they use baby talk, trying to be cute?

37. Do they use big words to try to impress people?

38. Do they often have trouble focusing on what they want to say?

39. Do they talk too much?

40. Do they ask too many questions?

41. Do they seem nosy, asking invasive questions?

42. Do they seem to be inattentively thinking about what they are going to say while another person is talking?

43. Do they seem to tune out when others are talking?

44. Do they use the word "I" a lot, talking about themselves excessively?

45. Do they seem to talk only to people who can benefit them?

46. Are they always selling people on who they are and what they do?

47. Do they know a great deal about many things and let others know it, even at others' expense?

48. Do they lecture people so that often they seem to be engaged in a monologue instead of a dialogue?

49. Do they always say self-deprecating things?

50. Do they make too many sarcastic comments about situations and people?

51. Is their tone usually angry?

52. Is talking to them like pulling teeth?

53. Do they often go on and on when they tell a story?

54. Do they have trouble saying nice things to others?

55. Do they seem uncomfortable complimenting someone?

56. Do they giggle nervously?

57. Are they at a loss for words?

58. Do they enjoy the sound of their own voice?

59. Are there times when they don't seem to make sense?

60. Do they have trouble backing down from an argument even though they know they are wrong?

61. Do they have difficulty apologizing when they have done something wrong?

62. Do they often put their foot in their mouth?

63. Do they raise their voice or begin to argue at the slightest provocation?

64. Are they blunt with people and undiplomatic when they have to say something negative?

65. Do they receive a compliment uncomfortably?

66. Do they have difficulty hearing nice things about themselves?

67. Do they usually talk in stream of consciousness, in essence saying everything they are thinking?

68. Do they shout and yell when angry?

69. Is most of their conversation teasing or flirtatious?

70. Do they find it difficult to ask for assistance when they need it?

71. Do they often tease about things they know others are particularly sensitive about?

72. Do they find it difficult to communicate with someone who has apologized to them, as they still hold a grudge?

73. Do they often force their opinions on others?

74. Do they clam up when something bothers them?

75. Do they expect close friends to know what they are thinking and how they feel?

76. Do they often cry when they have to confront a difficult situation?

77. When answering questions, do they usually offer minimal responses, such as "Yep," "No," or "Fine," instead of elaborating?

78. Do they tend to monopolize a conversation, giving others little chance to speak?

APPLYING THE TOXIC IMAGE INVENTORY

•

Knowledge is power. Even if you substituted the word "you" for "them" and saw things in yourself that others may find toxic, you definitely have the power to change many of these things, so don't get depressed. Being more conscious of your hygiene or dress, or changing your vocal or communication skills, can improve how you come across to others. Some of these areas are beyond your control, but being aware of potential problems will assist you in presenting a non-toxic image.

In essence, if you answered *yes* to any of the questions, you must change certain things about yourself.

Often the awareness that you are doing negative things can be the catalyst to turning them around. Just by paying attention to these toxic behaviors, you can often correct them. If you still have difficulty controlling these behaviors, you may want to seek psychological counseling with a reputable therapist. The American Psychological Association can assist you by recommending a licensed therapist in your area.

If you applied the Toxic Image Inventory to a specific toxic person and now know what it is that turns you off about him or her, you may just be satisfied with simply knowing. Indeed, your awareness of the problem could be enough to dissipate your negative feelings so that you don't keep all those ill feelings inside you.

On the other hand, now that you clearly see the problem, you may very well want to tell the toxic person what it is that annoys you. In Chapter 11, you will learn specific techniques for doing so.

REVITALIZING THE TOXIC RELATIONSHIP

- **Starting Over**

- **Asking for Help from the Person You've Been Toxic To**

- **Watching Your Words**

- **A Pat on the Back Is Only a Few Vertebrae from a Kick in the Pants**

- **Setting Up New Rules for a Formerly Toxic Relationship**

Before you decide whether or not to revitalize a toxic relationship, you have to ask yourself a number of things:

1. **Are you willing to give it another try?**

2. **Can you ever forgive them, or do you think they can forgive you?**

3. **Is your life empty or less effective without them?**

4. **Are you willing to make the first move?**

5. **Are you willing to let bygones be bygones and start all over again?**

If you answered *yes* to any of these questions, you have a good chance of renewing your relationship.

This chapter will show you how to do it effectively, whatever your side in a toxic relationship. You may feel awkward, but you will learn how to feel more comfortable when reaching out.

PEOPLE CAN CHANGE

•

We have all heard the expression "Never say never." Finding somebody toxic today doesn't mean you will find the person toxic tomorrow. Look at what is happening around the world. Enemies have become friends as peace attempts to flourish. Arabs and Jews are sitting down together, breaking bread and negotiating with one another in hopes of reconciliation. U.S. and Russian leaders meet regularly and the walls between West and East Germany have come tumbling down.

Who would have supposed that these things would happen in our lifetime? If political walls can come tumbling down, why not the walls that toxic people build up?

It is true that leopards never change their spots. But human beings are not leopards.

Human beings *can* and *do* change, especially if they want to and, most important, if they achieve a greater degree of awareness and knowledge. True, there are people who do not want to change, but most people do want to change, and for the better. They simply don't know how.

There's another expression: "Ignorance is bliss." That one *isn't* true. *Knowledge* is bliss. In fact, knowledge is power. Only by acquiring knowledge can you achieve the power to change. Sometimes the most toxic of people can be educated so they will change their entire outlook on life, thereby becoming less toxic to others as well as to themselves.

Only when you have the knowledge do you have the power to change. The basic reason people hate other, different people is that they are ignorant. This is most evident in biases against particular nationalities.

As people become more educated and more aware, they realize that it is ridiculous and futile to hate other people for something their ancestors did hundreds of years ago. Perhaps one of the most poignant examples of reawakened awareness is how Lutherans, though they honor most of the insights of the sixteenth-century church reformer Martin Luther, recently renounced his slurs on Jews and Judaism.

It took four centuries to do this, but the act nevertheless provides new hope for bridging gaps between religions and systems of belief.

The knowledge of our similarities as human beings can perhaps abolish the ugly prejudices we harbor against people who seem different from us.

KNOWLEDGE IS POWER

•

Knowing how to handle toxic people can defuse your animosity and, most important, change not only your behavior toward them but theirs toward you. The Ten Techniques in Chapter 6 can definitely help you repair a previously toxic relationship.

One of my clients, Marissa, had never gotten along with her father, but having learned the techniques, she visited him at Thanksgiving and, for the first time in her life, was able to carry on a decent conversation with him. By using the Direct-Confront, Tension-Blowout, Calm Questioning, and Give-Them-Love-and-Kindness Techniques, she learned things about her father that she'd never known before and found out that he was "a pretty cool guy," as she put it. All she had remembered from growing up was that he was a macho disciplinarian. Now he had mellowed into an understanding, liberal, and open man. As Marissa learned, communicating through the techniques can shed a new light on a previously toxic person.

Knowledge is definitely power when you have new options and tools that can turn situations around. When we understand the underlying reasons for people's actions, we can gain compassion and in turn forgive them.

Another client of mine who had a tumultuous relationship with her father was Kelly. She felt his volatile behavior toward her had damaged her tremendously. About to get married, she confronted him because she wanted to resolve all her ill feelings toward him before starting a new life with her husband.

Discussions with her father revealed that he had suffered many atrocities while a prisoner during the Vietnam War, which caused him great psychological damage. Unable to trust anyone, he became paranoid. Unfortunately, this was manifested in violent outbursts toward his daughter. Hearing about the pain he had suffered, she gained a better understanding of his actions and gave their relationship another chance. Today they are extremely close, and he recently gave her away in a very emotional wedding ceremony.

You will never know why a person is toxic to you unless you

ask questions, confront, and communicate. You may be surprised by what you discover. You may see a side that you never before considered. It may help to free you from years of internal pain, as you discover that people can and do change.

I have seen countless examples of estranged individuals reuniting because they were willing to communicate and try to understand one another. Being willing to see things from a point of view other than their own made them a lot more compassionate and tolerant.

When we are able to open our minds and understand a person who seemed toxic, we end up opening our hearts as well.

Growing up, Charles and Brad were close. Charles was the big brother, the macho athlete, while Brad was slight and delicate. As they grew older, Charles suspected that Brad might be gay, but he never said anything to him. Although Brad emulated his older brother by going into the armed services, marrying, and having children, he couldn't suppress the reality of his homosexuality. When finally he came out of the closet, the first person he told was Charles, who punched Brad in the mouth, knocking out two front teeth.

The brothers became estranged, Charles hating Brad with a passion and never wanting to speak to him again. One day Charles saw a PBS documentary about a caring, loving gay couple who were both suffering from AIDS. Charles sobbed uncontrollably as he watched the show, for he realized how much he truly loved his brother. He saw how when someone's life was in jeopardy all prejudices flew out the window. He immediately called Brad, and they met for a very emotional reunion. Despite their differences, they renewed their once close relationship. Although Charles couldn't embrace Brad's lifestyle, he loved and accepted Brad totally.

MAKING CONTACT

•

If you want to revitalize or renew a once toxic relationship, you can attempt it in a number of ways. You can make contact by writing a letter, phoning, or meeting face-to-face. Whatever channel you use, you should *never accuse or abuse* the person. Your intention must not be to pronounce them wrong. Rather, express your feelings in an attempt to gain a new understanding of that person's behavior.

Letter Writing

Perhaps the best medium for initial contact is a letter. Once again, keep in mind that your intention is to open up channels of communication, not close them—so *do not attack.* Allow the recipient to feel open enough and safe enough to make the next move and respond to your letter. Here is a letter one client of mine wrote to his estranged father.

Dear Dad,

I am writing you this long-overdue letter because I need to resolve some issues that have bothered me for as long as I can remember. I have been carrying around some heavy emotional baggage, and it is seriously affecting my personal and my professional life.

My intention in this letter is not to cause guilt or to determine right or wrong, but to understand the reasons behind your actions, so I can get on with my life.

You may ask yourself why, at the age of forty-six, I am thinking about these things. It is because I have come to realize that many of the problems I have, including the fear of public speaking, stuttering in stressful situations, and being overly sensitive to other people's impressions of me, especially those in positions of authority, are directly related to my relationship with you.

Every child needs and wants the support and admiration of his father. He looks up to his father and is validated by his father's love and belief in him. When I was very young, I thought you were the greatest. But I always felt that my efforts were never good enough. I never felt that I got the validation I needed or even loving acceptance. I felt you were never there for me emotionally. You never encouraged me or even said a kind word when I excelled in sports or at school. You never showed up at any of my school events, which I interpreted as your not caring. You always made me feel nervous and uptight, and whenever you asked questions, you used such a demanding tone that my stomach churned. You once beat me with a belt just because I couldn't get the words out fast enough for you. Whenever I made any attempt to talk to you, you would belittle and negate every thought, calling me names and cursing at me.

Although I've tried my best to hide them, these memories still haunt me, and I can never forget the hurt and pain I suffered at your hands. I now know that your abuse of alcohol at that time was a major contributing factor in your actions, but I need to understand what in your life drove you to such extremes of behavior. I sometimes see a bit of that person in myself, and it terrifies me!

I know you have often wondered why I have never gone out of my way to call you. It is because we never resolved *anything*. We just tried to forget it. I can't forget it any longer.

So I had to take the risk that this letter could just make things worse. I *truly* hope it doesn't. I *need* to understand you, just as I need to understand myself. I hope that sometime soon we can talk about this and, hopefully, bury some demons.

I do love you and want to be close with you.

> Your loving son,
> Terrance

As you saw in the letter, Terrance didn't attack or verbally abuse. He discussed his pain and his hurt and asked for the reasons his father did what he did. He left the door open for further contact.

At first his father was so stunned by the letter that he could not acknowledge it.

Finally, after months had passed, he called Terrance and said in a sheepish voice, "I got your letter."

His son stayed calm, and they agreed to meet at the father's home. After yelling and tears on both sides, Terrance gained an awareness of why his father had acted the way he did. They ended up fishing buddies and the best of friends.

Until they communicated, neither of them would have thought this possible.

Telephoning

When you undertake a phone confrontation, you may be met with silence or anger on the other end. In any case, it is imperative that you not *react* but *act,* keeping your cool. Do the Tension-Blowout Technique to help keep control of your voice. Your remaining calm will usually calm down the toxic person, who will then listen to what you have to say.

You may want to prepare a list of important points you want to discuss. Keep your notes in front of you so you will be more organized in your thoughts and in your intentions.

Once again, it is important to remember: *Do not accuse—do not abuse.* Instead let the person speak his or her mind as well. Make it clear that you have made the first move in an attempt to work out your previous misunderstandings.

Confronting in Person

Sometimes hearing and seeing the individual can restimulate your toxic feelings. Perhaps the person's body or facial language is off-putting or unapproachable.

Do not pay attention to this, as it may just be protective. It is up to you to make the first move, so take charge. If you want to change the entire mood and make the situation a pleasant one, you can break the ice with a smile, a handshake, and a warm hug, in that order.

Touch is a very powerful thing, as anthropologists have discovered. A gentle touch lets someone know that you want to make contact and want to make peace.

Being Open to Any Reaction

Whatever means you use to make contact, you must be prepared for any response. The person you contact may be defensive, accusing, hostile, or noncommunicative—or open, apologetic, compassionate, and equally willing to renew the relationship.

No matter what the outcome is, the fact that you made the first move and tried to reestablish communication lines means a lot.

You have no control over how others react, but you can control your own actions. If you act openly, honestly, in good faith, and with sincerity, you have done your best and could not have done any more. Whether your attempts to reconcile are reciprocated or not, you should feel very proud of yourself, for it takes a very big person with an open mind and an open heart to make that first move.

LOVE IS HAVING TO SAY YOU'RE SORRY FOR BEING TOXIC

•

Just as it takes a big person to make the first move, it takes a big person—a person with a lot of inner strength—to admit to error and to really feel remorse.

The popular bromide of the 1970s that arose from the movie *Love Story*—"Love is never having to say you're sorry"—is outmoded. Today, love is *definitely* having to say you are sorry.

I can't begin to tell you how many times I have heard a client say, "If only he/she would apologize, then I could go on with my life."

If you have done someone wrong, you owe it not only to that person but to yourself to cleanse your soul—to say you are sorry and try to make amends.

This is the only way you can really change and forgive yourself for the toxic actions of your past. Many twelve-step programs employ the technique of making amends so that people can begin on the road to recovery.

One of my clients, who had a tumultuous relationship with his alcoholic mother, came to me in tears and shared the happiest day of his life, which had occurred the day before. He confronted his mother, telling her how horrible it had been to be her son, living in constant insecurity, not knowing what kind of man she would bring home or if he would have any food or even a home to come back to each day as he left for school.

Her eyes filling with tears, his mother looked directly at him and said, "Look, John—I was a total mess. I had no right to put you through the hell I did. I was wrong, and I have punished myself every day of my life for the way I treated you. I hope you can find it in your heart to forgive me." He did, as these were the exact words he had dreamed of hearing from his mother for the past thirty years. John was able to establish a closer relationship with his mother and feel more peace and less anger in his heart.

MAKE IT UP TO THEM

•

When you have made the first move to inform someone that you know you have been toxic, you have to be prepared for the person's reaction. He or she may forgive you, reject your apology, become angry, or ignore you. The reaction is not important. What *is* important is that you made the first move—that you were big enough to do something to try and rectify the situation and make amends.

One of my clients, Connie, came to realize that she must have done her daughter a lot of damage with the high expectations she placed on her while Sylvie was growing up. When she openly and emotionally apologized for her toxic behavior, her daughter was so happy that she embraced Connie and forgave her. All her life, all she had ever wanted to hear from her mother was the same thing that John wanted to hear—that she was sorry. Just hearing her mother say, "I was wrong and I really am proud of the way you turned out," made all the difference in her life. Today they are the best of friends, they have a wonderful working relationship, and they are able to communicate. From time to time Connie does slip and go back to her old negative ways, but now she is able to catch herself so that she won't alienate Sylvie ever again.

On the other hand, I had another client, Gail, who was very toxic to an old boyfriend. She was jealous and vindictive, and she spread rumors about him all over town. As she grew older, she realized how wrong her behavior was, so she located him and attempted to make amends. It did not work: he cursed her out, telling her that she had ruined his life. Then he hung up on her.

Though this was painful for her, she did feel that she deserved it, and she was able to purge what she had been carrying in her heart for years.

If you take the time to right your wrongs, it says a lot about you as a person—that you are willing to look at yourself objectively and grow from the experience as you mend your toxic ways.

REBUILDING A TOXIC RELATIONSHIP

•

Now that you are back together again, what do you do? How do you act? What do you say?

You must realize that rebuilding a relationship will not happen overnight. It probably took a long time for the relationship to deteriorate.

The process of restoration will require a great deal of patience. The Tension-Blowout and Stop-the-Thought Techniques can be big lifesavers. They will keep you from beating yourself up and will help you deal with any negative reaction from the other party.

Take it slowly. Initially you may just need to spend a few minutes on the phone together to touch base. Periodic brief calls will help you reintroduce yourself into the other person's life. The phone conversations can gradually lengthen. Next you may want to go to lunch together, or you may just have the person over for tea or go out for coffee. Make sure that this initial meeting doesn't last more than an hour.

Finally, you may want to extend your time together, having lunch, then dinner, and eventually spending an entire evening with each other.

It is very important that you take your time when you want to reconstruct a relationship. The longer you rebuild, the more chance you will have of cementing a broken relationship and making it a lasting one.

STARTING OVER

•

You cannot begin where you left off, continuing your old ways, because then you will reactivate the negative situation and alienate the person all over again. Instead you need to set up rules for a new way of communicating. You must have a new relationship, in which you do not act the way you did before. Obviously something didn't work, so it is up to *you* to change your toxic communication patterns.

The first thing you need to do is let go of *guilt* or any bad feelings you have. Since you already said you were sorry and meant it, your soul is purged. Stop beating yourself up! It is essential that you go into the relationship with a clean slate, mentally, physically, and emotionally.

If you do find yourself thinking self-destructively of the negative things you have done, use the Stop-the-Thought Technique. This will prevent you from rehashing the past. Next you need to smile more and be more animated.

If you do want to criticize or say something negative, take a breath in, hold it, and silently scream at yourself: "Stop the thought!" As you do this, flatten your tongue and bit down on the sides, to stop yourself from saying something you may later regret. You don't have to bite your tongue so hard that it bleeds, but you do need to apply enough pressure so that you won't move it, wag it, or say anything that will put a damper on your now tender and fragile relationship.

ASKING FOR HELP FROM THE PERSON
YOU'VE BEEN TOXIC TO

•

Sometimes you have treated someone poorly and you don't really know what to do, what to say, or how to treat the person.

Let's say you've been in a recovery program, you have changed your ways, and you realize how horrible life has been without a certain person. You may want to ask that individual for help.

In order to open up a line of communication, say: "If I have done or said anything that upsets you, please let me know about it right away. Help me become aware of my actions so that I don't continue acting the way I did toward you, and tell me *immediately* so that we don't continue to have hard feelings toward each other."

When the person does take heed and begins telling you when you have offended, *do not defend yourself.* Let that person talk and air his or her feelings. You just sit quietly and *listen!*

The next thing you may want to do is ask for help from a professional. If you do have a problem that contributes to your toxicity, often a professional can show you various behavioral or psychological techniques you can use to modify your toxic behavior patterns.

WATCHING YOUR WORDS

•

Be careful not to use the toxic word triggers that we discussed in Chapter 2. The "You should"s, "You ought to"s, and commands need to be replaced with suggestions, such as "Why don't you" or "Perhaps it may work if" or "Would you consider."

It can be very hard for a parent who is rekindling a relationship with a grown child not to use toxic word triggers. When you feel these words coming, it is in your best interest to call upon the Stop-the-Thought Technique and bite your tongue.

If you find yourself getting angry, irritated, or exasperated at the person you were toxic to, the Tension-Blowout Technique will aid you in controlling any negative reaction. It also helps you not to take everything they say personally or too seriously. You can let negative thoughts go by breathing them out.

In the course of seeking to revitalize a relationship, you may understand clearly why you were so toxic to the other person and realize that the relationship is unavoidably noxious. It is in your best interests to let go.

Being honest with yourself and willing to accept the fact that you are incompatible will enable you to use the Unplug Technique and release them with love instead of hate.

A PAT ON THE BACK IS ONLY A FEW VERTEBRAE FROM A KICK IN THE PANTS
•

Often when toxic people irritate you, it may be not only *their* problem but *your* problem as well. Perhaps your low threshold of tolerance for them renders you incapable of handling their actions. So whenever you want to say something negative to them, why don't you turn it around and say something positive?

You may not like what they're doing, but instead of yelling at them or making demands, you might ask a calm question.

You may want to focus on the good things they have done in their life, which make you like and respect them. Practice saying nice things to them.

The tone of your voice is important when you are making amends. A whining, staccato, griping sound will never get you the results you want. Instead you need to have flowing, breathy tones that reflect a positive, loving image. If you need help in acquiring the tone, you can write to me (see the information section at the end of this book), and I will provide you with information that can help you to achieve a better-sounding voice.

SETTING UP NEW RULES FOR
A FORMERLY TOXIC RELATIONSHIP

•

If you are going to revitalize a formerly toxic relationship, you have to come up with a new set of rules. You cannot continue the old ways. There has to be a means of communicating that allows both of you to save face and preserve dignity and respect. The following ten rules are essential for establishing open communication in a formerly toxic relationship:

Don't Blame

Let go of the blame and forget about whose fault it was. After all, you are both trying to revitalize a once toxic relationship. You cannot blame yourself for what happened, just as you cannot blame the other person.

Apologize Readily If It's Your Fault

If there has been any miscommunication or misunderstanding, it is essential that it be brought out in the open immediately. That way an apology can be made—and accepted—as soon as possible. This is the only way an honest, open flow of communication can ever be established.

Don't Hold Back—Say It All

One of the reasons toxic relationships become toxic is that the parties involved did not confront each other with what was on their minds. They held back because they either didn't want to hurt the other person or did not want to "make waves." If you are going to revitalize a toxic relationship, you can never hold anything back. You have to say it all. You have to say what bothers you. Although you cannot blame or accuse, you can clarify how the person's actions have affected you. For example, you can say, "When you talk to me like that, it really hurts my feelings." This way, not only will you allow the person to save face but you will say exactly how you are feeling. By putting all your cards out on the table, you will be allowing for a more open and honest interaction.

Don't Attack

You cannot attack the other person verbally. Period.

Don't Threaten

You can never say, "If you don't do this, I'll leave" or "If you say that again, I'll leave." If you paint a person into a corner and make him or her feel defensive, there will never be open channels of communication.

Don't Hit Below the Belt

Hitting a person's vulnerable spot can be devastating. Revitalizing the relationship is about trying to rebuild, not punishing. Often people make the mistake of bringing up something that they know will hurt the other. This is not ever going to add to the healing process. Put on the defensive, someone will resist the effort of reconciliation.

Don't Use Sarcasm or Belittle

You cannot use sarcasm or put someone down in order to get your point across. People can definitely detect sarcasm in your tone of voice. If something is bothering you, get it out in the open. Don't be clandestine about it. Don't say something nasty and then temper it with "I was only kidding." Instead be up front and direct.

Stick to the Issues

When people try to revitalize a relationship, they often bring up things from the past and go over and over them. This solves nothing. It only restimulates animosity. Don't say, "This is exactly what you did four years ago. This is why I couldn't stand to be around you for so many years." Instead say, "You know, this situation really bothers me. I would prefer if you didn't do that." Don't mention anything that may have taken place in the past.

Watch Your Tone of Voice

Do not yell, shout, or scream. Rather, speak in a manner that is calm and collected. When you get emotionally volatile, it will encourage the other person to follow suit and will result in a heated argument.

Show Compassion

Try to see things from the other person's point of view. Though it may be difficult for you to understand where another is coming from, seeing another side can open your mind and your heart. Remember, you cannot judge people unless you have walked a mile in their shoes. So don't be too quick to judge.

CHAPTER 12

GETTING ON WITH YOUR LIFE

- Taking Good Care of Yourself

- Hermit Time

- Pampering Your Body

- Pampering Your Mind

- Pampering Your Soul

- Taking Inventory

- Coming Out

- Redecorating Yourself

- Have a Mission in Life

- Meet New and Different Kinds of People

- **Start Saying Nice Things to Yourself**

- **Be True to Yourself**

TAKING GOOD CARE OF YOURSELF

•

If all attempts at reconciliation have failed, or if you have decided that to renew a toxic relationship would be too self-destructive, you must enter upon a healing process. Since you are emotionally tender, you have to do whatever you can to be nice to yourself and treat yourself with the respect and dignity you so richly deserve.

Just because you were never treated well in the past doesn't mean you can't be treated well now. You must start by treating yourself right—by being good to yourself and even by saying nice and kind things to and about yourself.

If *you* don't treat you with respect, nobody else will either.

If I come over to your house and I see that you live in a pigsty and there is garbage thrown all over your living room, what would prevent me from crumpling up some paper and throwing it on the floor, thereby adding to the mess? After all, if you don't have enough respect for your own home to take care of it and to keep it clean, then why should anyone else?

On the other hand, if you have a clean home that is organized and litter-free, nobody would even dream of littering your floor. This same concept applies to your soul and to your being. If you treat yourself disrespectfully and are nasty to yourself, what would prevent other people from treating you the same way?

If you have been toxic to yourself, the first thing you have to do is stop taking it out on yourself. Stop beating yourself up! It is so easy to do that when you're angry at yourself. You will overeat, or drink, or pity yourself, and you won't exercise. You'll just walk around with a "poor me, I'm no good, nobody likes me, everybody hates me, I think I'll eat worms" attitude. Self-pity does not work; it only serves to create a bigger hole in your self-esteem.

Whenever you want to beat yourself up, you need to breathe out negative thoughts, using the Stop-the-Thought Technique. If you want to binge on chocolate cake, first ask yourself why you are doing it. If it's because you're angry, lonely, frustrated, or depressed, you need to be your own best friend and ask yourself honest questions, such as: "Am I eating this cake so it will immediately make me feel better because I am in so much pain?" "Will I feel worse an hour after I eat it?" "How else can I express my anger?" We read so many books about being our own best friends and loving ourselves, and it makes a lot of sense, because if *you* don't like you, neither can anybody else.

HERMIT TIME

•

Sometimes we need to be alone. As long as we don't feel this way all the time, like Norma Desmond in *Sunset Boulevard,* it is perfectly healthy. By occasionally shutting out all stimuli, staying away from people, we can regenerate.

After the husband of one of my clients died, she wanted to be by herself. Many of the people she knew felt alienated. But this is what she needed to do in order to heal. She spent months alone, crying. But when she did emerge from her cocoon, she was a stronger, more vibrant person. Because she felt so bad about shutting out all the well-wishers, she wrote them lovely notes expressing why she did what she did and how being a hermit helped her cope with the passing of her husband.

When you are recovering from the wrath of a toxic person or the pain of a toxic situation, being a hermit is one of the most healing things you can do, as it allows you to rejuvenate yourself by getting away from it all.

Sometimes you can do it by retreating into your bedroom for just a few hours. Perhaps this alone time can happen in your bathtub, where you light candles and just soak as you renew yourself, away from the world and its stimuli, all the telephones, televisions, and people.

Sometimes you have to regenerate for a few months. Sometimes you need to do it for a few years. Perhaps going out of town for a few days can do it. It doesn't have to be expensive. Even a trip to the park or the library may do the trick. Whatever it takes to be alone and to be able to reflect on your own thoughts and your own feelings, do it, so that you can emerge a stronger and happier person.

PAMPERING YOUR BODY

•

Numerous books tell you how to pamper your body, but the main thing you need to do is to take great care of yourself. You need to exercise. I can't stress this enough. Studies have shown that your endorphin levels increase when you exercise, which makes you feel better physically by putting you in a better mood. Whether it is for ten minutes a day or twenty minutes, get active. It will improve your mood and help you look better. Do things you have never done before. Get a manicure or pedicure. Do anything that is self-pampering and can get you on the road to recovery.

PAMPERING YOUR MIND

•

Stimulate your mind with new things. Read new books or magazines. Get interested in things you have never done before. For example, even if you have never been interested in sports, turn on a game and force yourself to watch it. You might be surprised to find that you like it. Take a class and learn something new. Talk to people and learn from them. Be open to new ideas. Try to see things from a different point of view.

PAMPERING YOUR SOUL

•

I am definitely not going to tell you what religion to follow or how to approach God. But I will tell you that when you have a sense of spirituality and a sense of belonging to the universe, you tend to feel a lot more secure in your life.

Your means of accomplishing this certainly depends on you, but you do need to seek solace in whatever belief system you have. This will often guide you toward a better path in your healing process. If you don't know how to proceed, or you want another dimension, you can explore various options at a spiritual or religious bookstore.

TAKING INVENTORY

•

Now that you have reserved some time to spend with yourself, it is important to take inventory of yourself—mentally, emotionally, physically, and spiritually.

Perhaps the best way to gain an understanding of where you are in your life is to take the Self-Inventory. On a piece of paper, list five aspects of your life in the left-hand column: Social Life; Work Life; Professional Life; Family Life; Physical Appearance. Across the top of the page list: Present Situation; Ideal Situation; Steps to Achieving the Ideal Situation.

In the first column, under Social Life, for example, consider whether you have enough friends, how often you socialize, how often you meet new people. Be honest and open with yourself.

Under Work Life, you need to write down what is happening in your present job and whether it is the job you want. Is your salary sufficient to make ends meet? In the third category, you need to evaluate the present status of your career. Are you accomplishing all your career goals? In the fourth category, Family Life, you should consider the present status of your relationship with people who are close to you: your children, your parents, your relatives, your boyfriend or girlfriend, your husband or wife.

In the last category, Physical Appearance, go down a list from head to toe, from hair and face to clothes and body, from your weight to your speech. It is important that you honestly examine yourself so that you describe yourself objectively and openly.

In the second column, write a fantasy about the ideal situation regarding your social life, your work life, your professional life, your family life, and your physical appearance. Pretend there is a fairy godmother to give you whatever you want.

In the third column, list all the steps that you would take in order to make the dreams from the second column come true.

For example, the reality of your present social situation may be that you have very few friends. You may feel lonely and dejected and completely empty. Your ideal situation may be to have the man of your dreams, someone who speaks kindly to you, treats you with respect, spends money on you, looks at you with love in his eyes.

The steps that you need to make this come true are to: tell all your friends that you are available; join a dating service or a singles organization; give dinner parties to which your women friends invite men who are their friends; go out more often, getting involved in classes or in sports. Ask your clergyman for assistance, and be more open and friendly to people whom you meet; be more assertive, smiling and saying hello.

This Self-Inventory has proved a most effective technique, which I have shared with readers of my book *Say It Right: How to Talk in Any Social or Business Situation.* Clients of mine have literally changed their lives for the better by using it.

COMING OUT

•

Now that you have regenerated yourself, you need to come out. But you don't have to come out all at once. In fact, it is best that you do so slowly. The fact that you are even out the door says a lot for your healing process. Sometimes it's hard to take that first step. Whenever you are feeling paralyzed, think of the old Nike commercials that said: "Just do it."

I'm saying the same thing to you. *Just do it!* Even though it is scary, do things you have never done before. Taking trips by yourself, going to the movies alone, or having a cup of coffee solo can give you a lot more self-confidence. Creating new adventures for yourself and doing things that are out of character will not only make your life much more exciting but also prevent you from wallowing in the self-pity mode.

When you take risks, don't be afraid to be rejected. Don't be afraid to feel stupid or awkward. Take a risk—the adage "Nothing ventured, nothing gained" is true.

I know a woman who had a good position but quit after working with a Bitchy, Bossy Bully boss. He told her that she would never get a good recommendation from the company and that he would see to it that she never got another job in her field. He also told her she would never amount to anything, that she needed him and would come crawling back to him, begging for her old job. Unfortunately he was right, as she found it impossible to get another job. Refusing to be defeated, she took up a new interest and learned all she could about handwriting analysis. She got to be pretty good at it and began to tell all her friends about their personalities, based on their handwriting. The next thing she knew, she was booked at parties as entertainment. She opened a booth at an open market on weekends. She ended up turning this little hobby into a major business and now makes six figures a year. She even has the police department as a client, analyzing handwriting samples to help their investigations. She has worked for private investigating agencies and has even discussed handwriting analysis on television.

In essence, she proved her toxic nemesis wrong. By doing something completely different in her life and refusing to put up with her boss's toxic behavior, she ended up earning more money than he ever would. She took a risk and would not allow herself to be destroyed by anyone.

REDECORATING YOURSELF

•

Now may be the time to do whatever you have always wanted to do to change your image. Perhaps it is to cut your hair or grow a mustache or a beard. You may want to do something completely different. Doing something different indicates that you have emerged from the period in which you knew the toxic person. A physical change may also pick up your spirits.

Bonnie, one of my clients, broke up with Mark, whom she loved but who was very, very toxic to her. He constantly told her what was wrong with her and put her down. She never felt good enough around him. Finally, she had enough sense to break up with him and to end their toxic relationship for good. She also ended her era of dowdiness. Taking every cent she had saved, she spent it on plastic surgery, getting a face-lift, liposuction, a nose job, her breasts enhanced, and her butt and stomach tightened. She bleached her hair, got blue contact lenses, went on an exercise program and lost twenty pounds, developing a great body. She had her teeth bonded and had long acrylic nails applied to her fingertips. Bonnie even splurged on a twenty-four-hundred-dollar Thierry Mugler suit, in which she looks like a million dollars. She has never felt better about herself.

HAVE A MISSION IN LIFE

•

The first step in making yourself a better person is to find something that gives your life meaning. There are a number of things you can do. You can start by finding spiritual solace in your religion or in doing some of the things that you enjoy and find comfort in. Why not look at life as having a lot more meaning? Perhaps the reason you are on this earth is to be kinder to other people, to make it a better world, or to do something unique for others. Find out what your mission is, and make a commitment to that mission. You may find that you do have a unique place in the world.

You may even realize the importance of other aspects of your life. When one of my clients, Matilda, did this, she realized that her main love in life was children. She went back to school, got a teaching degree, and became a special-education teacher. She loves it despite its demands, and she believes that she has found her mission in life.

When you are unhappy and wallowing in self-pity, worrying about what is going wrong in your life, lift your head up and look around. There may be somebody out there who is in more pain than you are.

You know about the man who was crying because he had no shoes and then looked up to see a man who had no feet. Sometimes we have to count our blessings. I have had too many clients who have been victims. They have been upset because of their toxic jobs or the toxic people in their lives. They have hated their toxic families, have hated their parents, hated their spouse; they feel that life is no good, nobody can help them, they are completely lost. They are the "yeah, but" people. They feel hopeless. But if they can be convinced to look outside themselves, their entire life takes on new meaning.

Just do something, and do it yourself! That is the true meaning of giving. Make every day Christmas, instead of being charitable and kind to others only once a year.

Go to a hospital and hold a baby who is addicted to crack. Visit a patient who is dying of AIDS or volunteer at the Braille Institute and read for the blind. Adopt a pet from an animal shelter. Giving is about that—not about sending off money to deduct from your taxes at the end of the year. The added value of giving unselfishly to others helps you to feel much better about yourself. When you do good things for others, it comes back to you tenfold.

I once had a client who was an unemployed actress. All she did was talk about how she didn't get this job and didn't get that job. Consumed with her own life, she didn't realize that other people had lives as well. I encouraged her to volunteer at the Braille Institute. She took my advice and read for the blind on a regular basis. She also volunteered with blind children, who in turn enriched her life. Giving her services to the blind changed her dramatically. She was no longer self-absorbed. Now when she went on casting calls she had something else to talk about—her work with the blind— which impressed a lot of people, especially casting agents. Her career rebounded.

MEET NEW AND DIFFERENT KINDS
OF PEOPLE

•

You need to take time out to be with others. The old Barbra Streisand song is so true: "People who need people are the luckiest people in the world."

But how do you meet new people? You can meet them anywhere—at the grocery store, walking at the mall, getting gas. All you have to do is smile. Get out of yourself, be assertive, and say hello. Sometimes your greeting won't be reciprocated. Sometimes people don't have time, or, frankly, they may not want to meet you. Perhaps they are shy. It doesn't matter. Just keep smiling anyway and keep saying hello. Eventually it will all pay off.

You need to be assertive. Get out of your own way so that you can take that first step and make the first move. Don't wait for somebody to come to you. A lot of people make the mistake of expecting others to come to them and, when they don't, feel even worse about themselves than before.

START SAYING NICE THINGS
TO YOURSELF

•

In order to heal the pain of a toxic interaction, you need to say the right things to yourself. Saying "Oh, I'm so stupid" or "I'm just horrible" perpetuates a poor self-image that may have been projected onto you by that toxic person, thereby creating a self-fulfilling prophecy. If you keep repeating such toxic statements, you will eventually come to regard them as factual. Instead, whenever you want to say something ugly to abuse yourself, use the Stop-the-Thought Technique and substitute a positive statement about yourself. Whatever you put out in the universe is what is revealed about you. You need to take charge and censor negative thoughts and words you say to yourself.

Just as saying negative things about yourself can bring on toxic reactions to you, saying positive things about yourself can affect how others think of you. Positive self-talk is one of the most important gifts you can give yourself.

I once had an amazing client, a very wealthy businessman from Texas, who wanted to become a more polished public speaker. He told me that upon waking up each morning, he looks in the mirror and, in his most positive, enthusiastic tone, says, "Good morning, Wayne. It's good to see you. We're going to have a terrific day, and all kinds of great things are going to happen. We're going to have fun and make a lot of money and a lot of friends."

His thirty-second pep talk has enabled him to become a multi-millionaire, as he doesn't allow toxic words or toxic thoughts, let alone toxic people, into his life. Just as he doesn't say negative things about others, he never allows anyone to say negative things to him.

Wayne is a great example of the power one holds in one's tongue. If you treat yourself well and say nice things to yourself, usually other people will follow your lead and treat you with the same respect you accord yourself.

BE TRUE TO YOURSELF

•

A lot of times you are subject to self-loathing because you aren't honest with yourself.

Think of Christmastime, when you feel obligated to be around a bunch of toxic people whom you can't stand.

Well, guess what? You have permission not to go and not to be there. Why subject yourself to an evening of pain and torture? "But it's a family obligation," you say. "I always do it, I always go." I reply,

"You always get sick after you return. You always get a headache while you are there from annoyance and holding your temper in. You end up eating and drinking too much out of frustration. You feel horrible about yourself after you are around these toxic people."

If you can't bring yourself to use any of the techniques described earlier in this book, then you must be true to yourself and not go. Do not be a hypocrite. Do not show up just because you feel guilty or obligated. *You no longer have to be a victim!* You are free to be true to yourself.

This extends beyond family obligations. In being true to yourself, you never have to be around people *just because of what they can do for you.*

You will often find that the people who are most toxic are those whom you associate with only because of what they can do to better your career or your personal or social life. You may be sticking around with a boyfriend because you think to yourself: "I can't find anyone else" or "He's better than nothing." You may fawn over a toxic boss because you think: "If I don't, he may fire me" or "I'll kiss up to him so he'll like me and I'll get ahead."

It is not worth being untrue to your feelings, because your boss may fire you anyway. Your boyfriend may cause you so much grief that it may be better to be alone than to be with somebody you don't respect. People are not stupid. They pick up on subtle signals in tone of voice and body language. They know if you like them or not. Therefore it's a big waste of time and energy to be phony and not react honestly to these people.

One of my clients couldn't stand a certain businesswoman, but he seduced her, thinking that if he slept with her she would be sure to give him some of her business. Needless to say, she gave it to somebody else.

The best business ventures involve people who genuinely like and respect one another. Therefore associate only with people with whom you can grow, whom you respect, and whom you admire. If you associate with people based only on what they can do for you, they may be able to open some doors, but the doors will quickly shut when they realize why you were being nice to them.

People are not stepping-stones to be walked on, used, and discarded.

Instead people are to be valued, cherished, and treated with respect and dignity. Being nice to people to their face and unkind behind their back only hurts you in the long run.

If you want to live an untoxic life, you have to be true to yourself in everything you do and say.

Let's Be Winners!

We live in a world in which people are scared to death of one another and rightfully so.

The world has changed, and *not* for the better. Years ago you could leave your doors open, for people were trustworthy. In those days, people were not punished for helping one another. They did not have to worry about possible lawsuits. If people fell down, you picked them up.

Nowadays we are afraid to say anything that might inadvertently offend or harm people and are equally afraid of doing something helpful for someone, for fear that the strong arm of the law will come down upon us.

Today we have taken anger to the limit. Nothing is sacred, no holds are barred. We can see and hear anything, as we watch rapists, transvestites, mothers who have murdered their children, and even chronic masturbators on our daily talk shows. Watching the constant parade of victims march across our television screens, we have become immune to their shock value. Everyone is telling a sob story, trying to outsob the next person. Many of us have begun to feel hopeless and victimized, full of hatred and anger. Everyone is talking, yet no one is listening.

Let's stop being victims.

Let's stop hating each other.

Let's stop hating ourselves.

Let's stop killing each other.

Let's stop saying such toxic things to one another that they cease to have meaning.

Throughout this book, I have emphasized that *knowledge is power!* If we have awareness—the knowledge of what is, what to do, and what the results will be—then and only then can we change our lives for the better.

Something *has* to change, and it has to change *immediately.* We need not only to put more love into people's lives but also to learn to cope with the toxic forces that infect our own lives.

Nobody is immune to exposure to toxic people. In fact, the richest, most famous, most successful people in the world have had to cope with them.

Superstar Madonna was told that she was untalented and would never make it. Needless to say, she proved the nay-sayers wrong, becoming one of the wealthiest female performers in the world.

Lauren Hutton was told that she couldn't be a model because she had a crooked nose and imperfect teeth. Ignoring the toxic comments, she went on to become one of the world's most prominent fashion models.

A talent manager felt that Oprah Winfrey had no talent and didn't look right. Did she ever prove him wrong!

Sylvester Stallone couldn't get a job in Hollywood for a long time. Now he seems to be one of the few Hollywood actors who work all the time.

Melanie Griffith came to see me after she was fired from a job because of her high-pitched voice. She was told she could never work in this town because she sounded like a little girl. She was later nominated for an Academy Award, little-girl voice and all.

Similarly, Academy Award–winning Dustin Hoffman talks publicly about the toxicity he experienced in his family when he announced that he was going to be an actor. One relative told him that he wasn't good-looking enough. This was also the opinion of various casting directors. Despite his looks and his small stature, there is no question that Dustin Hoffman is among the greatest movie actors of all time.

These accomplished people and countless others have endured slings and arrows from the mouths of toxic people but have gone on to greatness anyway.

They refused to be *victims*! They refused to let someone else's toxicity immobilize them. They refused to let anger and hate consume them. They, like so many other winners, fought back against those people in their lives who made them miserable.

We should derive our inspiration not from the parade of hopeless victims we see daily on television but from those who can inspire us. We need to stand up and say, "I *refuse* to be a victim anymore."

This book offers the tools to fight back effectively, so that we can become winners too—surrounded by other winners.

Let's *stop* looking at the victims and start looking at life's *winners*—at people who can inspire us. Instead of looking at pain and suffering, let's look at pain and *healing*.

Look at what happened in California during the Malibu fires and during the earthquake. Strangers went out of their way to help other strangers. Look at how many strangers lent one another a helping hand after the debilitating hurricane in Miami. Look at how giving and loving people were to one another during the horrible floods in the Midwest. Strangers readily gave food and shelter to others, while they helped them place sandbags around their homes in efforts to salvage them.

Entire communities have joined forces when a child has been kidnapped or has vanished. Strangers readily volunteer to have their blood drawn and examined to see whether they are a compatible donor for a bone marrow transfer to save the life of a person they don't even know. There are *good* stories on the news, about *good* people, but unfortunately we all too often focus on negative stories and sensationalize evil and toxic people.

It is people who perform acts of kindness and goodness who should be the main focus of our newscasts, so that they can inspire others to follow suit. People like Chuck Wall, a college professor who assigned his class to perform one act of senseless kindness. This literally changed his students' lives. As they unselfishly gave to others, people who were in need, they felt much better about themselves.

People can be kind—like the veterinarian who gives homeless people's pets free veterinary help. And like the person who went to a children's hospital each day and gave gifts to young cancer patients. A note said the gift was from the child's "special angel." He never let them know who he was. He gave generously so that a dying child could smile each day and have something to look forward to.

There are good and kind people in every neighborhood, and their actions don't go unnoticed.

One morning, while purchasing some muffins at the Muffin Oven in Beverly Hills, I saw a homeless man walk in. My first inclination was to buy him a few muffins, but the lovely European couple who own the shop said, "Oh, you don't have to do that—we give him free coffee and muffins every morning." I got choked up, touched by their gesture of kindness toward a fellow man in need.

There are kind people like the man who put on a magic and comedy show for the residents of a nursing home and visited every resident each week—he sent flowers on their birthday—just so these elderly people would know that someone cared about them.

These are our heroes, our role models—not some vulgar, drugged-out singer, promiscuous athlete, wife-beating celebrity, or heroin-taking actor.

We all need to be each other's heroes—generously doing good for each other and treating one another with the respect and dignity that each of us so richly deserves.

It is the attitude of these heroes that represent what America is all about—that represent the American Dream: with a lot of hard work, compassion, and help from your fellowman, you *can* survive. This was the philosophy that allowed our forefathers who pioneered their way across the United States to survive. It was all about people helping one another.

If we continue this great tradition set forth by our ancestors, we *can* and *will* survive. After all, this is what our great country is based on.

YOU DON'T HAVE TO BE VICTIMIZED

•

Now you have choices, you have options, and you never again have to feel hopeless, convinced that you want to curl up and die. You no longer have to be destroyed by toxic people.

The philosopher Nietzsche once said, "That which does not destroy you makes you stronger."

How right he was! When you are able to handle the people in your life who make you miserable, you will definitely become a much stronger and more secure person. Your inner strength will allow risk taking in your career and in your social life, thereby creating a richer, fuller, and more adventurous journey through a life that is filled with positive, good, and exciting things.

Perhaps nothing illustrates this point more clearly than the following ancient story:

One day a teacher asked his students how they could tell when the night ended and the day began. One student said, "It is when you see an animal in the distance and can tell if it is a dog or a cat." "No," answered the teacher. Another child answered, "It is when you look at a tree in the distance and can tell if it is an apple tree or a fig tree." "No," replied the teacher.

"Well, when has the night ended and the day begun?" the students demanded to know.

The wise old teacher answered, "It is when you look at the face of any man or any woman or any child and see that it is your sister or your brother. Because if you cannot see this, it is still night!"

Though it may still be night for many people, perhaps someday we will be able to see and embrace any man, woman, or child, no matter who they are, what color their skin is, or what their belief system is. Perhaps the guidance of this book will help some of us finally to see daylight!

Those of us who learn when the night has ended and the day has begun will see that each man is our brother, each woman our sister—that we are the same and there is no difference! No matter what color our skin is, how we look or what we wear, everyone else is exactly like us. *All* of us want the same things in life. We all want enough food, and jobs so that we can earn enough money to support our families. We want a safe place to live, and we want self-respect and the respect of others.

A perfect illustration of how alike we really are is provided by South African leaders Nelson Mandela and F. W. de Klerk. Although they may differ in their physical appearance—basically, their skin colors—they are alike in numerous ways. They are both loved by many people. Both have families and children whom they adore. Both are brilliant, are men of integrity, and great leaders. Both nurtured the dream of peace, so much so that they were recently given a joint Nobel Peace Prize.

When you look at these two men and their similar dreams for peace in South Africa, you see no color, no supremacy, no inferiority—you see only equality, as these men try to live out their dream of peace, working together as equal partners.

These two great men symbolize the fact that no one is better than anyone or worse than anyone, despite his or her appearance or ancestral origins.

There will always be people in the world whom we may find toxic, but we have options available that equip us to overcome their toxic influence. We need to stop the hatred and prejudice and jealousy and victimization and start pulling together as a people, as a nation, and as a world!

WHERE TO GET MORE INFORMATION

For additional information, please send this page along with a self-addressed stamped envelope to:

Dr. Lillian Glass
C/o Your Total Image, Inc.
435 N. Bedford Drive, Suite 207
Beverly Hills, CA 90210

(310) 274-0528 phone
(310) 274-0269 fax

Name:

Address:

City, State, Zip Code:

Phone Number: (   )

Fax Number: (   )

Check Those That Apply:

_____Books

_____Audiotapes

_____Videotapes

_____Seminars

_____Consultations

REFERENCE SOURCES

Abramson, Rudy. "Has the Bobbit Case Escalated the War Between the Sexes?" *LA Magazine,* 22 November 1993.

Bach, George R. *Stop, You're Driving Me Crazy: How to Keep the People in Your Life from Driving You up the Wall.* New York: Berkley Books, 1981.

Bach, George R., and Torbet, Laura. *The Inner Enemy: How to Fight Fair with Yourself.* New York: Berkley Books, 1985.

Bernstein, Albert J., and Rozen, Sydney Craft. *Dinosaur Brains: Dealing with All Those Impossible People at Work.* New York: Ballantine, 1989.

———. *Neanderthals at Work: How People and Politics Can Drive You Crazy and What You Can Do About Them.* New York: Ballantine, 1992.

Berry, Carmen R. *When Helping You Is Hurting Me.* New York: Harper Paperback, 1989.

Braiker, Harriet B. *Lethal Lovers and Poisonous People: How to Protect Your Health from Relationships That Make You Sick.* New York: Pocket Books, 1992.

Bramson, Robert M. *Coping with Difficult People.* New York: Anchor Press / Doubleday, 1981.

Bukkyo Dendo Kyokai. *The Teaching of Buddha.* Tokyo: Toppan Printing, 1990.

Carter, Jay. *Nasty People: How to Stop Being Hurt by Them Without Becoming One of Them.* Chicago: Contemporary Books, 1989.

Carter-Scott, Cherie. *The Corporate Negaholic: How to Deal Successfully with Negative Colleagues, Managers, and Corporations.* New York: Fawcett Crest, 1992.

Cava, Roberta. *Dealing with Difficult People.* London: Piatkus, 1990.

Chopra, Deepak. *Ageless Body, Timeless Mind.* New York: Harmony, 1993.

Cleary, Thomas. *The Essentials of Confucius: The Heart of Confucius' Teachings in Authentic I Ching Order.* New York: HarperCollins, 1992.

Cornell, George W. "Founder's Slurs on Jews Renounced by Lutherans." *Los Angeles Times,* 21 October 1993.

Cowley, Geoffrey, and Hall, Carol. "The Genetics of Bad Behavior: A Study Links Violence to Heredity." *Newsweek,* 1 November 1993.

Deep, Sam, and Sussman, Lyle. *What to Ask When You Don't Know What to Say.* Englewood Cliffs, N.J.: Prentice Hall, 1993.

————. *What to Say to Get What You Want.* New York: Addison-Wesley, 1992.

Dewar, Helen. "Senator Feinstein Gives Idaho Colleague a Barrelful." *Washington Post,* 11 November 1993.

Dore, Henry, and Mikennelly, S. J. *Chinese Customs.* Singapore: Graham Brash, 1990.

Dunne, Dominick. "Dominick Dunne's Courtroom Notebook from the Menendez Murder Trial." *Vanity Fair,* October 1993.

Elgin, Suzette Haden. *The Gentle Art of Verbal Self-Defense.* New York: Dorset Press, 1980.

Felder, Leonard. *Does Someone at Work Treat You Badly?* New York: Berkley Books, 1993.

Glass, Lillian. *He Says, She Says: Closing the Communication Gap Between the Sexes.* New York: Putnam, 1992.

————. *Say It Right: How to Talk in Any Social or Business Situation.* New York: Putnam, 1991.

————. *Talk to Win: Six Steps to a Successful Vocal Image.* New York: Putnam, 1987.

Hewitt, Bill, and Bell, Bonnie. "The Cruelest Hoax: A Cold-Blooded Mother-to-Be Toys with the Yearning of Couples Desperate to Adopt Her Baby. " *People,* 10 May 1993.

Jenkins, Sally. "Persona Grata: Because of His Abuse of His Daughter Mary, Jim Pierce Is No Longer Welcome on the World Tennis Circuit." *People,* 13 September 1993.

Larrabee, John. "New Hampshire Teens Cry for Help." *USA Today,* 26 October 1993.

Leland, John. "Criminal Records: Gangsta Rap and the Culture of Violence." *Newsweek,* 29 November 1993.

Mackay, Harvey. *Swim with the Sharks Without Being Eaten Alive.* New York: William Morrow, 1988.

Marsh, Peter. *Eye to Eye: How People Interact.* Topsfield, Mass.: Salem House, 1988.

Martin, Marty E. "Skinheads: When Violence Feeds on Chaos." *Los Angeles Times,* 25 July 1993.

People magazine. "For Hervé Villechaize There Was No Island of Escape from His Own Tortured Life: Laying Down the Burden." 20 September 1993.

Perret, Gene. *Great One Liners.* New York: Sterling, 1992.

Reed, Stanley Foster. *The Toxic Executive.* New York: Harper Business, 1993.

Reed, Susan, and Bacon, Doris. "Fed Up with Violence, Chuck Wall Calls for an Outbreak of Random Kindness." *People,* 13 December 1993.

Rogan, David. "Even Superstars Get Rejected." *Cosmopolitan,* November 1991.

Rosen, Carol. *Maybe He's Just a Jerk.* New York: William Morrow, 1992.

Rubin, Theodore Isaac. *The Angry Book.* New York: Macmillan, 1987.

Safiar, Louis A. *The Giant Book of Insults.* Secaucus, N.J.: Castle Books, 1967.

Shinn, Florence Scovel. *The Wisdom of Florence Scovel Shinn.* New York: Simon & Schuster, 1989.

Solomon, Muriel. *Working with Difficult People.* Englewood Cliffs, N.J.: Prentice Hall, 1990.

Stolberg, Sheryl. "Researcher Links Gene to Aggression." *Los Angeles Times,* 22 October 1993.

Tanner, Mary. "The Green-Eyed Monster." *Allure,* December 1992.

Temoshok, Lydia. *Type C Connection: The Behavioral Links to Cancer and to Your Health.* New York: Random House, 1992.

Williman, Chris. "Jackie Mason: Mining the 'Political Incorrect.'" *Los Angeles Times,* December 1993..

Index

Dr. Lillian Glass, known as "America's First Lady of Speech," is recognized as one of the world's foremost authorities on communication skills and self-image. In popular demand as a motivational speaker, she makes her message known worldwide on such topics as: The Power of Influence, Speaking for Success, Improving Your Total Image, Confident Conversation, Gender Differences in Negotiation, Closing the Communication Gap Between the Sexes, and Toxic People.

Dr. Glass also has a very successful private practice in Beverly Hills, California, where she helps people gain more confidence in the way they communicate, and has worked with corporate executives, sports figures, politicians, and countless celebrities.

She has authored numerous books and tapes including *How to Deprogram Your Valley Girl, Speak for Success, Talk to Win, Say It . . . Right, Confident Conversation, World of Words,* and *He Says, She Says: Closing the Communication Gap Between the Sexes.*

A frequent guest on national television and radio shows, she has written newspaper and magazine articles worldwide.

Dr. Glass's mission is to help achieve "global peace through communication." She believes that only by learning how to communicate effectively with those around us can we make a better world for ourselves and for future generations.